M000287123

A 'must-read' for students embarking on their fi... ..... stepping up to the challenge of teaching Computing at school. This is not just a book about programming, more a template for teaching. Karl Beecher speaks in plain English. Incisive insight and practical advice, standing independent of the Python exemplars used, predicated as it is on a holistic understanding of the subject terrain.

Roger Davies, *Director of IT, Queen Elizabeth School, and Editor, Computing At School, Tenderfoot Training Project*

I really enjoyed this book - it bridges the gap between the very practical, but perhaps narrow, field of computer programming with the real world problems that computer scientists might need to solve. The issue with encouraging young people to learn 'coding' is that they often struggle to understand how and when to use specific concepts and ideas. The underlying principles and real world applications are essential, and much harder to put across, than remembering the syntax for an IF statement. The discussions are presented in a readable format that would be suitable for bright GCSE students and should be essential reading for all A Level computer scientists.

With the shift in focus at GCSE and A Level alike, from 'programming' to 'computational thinking', explanations and examples of abstraction, decomposition and generalisation, along with modelling, logic and efficiency are both engaging and useful.

Mark Clarkson , *Subject Leader and CAS Master Teacher*

Computational Thinking is a sprint through the theoretical underpinnings of computation through to their application and the creation of software. The thirteen chapters start with an explanation of what is computational thinking, move through logical and algorithmic thinking, abstraction and modelling, to then focus on how to apply these concepts. The middle set of chapters cover how to create software with a focus on object-oriented solutions with a relatively short discussion on testing. Python is used as the programming language to demonstrate the use of the various techniques introduced in the early chapters but it would be straight forward to convert the examples to other similar languages such as Java, C#, etc. The final chapter provides a guided example based on the creation of a computer-controlled home automation system. Each chapter has a set of exercises to work through and model answers for these are supplied in an appendix.

This is a very good overview of a very large field. While all of the topics are deserving of their own book the strength of this book is the explanation and demonstration of their close relationships. This book is an excellent complement to the many books on the Raspberry Pi and Python programming because it starts to explain some of the theoretical underpinnings. The seasoned software developer should not be discouraged by the beginner's guide sub-title as this is also a good refresher on some of the basics.

Colin Smythe, *Dunelm Services Limited, Principal Consultant*

A scholarly book albeit written from a pragmatic perspective distilling the knowledge and expertise of an experienced software developer into a form that is accessible for beginners. It's engaging exercises and comprehensive references make it an invaluable learning resource. I would recommend it to anyone who wishes to gain an understanding of computational thinking and best practice in modern software development.

Professor Cornelia Boldyreff, *University of Greenwich*

This book will prove an excellent companion to more general texts on Computing, especially for teachers who are new to the subject. And with exercises at the end of each chapter, there is much to challenge students also. Highly recommended.

Terry Freedman, *independent education technology writer and consultant, and publisher of the ICT and Computing in Education website at www.ictineducation.org*

COMPUTATIONAL THINKING

BCS, THE CHARTERED INSTITUTE FOR IT

BCS, The Chartered Institute for IT, champions the global IT profession and the interests of individuals engaged in that profession for the benefit of all. We promote wider social and economic progress through the advancement of information technology science and practice. We bring together industry, academics, practitioners and government to share knowledge, promote new thinking, inform the design of new curricula, shape public policy and inform the public.

Our vision is to be a world-class organisation for IT. Our 75,000-strong membership includes practitioners, businesses, academics and students in the UK and internationally. We deliver a range of professional development tools for practitioners and employees. A leading IT qualification body, we offer a range of widely recognised qualifications.

Further Information
BCS, The Chartered Institute for IT,
First Floor, Block D,
North Star House, North Star Avenue,
Swindon, SN2 1FA, UK.
T +44 (0) 1793 417 424
F +44 (0) 1793 417 444
www.bcs.org/contact

http://shop.bcs.org/

COMPUTATIONAL THINKING
A beginner's guide to problem-solving and programming

Karl Beecher

© BCS Learning & Development Ltd 2017

The right of the author to be identified as author of this work has been asserted by him in accordance with sections 77 and 78 of the Copyright, Designs and Patents Act 1988.

All rights reserved. Apart from any fair dealing for the purposes of research or private study, or criticism or review, as permitted by the Copyright Designs and Patents Act 1988, no part of this publication may be reproduced, stored or transmitted in any form or by any means, except with the prior permission in writing of the publisher, or in the case of reprographic reproduction, in accordance with the terms of the licences issued by the Copyright Licensing Agency. Enquiries for permission to reproduce material outside those terms should be directed to the publisher. All trademarks, registered names etc. acknowledged in this publication are the property of their respective owners.

BCS and the BCS logo are the registered trademarks of the British Computer Society, charity number 292786 (BCS).

Published by BCS Learning & Development Ltd, a wholly owned subsidiary of BCS, The Chartered Institute for IT, First Floor, Block D, North Star House, North Star Avenue, Swindon, SN2 1FA, UK.
www.bcs.org

Paperback ISBN: 978-1-78017-36-41
PDF ISBN-13: 978-1-78017-36-58
EPUB ISBN-13: 978-1-78017-36-65
Kindle ISBN-13: 978-1-78017-36-72

Ebook
available

British Cataloguing in Publication Data.
A CIP catalogue record for this book is available at the British Library.

Disclaimer:
The views expressed in this book are those of the author and do not necessarily reflect the views of the Institute or BCS Learning & Development Ltd except where explicitly stated as such. Although every care has been taken by the author and BCS Learning & Development Ltd in the preparation of the publication, no warranty is given by the author or BCS Learning & Development Ltd as publisher as to the accuracy or completeness of the information contained within it and neither the author nor BCS Learning & Development Ltd shall be responsible or liable for any loss or damage whatsoever arising by virtue of such information or any instructions or advice contained within this publication or by any of the aforementioned.

Typeset by Lapiz Digital Services, Chennai, India.

CONTENTS

LIST OF FIGURES AND TABLES

AUTHOR

Karl Beecher lives a double life as a writer and software specialist.

When being a writer, he focuses on science and technology. He especially likes to take meaty, complex ideas and present them in ways that are easy to understand.

As a software specialist, Karl has worked as a software engineer, earned a PhD in Computer Science, and co-founded a company specialising in the management of large-scale IT operations.

He lives in Germany with his wife and his small ~~monster~~ daughter.

ACKNOWLEDGEMENTS

My thanks go to Rebecca Youé and others at BCS for giving me the opportunity to write this book with them and for working with me to develop it.

Thanks go also to those who reviewed early drafts and gave valuable feedback; in particular, Marie-Luise Kochsiek and, of course, my favourite sounding board, my alpha (and omega) tester, Jennifer Beecher.

GLOSSARY

Abstraction   Way of expressing an idea in a specific context while at the same time suppressing details irrelevant in that context.

Algorithm   A sequence of clearly defined steps that describe a process to follow a finite set of unambiguous instructions with clear start and end points.

Assignment   The process of setting the value of a variable.

Biconditional   Relationship between logical statements that tells us the second logically follows from the first and the first logically follows from the second.

Cardinality   Property describing the number of elements in something.

Conditional   Programming construct that alters the flow of execution in a program depending on the truth value of a condition.

Conjunction   (aka logical **and**) Operation that connects two logical statements and identifies whether both are true.

Deductive reasoning   Applying a chain of reasoning whose conclusion necessarily follows from its premises (so long as it has been constructed properly and the premises are incontrovertibly true).

Disjunction   (aka logical **or**) Operation that connects two logical statements and identifies whether one or both are true.

Function signature   A function identifier made up of the function's name and an ordered list of the parameters it accepts.

Heuristic   Problem-solving technique that yields a sub-optimal solution judged to be sufficient.

Immutable   See **mutable**.

Implication   Relationship between logical statements that tells us the second logically follows from the first.

Inductive reasoning   Applying a chain of reasoning whose conclusion follows as a measure of probability from its premises.

Information hiding Concealing the structure of some (potentially unstable) parts of a program behind a stable interface.

Library Collection of data and routines hidden behind an interface, intended for use by other programs.

Loop Sequence of statements that are executed potentially numerous times in succession.

Mutable Object whose value can be modified after creation, as opposed to an immutable object, whose value is fixed at creation.

Negation Operation applied to a proposition that inverts its value.

Parameter Value passed to a function.

Pixel Smallest addressable unit on a computer screen.

Premise Proposition used in an argument.

Proposition Statement that has a true or false value.

Script Executable program, usually small (up to a few thousand lines of code) and interpreted (as opposed to compiled).

Signature See **function signature**.

Subroutine Callable sequence of program instructions packaged as a distinct unit.

Tree (structure) Hierarchical data structure where each node may have any number of child nodes, but only one parent node (with the exception of the root node, which has no parent).

Truth value Property of a logical statement that denotes whether it is true or false.

INTRODUCTION: WHY STUDY COMPUTATIONAL THINKING?

Computers are everywhere in the modern world. They help run almost every aspect of our lives and our society.

Some of the ways they help us are obvious. We control our finances using computers. We use them to handle our social interactions, get the latest news or arrange travel. They've enabled new modes of political participation, and it's impossible to conceive of modern office life without computers.

However, many other parts of modern society depend on computation in ways you might never have considered. Your personal finances, healthy as they may be, are just a drop in the ocean compared to the billions processed daily by computers in banks and stock exchanges around the world. The content you consume online is delivered to you from huge data centres and is created using software like word processors, graphical editors and databases. Computers power our global communication networks. Computerised farm machinery produces the food you eat. Your consumer goods are assembled in automated factories. Billions of texts and online messages are shuttled around the world by software daily. Clearly, computers are deeply embedded in society and we humans are highly dependent on them.

And yet, there's a flip side to the computer revolution that exposes us to numerous risks. Cybercrime increases as more of our lives are lived online. Privacy issues continue to be fought over. More and more it's algorithms,[1] not humans, which decide things like what news you read and what potential danger you pose. 'Computer says no' becomes less of a punchline and more an ominous phrase from our computer-controlled future.[2] Just as clearly, then, society has a duty to prepare everyone for living in such a world.

Computers are our tools. They should be subservient to us and not the other way around. They should enable us, inspire us and be a beneficial force in our lives. To help ensure this, it's important we understand how they work and what they're capable of doing. To this end, computational thinking (often shortened to CT) distils important lessons and principles from computer science (CS), the subject area that teaches us how to bend those machines to our will. These lessons and principles include how pick out the essential details of a problem, how to formulate a problem in ways a computer can understand, and how to follow a problem-solving process in ways that the process can be automated. These should be important to anyone, regardless of whether they work in computing or not, because the ultimate aim of distilling them (beyond just understanding them) is to empower everyone to be able not only to solve a problem, but also to incorporate a computer in a solution to carry out the task more quickly and efficiently.

If you don't know what a computer is capable of, then you can't very well make it do things for you.

For those who intend to pursue a career in software development, there are obvious benefits of learning CT. It links a problem analysis method with the knowledge and technology from CS, giving you core problem-solving skills relevant to producing high-quality solutions. By studying CT, you'll learn ways to make the software you develop more robust, powerful, well designed, widely applicable and error-free.

But even if you're not set on a programming career, CT still has important lessons for you to learn. You may not become a professional programmer, but you will likely encounter programming in some capacity. Numerous research papers[3] discuss the importance of computational thinking in many diverse careers, such as:

- natural sciences:
  - computational biology;
  - genomics;
  - applied physics;
  - climate change;
  - astronomy.
- social sciences:
  - social studies;
  - population analysis.
- medicine:
  - disease analysis;
  - medical imaging;
  - clinical practice.
- linguistics;
- law;
- music;
- teaching.

'It is nearly impossible to do research in any scientific or engineering discipline without an ability to think computationally. (Carnegie Mellon, 2016)

Finally, as well as being important in a diverse range of fields, CT is even promoted as a life skill. Jeannette Wing, who has done much to push the idea of computational thinking since her landmark talk in 2006 (Wing, 2006), emphasises the importance of CT to everyday life and suggests that everyone can get something out of studying it:

I argued that the use of computational concepts, methods and tools would transform the very conduct of every discipline, profession and sector. Someone with the ability to use computation effectively would have an edge over someone without. So, I saw a great opportunity for the computer science community to teach future generations how computer scientists think. Hence 'computational thinking.'... Computational thinking will be a fundamental skill used by everyone in the world by the middle of the 21st century. By fundamental, I mean as fundamental as reading, writing and arithmetic.

(Wing, 2014)

This book is a guide to the subject of computational thinking and how it can aid you in learning software development. It will take you through all the subject's core concepts, explaining each one using definitions, discussions and examples. The material is supplemented with numerous rules, tips, advice and references to further reading. And you will get the opportunity to put your newfound knowledge into practice by using the exercises at the end of each chapter.

Read on and enjoy.

PART I
COMPUTATIONAL THINKING

The first part of this book introduces computational thinking as an approach to problem-solving. It introduces the basic concepts and helps the reader to build up a solid understanding of them. As well as the theoretical concepts, you'll find definitions, tips, warnings, golden rules and opportunities for further reading elsewhere.

This part doesn't assume any programming skill on the part of the reader. Illustrative examples are based around everyday concepts that come from a broad range of domains. At the end of each chapter, you'll have the opportunity to put your newfound knowledge to the test by trying out some exercises. Like the examples, the exercises require no prior programming skill.

After reading this part, you will have an understanding of all the topics that make up computational thinking. You'll then be ready for Part II, where you'll learn how to put those skills into practice as a programmer.

PART I
COMPUTATIONAL THINKING

1　WHAT IS COMPUTATIONAL THINKING?

OBJECTIVES

- Define computational thinking.
- Show how it can be used in different fields.
- Explain the current limitations of computational thinking.

WHAT IS COMPUTATIONAL THINKING?

Answering this question is actually quite challenging. Proponents of computational thinking (CT) have until very recently spent a lot of time debating over how to define it.

As recently as 2011, a workshop was organised where numerous individuals came together to explore what the nature of CT should be. Some at this workshop argued in favour of a rigorous and consistent definition (Committee for the Workshops on Computational Thinking, 2011). Conversely, others have argued that trying to **strictly** define CT is unnecessary (Voogt et al., 2015).

In the latter's view, understanding CT should not be done by coming up with a definition in the usual sense (in other words, creating a list of conditions that something must meet before being considered a match). Voogt et al. argue that defining CT shares similar difficulties with defining what a 'game' is. (Must every game pit at least one player against another? Does every game have the concept of winning? Should every game include some element of luck or randomness?) Like our understanding of a game, they say, the approach to defining CT should be fuzzier and considered as a series of similarities and relationships that criss-cross and overlap.

Other reasons exist to make defining CT a challenging endeavour. First, computational thinking is strongly related to computer science (CS), which itself can be problematic to define satisfactorily. Like CS, CT includes a range of both abstract and concrete ideas. They both share a universal applicability, and this broadness, while making it powerful, also makes CT hard to define concisely.

CT is also an idea that's both new and old. It's new in the sense that the subject suddenly became a hotly debated topic in 2006 after Wing's talk (Wing, 2006). However, many of its core ideas have already been discussed for several decades, and along the way people have packaged them up in different ways. For example, as far back as 1980,

Seymour Papert of the Massachusetts Institute of Technology pioneered a technique he called 'procedural thinking' (Papert, 1980). It shared many ideas with what we now think of as CT. Using procedural thinking, Papert aimed to give students a method for solving problems using computers as tools. The idea was that students would learn how to create algorithmic solutions that a computer could then carry out; for this he used the Logo programming language.[4] Papert's writings have inspired much in CT, although CT has diverged from this original idea in some respects.

Nevertheless, during the 10 years following Wing's talk, a number of succinct definitions were attempted. A small sample of them features in Table 1.1. While they hint at similar ideas, there appears to be some diversity in what these people say. Perhaps Voogt et al. were right, and our best hope of understanding CT is to build up those overlapping, criss-crossing concepts. As luck would have it, this work was already done by Cynthia Selby (Selby, 2013), when she scoured the CT literature for concepts and divided them into two categories: concepts core to CT, and concepts that are somehow peripheral and so should be excluded from a definition.

Table 1.1 A list of definitions of computational thinking

Definition	Source
'Computational thinking is the thought processes involved in formulating a problem and expressing its solution(s) in such a way that a computer—human or machine—can effectively carry out.'	(Wing, 2014)
'The mental activity for abstracting problems and formulating solutions that can be automated.'	(Yadav et al., 2014)
'The process of recognising aspects of computation in the world that surrounds us, and applying tools and techniques from Computer Science to understand and reason about both natural and artificial systems and processes.'	(Furber, 2012)
'A mental orientation to formulating problems as conversions of some input to an output and looking for algorithms to perform the conversions. Today the term has been expanded to include thinking with many levels of abstractions, use of mathematics to develop algorithms, and examining how well a solution scales across different sizes of problems.'	(Denning, 2009)
'[Teaching CT is teaching] how to think like an economist, a physicist, an artist, and to understand how to use computation to solve their problems, to create, and to discover new questions that can fruitfully be explored.'	(Hemmendinger, 2010)

In this book, I will follow a very similar approach to Selby. Certain concepts are considered as 'core' to CT and are covered in great detail. Others are included, but treated as peripheral and covered in much less detail.

This book considers the core concepts of CT to be:[5]

- logical thinking;
- algorithmic thinking;
- decomposition;
- generalisation and pattern recognition;
- modelling;
- abstraction;
- evaluation.

Other peripheral concepts will be mentioned, but not treated as essential to the topic of CT. They include:

- data representation;
- critical thinking;
- computer science;
- automation;
- simulation/visualisation.

I will define individual concepts as they are introduced over the course of the book.

HOW IS COMPUTATIONAL THINKING USED?

CT can be applied by anyone who is attempting to solve a problem and have a computer play a role in the solution. To give us some idea of how CT is used, not just in computer science but in a range of subject areas, we can look at examples (sourced from Barr and Stephenson (2011)) of the core computational thinking concepts just listed.

For example, what could algorithmic thinking mean in different situations? To a computer scientist, it means the study of algorithms and their application to different problems. To a mathematician, it might mean carrying out long division factoring or doing carries in addition or subtraction. A scientist might think of it as the process of doing an experimental procedure.

Similarly, abstraction has application beyond the computer scientist's view of it. When a linguist uses simile and metaphor, or writes a story with branches, they're using abstraction, as are social scientists who summarise facts and use them to draw conclusions. When a scientist builds a model or a mathematician uses algebra, they too have introduced abstraction into their work.

The following are examples from other sources discussing specific examples of CT in action.

Example: Pipelining a graduation ceremony

Dean Randy Bryant was pondering how to make the diploma ceremony at commencement go faster. By careful placement of where individuals stood, he designed an efficient pipeline so that upon the reading of each graduate's name and honors by Assistant Dean Mark Stehlik, each person could receive his or her diploma, then get a handshake or hug from Mark, and then get his or her picture taken. This pipeline allowed a steady stream of students to march across the stage (though a pipeline stall occurred whenever the graduate's cap would topple while getting hug from Mark).

(Wing, 2011)

Example: Predicting climate change

Predicting global climate change is only possible because of advanced computer models. According to the UK Met Office, 'The only way to predict the day-to-day weather and changes to the climate over longer timescales is to use computer models.'

(Furber, 2012)

Example: Sorting music charts

I showed up to a big band gig, and the band leader passed out books with maybe 200 unordered charts and a set list with about 40 titles we were supposed to get out and place in order, ready to play. Everyone else started searching through the stack, pulling out charts one-at-a-time. I decided to sort the 200 charts alphabetically $O(N \log N)$[6] and then pull the charts $O(M \log(N))$. I was still sorting when other band members were halfway through their charts, and I started to get some funny looks, but in the end, I finished first. That's computational thinking.

(Roger Dannenberg in Wing, 2011)

Example: Assisting police, lawyers and judges

Computational Thinking has a long tradition in influencing the law, especially in the dream of providing a set of logical rules that can automate the process of reaching a verdict, [underpinning] its desire to minimise human discretion and maximise predictability of outcome... legal reasoning systems have been making inroads where they merely try to assist those making legal decisions. For instance, researchers at the Joseph Bell Centre have built a system that constructs a space of hypotheses to explain the evidence in a crime scene. This has been used to remind detectives of hypotheses they might otherwise have missed.

(Bundy, 2007)

DISCLAIMERS

This section discusses common misunderstandings about CT, as well as its current shortcomings.

What is computational thinking not?

There is bound to be some confusion over what CT is and is not. For one thing, it's closely related to other subjects, like computer science and programming, and distinguishing between them may present difficulties. For another, its definition is broad and has been subject to debate for several years. This section will discuss something that some people might have been led to believe about CT which isn't necessarily the case. In the process, more details about CT's nature will be revealed.

First, teaching computational thinking is not the same as teaching computer science. The main aim of teaching the latter is to educate students in the study and application of the principles of mathematical computation. Perhaps to counter this impression, some, including Jeannette Wing, have said that computational thinking is 'thinking like a computer scientist'. However, others have criticised this phrase (for example, Denning, 2009; Hemmendinger, 2010) because it leaves in place a strong association with computer science, which runs the risk of people seeing it not as an everyday skill, but merely as a repackaging of CS.

Teaching programming (a subfield of CS) is mainly done to educate students in how best to write programs, and it focuses on the production of high-quality software. CT, while sharing some aspects with these other subjects, is better described as an approach to problem-solving. What makes it distinct from other problem-solving approaches is that CT assumes a computer will execute the eventual solution.

CT teaches an approach to problem-solving where the ultimate aim is to provide a solution whose form means it is ready to be programmed into a computer.

CT takes a relatively small subset of concepts – which just happen to be important to CS – and uses them to construct a widely applicable, problem-solving approach.

These distinctions are important. Teaching computing skills as a mandatory part of the school syllabus has already been attempted in many places around the world. While these endeavours are noble and worthwhile, evidence is inconclusive about whether or not they succeed in their aim of teaching **transferable** skills (Voogt et al., 2015); that is to say, skills that students can intuitively take with them into various domains. CT attempts to perform better in this regard. By distilling some of the core aspects of CS that are relevant in many other fields, CT can be a course in the core school syllabus that is relevant to everyone. In the UK computing curriculum for example, CT already plays a big role (Department for Education, 2013). It can even be part of a CS or programming course that focuses exclusively on computer-based problem-solving.

In stressing the differences between computer science and computational thinking, it's worth pointing out that CT concepts are hardly exclusive to CS. As David Hemmendinger

(2010) points out, 'Constructing models, finding and correcting errors, drawing diagrams, analyzing – these are all parts of scientific (and other) activities.' Natural scientists, for example, have long been advocating that computation is a 'third leg' of the scientific process (alongside theory and experimentation) and that computational thinking is essential to their work (Denning, 2009).

> [The] ultimate goal should not be to teach everyone to think like a computer scientist, but rather to teach them to apply these common elements to solve problems and discover new questions that can be explored within and across all disciplines.
> (Barr and Stephenson, 2011)

Current shortcomings

We'll very soon proceed to consider the details of computational thinking. Before that happens, however, an honest discussion of the subject in its current form should be up front with any shortcomings. Keep in mind that these may disappear as CT matures.

Maturity

Although it has influences and predecessors dating back several decades, CT as a formal concept is still relatively immature. Workshops were organised to explore the meaning of CT only five years prior to this book being written. As little as three years ago, Cynthia Selby wrote an important paper proposing a definition for CT (Selby, 2013), because definitions at the time were still vague. Most other disciplines have long since stopped organising gatherings to decide what exactly it is they do. Nevertheless, a consensus is now emerging on what to include in a definition, largely in line with Selby's proposal of CT as 'a focused approach to problem solving, incorporating thought processes that utilize abstraction, decomposition, algorithms, evaluation, and generalizations' (2013). ('What is computational thinking?' on p. 7.)

Efficacy

A further consequence of CT's youth is the relative paucity of evidence for how effective teaching CT actually is. It has so far not been taught widely for an extended time. Nevertheless, the body of evidence will grow as studies into its efficacy are conducted. Experience reports and testimonials provide a more immediate form of evidence.

Perceived imperialism

Other commentators have cautioned that proponents of CT risk being imperialistic and off-putting. Their claims like 'you should think like a computer scientist' or 'computational thinking is X' (where X is something they approve of) appear territorial. As David Hemmendinger (2010) said, proponents should be careful that CT doesn't get into the habit of saying, 'If it's a good way of thinking, then it's ours.' It should be noted that many practices in CT are not original to the subject. In fact, they're not all original to computer science; many of them have been used in other fields as well as everyday life for a long time. They do not simply become computational by virtue of finding application in computing.

However, it does somewhat mitigate CT's immaturity when you realise that its constituent parts (such as logic, algorithms and decomposition) are individually tried, tested and mature.

SUMMARY

Computational thinking is an approach to problem-solving that involves using a set of practices and principles from computer science to formulate a solution that's executable by a computer. It's not just for programmers. In fact, it's applicable in a diverse array of fields.

EXERCISES

EXERCISE 1

List the core concepts of CT.

EXERCISE 2

Give an example of how you think people in each of the following occupations think computationally:

- A. mathematician;
- B. scientist;
- C. engineer;
- D. linguist.

EXERCISE 3

Think of everyday activities in which you participate that involve computational thinking.

2 LOGICAL AND ALGORITHMIC THINKING

OBJECTIVES

- Learn the importance of logic to computational thinking.
- Appreciate the difference between deductive and inductive reasoning.
- Understand Boolean logic and its importance to computation.
- See the importance of using logical and mathematical notation instead of natural language.
- Learn the properties of algorithms: sequence, iteration, selection.
- Understand the importance of state in algorithms.
- See common mistakes made in logical and algorithmic thinking and learn how to avoid them.

APPROACH

Logic and algorithms are essential to CT. They underpin the subject and rear their heads repeatedly throughout its application. The good news is: humans already have an innate, intuitive understanding of both logic and algorithms. The bad news is: they are both mathematical concepts in nature. Consequently, each has its own set of rules, procedures and definitions, which are very precise and systematic. That means you can't rely solely on your intuition when dealing with these topics, otherwise you'll make mistakes.

The best way to overcome this is to learn the precise, yet difficult core concepts. One could write a whole book just on logic or algorithms (many already have), but such a comprehensive treatment lies far out of scope for this volume, where they are just one topic of many. Consequently, this chapter must narrow its focus.

Research exists that shows us where newcomers tend to make mistakes (Pane et al., 2001), which will allow this chapter to concentrate on the more troublesome spots. I will focus on just a few core elements relevant to getting you into the habit of thinking logically and algorithmically. By the end of the chapter, you will have learned how to apply logic and algorithms to problem-solving. With some practice, they should become second nature.

LOGICAL THINKING

This section shows how important logic is to computational thinking. It introduces logical reasoning, along with Boolean and symbolic logic, and shows how to turn intuitive ideas into mathematically sound, logical expressions.

In brief: Logic

Put simply, logic is a system used for distinguishing between correct and incorrect arguments. By 'argument', I'm not referring to two people in a shouting match. I mean the philosophical idea of an argument; namely a chain of reasoning that ends up in a conclusion.

Logic includes a set of principles that, when applied to arguments, allow us to demonstrate what is true. You need no special training to begin doing this, as this classic introductory example of a logical argument demonstrates:

1. Socrates is a man.
2. All men are mortal.
3. Therefore, Socrates is mortal.

Even those of us without philosophy degrees understand this argument. We perform this particular brand of reasoning all the time (there's a draught in the room; a window is open; therefore, the draught is coming from the window). However, we don't always carry it out **correctly**, which can lead us to form wrong conclusions. And since we use computers essentially to automate our reasoning, we must learn to perform logic correctly before writing a computer solution.

In a sense, applying logic is a way of developing and testing a hypothesis. Using this way of thinking, applying logic assumes you already know at least some things for sure and allows you to use that knowledge to arrive at some further conclusions.

In a logical argument, each individual thing you already know (or assume) is called a **premise**. A premise is like any ordinary statement you or I might make, except that it can be evaluated to obtain an answer of 'true' or 'false'. A premise, therefore, has a **truth value**. In the Socrates example, our premises fit this requirement. It is either true or not that all men are mortal. The same goes for whether Socrates is a man or not. Other forms of expression, like questions or commands, can't be premises to an argument. It's neither true nor false to say 'Break a leg!' or ask 'What time is it?', for example.

Once all the premises are stated, the next step is to analyse them and react accordingly with a conclusion. Most of the magic lies in this step and this is what we will focus on.

Inductive vs deductive arguments

It's important to realise that some logical arguments are stronger than others. In fact, you can categorise arguments based on their certainty. The two best-known categories are **deductive** and **inductive**.

A deductive argument is the strongest form of reasoning because its conclusion necessarily follows from its premises (so long as it has been constructed properly and the premises are incontrovertibly true). We've already seen an example of deductive reasoning: the assessment of Socrates's mortality. While deductive arguments are strong, they have very strict standards, which makes them hard to construct. A deductive argument can fail in one of two ways.[7]

First, one of its premises could turn out to be false. For example:

1. Missie is a dog.
2. All dogs are brown.
3. Therefore, Missie is brown.

Premise 2 is false: not all dogs are brown. Even though the argument follows the exact same form as the Socrates example, it fails because at least one of its premises is false. Any argument with false premises fails. In computer jargon, this is an example of 'garbage in, garbage out'.

You can express the form of an argument by substituting symbols for objects. This helps when trying to work out if your reasoning is valid. The form of the Socrates example is: 'A is a B; All Bs are C; Therefore, A is C.' We'll see later how to handle logic symbolically.

The second way a deductive argument fails is when the conclusion doesn't necessarily follow from the premises. For example:

1. All tennis balls are round.
2. The Earth is round.
3. Therefore, the Earth is a tennis ball.

This argument fails because of faulty logic. Yes, all tennis balls are round, but so are lots of other things. In symbolic terms, this argument follows the form, 'All As are B; C is B; Therefore C is an A', but since this is in an invalid form, the argument is automatically invalid too.

Many books and online resources explain faulty forms of reasoning (i.e. fallacies). A good starting point is *Attacking Faulty Reasoning*, by T. Edward Damer (2005).

In reality, deductive arguments are relatively rare. You'll usually encounter them only when the knowledge you're dealing with is nice and neat. However, the real world often presents us with knowledge that's patchy, messy or provisional. Real-life issues are often nuanced (despite what you might read on social media). For this, we have inductive reasoning, which deals in probabilities rather than hard, black and white rules.

The premises in an inductive argument are not unquestionably true. Rather, we have some level of confidence in them. The form of the argument doesn't guarantee that the conclusion is true, but it probably results in a trustworthy conclusion. For example:

1. A bag contains 99 red balls and one black ball.
2. 100 people each drew one ball from the bag.
3. Sarah is one of those 100 people.
4. Therefore, Sarah probably drew a red ball.

This is a perfectly fine inductive argument, so long as you acknowledge the aspect of probability involved.

These aspects of reasoning are important in CT because computers are involved. The answer a computer gives is only as reliable as its reasoning, and since a computer is automating your reasoning, it's your responsibility to make sure:

1. that reasoning is valid;
2. you give the computer reliable input;
3. you know how to interpret what conclusion the computer reports, that is, is the result unquestionably true (the reasoning was deductive) or probably true (the reasoning was inductive)?

Boolean logic

Even though much of our reasoning is inductive, computers are not well equipped to deal with shades of grey. Their binary nature makes them more apt to deal with black and white issues. In order to instruct computers to make logical decisions, we need a system of logic that maps well onto this way of thinking. Boolean logic is such a method. It's a form of logic that deals with statements having one of only two values: true or false (usually). Different corresponding values could be used in other contexts: 1 or 0 for example, on or off, black or white.

Propositions

Statements in Boolean logic are also known as **propositions**, which have several basic properties.

First, a proposition can only have one value at any one time. In other words, a single proposition can't be both true and false simultaneously. There is no way to express levels of certainty. True means true; false means false. Consequently, you should keep in mind what was said earlier about deductive and inductive arguments: whereas real-life problems often present us with probabilities, the basic Boolean world deals in certainties. Some of your efforts will go into mapping real-world, grey areas onto Boolean black and white.

Second, propositions must have clear and unambiguous meaning. For example, a statement like: 'It is travelling fast', can certainly be evaluated as either true or false. However, it's ambiguous as stated. If 'it' is a car travelling at 150 mph along the motorway, that's certainly fast. But if 'it' is a spacecraft travelling towards Mars at 150 mph, that's undoubtedly slow.

> Qualify statements where necessary to avoid ambiguity. For example, you could restate the example above as: 'It is travelling fast, where "fast" is 70 mph or greater.'

Third, it's possible to combine individual propositions to make more complex ones (called **compound** propositions). For example, 'Jenny is wearing the shirt and the shirt is red.' This is helpful because we often want to evaluate several statements before reaching a conclusion. We make compound propositions by connecting single propositions together using **logical operators**.

Logical operators

Imagine you say, 'If the weather is sunny and I'm on holiday, then I'm going to lie in the garden.' You've just used logical operators. That statement contains two propositions, which serve as conditions for whether, or not, you decide to lounge on the grass:

1. The weather is sunny.
2. You're on holiday.

If both are true, then you can lie in the garden. If **either** of them are false (say, the weather is lousy or you have to go to work), then sunning yourself is not an option. That's because you joined them using the logical operator **AND**, which demands that both propositions should be true for the conclusion to be true.

Many different logical operators exist. It's worth looking at the most important ones in more detail because, even though we use them daily in informal speech, they have specific meanings in logic that occasionally run counter to our intuitive understanding.

To provide illustrative examples, we'll use the operators to describe the rules of a simple game: Noughts and Crosses.[8]

AND: the technical name for this operator is **conjunction**. (We just saw an example of a conjunction when we reasoned about whether to lie in the garden.) It chains propositions together in a way that **all** of them must be true for the conclusion to be true. If any of them are false, the conclusion is rendered false also. In classical logical arguments like we've seen so far, the presence of AND between propositions is implicit, but we can (and should) include them explicitly. So, for example:

1. At least one square on the board is still empty.
2. Neither player has achieved a row.
3. Therefore, the game is still in progress.

This can be expressed as:

> If at least one square on the board is still empty and neither player has achieved a row, then the game is still in progress.

OR: the technical name for this operator is **disjunction**. This operator chains propositions together in a way that **at least one** of them must be true for the conclusion to be true also. The only way that the conclusion is falsified is if all propositions are false. For example:

> If player 1 achieves a row or player 2 achieves a row, then the game is over.

In this case, only one condition needs to be true to end the game. In fact, due to the nature of the game, a maximum of one of these conditions can be true simultaneously. OR can also be used in cases when both conditions can be true at the same time:

> If a player achieves a row or all squares become occupied, then the game is over.

NOT: the technical name for this operator is **negation**. This operator doesn't chain propositions together itself, rather it modifies a single proposition. Specifically, it flips the truth value. Sometimes, negating a proposition can make it easier to express the chain of reasoning. For example:

> If a square is not occupied, then a player may add their symbol to that square.

IMPLIES: the technical name for this operator is **implication**. Using this operator is to state that there is a correlation between the two statements. If the first statement is true, then the second must be true also. Keep in mind, this is a correlation **not** a causation. Therefore, you can't necessarily work backwards from the conclusion of an implication. Consider this:

> If a player achieves a row, then the game is over.

It's true that a game ends when a player achieves a row, but it's not the only way to end a game. Saying 'the game is over, therefore a player achieved a row' is not always true.[9] The game could be over because it ended in a draw.

IF AND ONLY IF: the technical name for this operator is **biconditional**. This behaves very similarly to implication, but a biconditional means that the second proposition is influenced **solely** by the first. If the first is true, the second is true. If the first is false, the second is false. No exceptions. For example:

> If and only if all squares are occupied, then no more moves are possible.

In this case, we **can** work backwards. The only reason no more moves are possible is because all squares are occupied.

Symbolic logic

Logic requires precision and an absence of ambiguity, but it can be difficult to meet these requirements when using natural language. Not only can statements grow wordy and confusing, but their meaning can become almost unavoidably ambiguous.

Saying 'she's a fast reader or she's read the book before' raises the question: could both be true? I would say so. But what about 'Starter is a soup or a salad'? In this case, both can't be true. Notice, however, that in each case we used the word 'or' to join two propositions, but its use implied different meanings in both cases. The other logical operators can similarly be misused to mean different things.

To help us manage our reasoning, mathematics gives us symbolic logic, which recommends using symbols instead of natural language sentences. The earlier example, 'If at least one square on the board is still empty and neither player has achieved a row...' contains two propositions that are replaceable with symbols. If,

P = at least one square on the board is still empty

Q = neither player has achieved a row

S = the game is still in progress

then we can say:

If P and Q, then S

Not only does that reduce the clutter, but it becomes more intuitive to treat each proposition as a variable. After all, each proposition has a value that can be true or false at different times.

The operators, too, are often replaced by symbols (see Table 2.1).

Table 2.1 Logical operators and their symbols

Operator name	Symbol	Example
AND	$\land$	$A \land B$
OR	$\lor$	$A \lor B$
NOT	$\neg$	$\neg A$
IMPLIES	$\rightarrow$	$A \rightarrow B$
IF AND ONLY IF	$\leftrightarrow$	$A \leftrightarrow B$

Our example can then further be reduced to:

$$P \land Q \leftrightarrow S$$

(Rather than overload you with symbols just now, I'll continue to use the operator name rather than the symbol. When you see the operator name in upper case letters, it specifically means the logical operator.)

Symbolic logic also gives each logical operator formal rules, which promote precision and eliminate ambiguity. The meaning of each logical operator is specified in precise mathematical detail. The standard way to do this is to use a truth table. This lists all the possible combinations of values of the propositions. The truth table states whether each combination is logically valid or not. Let's start by looking at the truth table for conjunctions.

To read a truth table, take it one line at a time. The first line of Table 2.2 says that if both propositions are individually valid by themselves, then it's valid to say they are both true together. In the three other eventualities, it is invalid to say they are both true together because one or both propositions are false.

Table 2.2 Truth table of conjunction (logical AND)

P	Q	P AND Q
True	True	True
True	False	False
False	True	False
False	False	False

Keep in mind that the use of 'True' and 'False' can be replaced by other pairs of opposing symbols. Table 2.3 shows the same information as Table 2.2, except that it uses 1 and 0 instead of True and False.

Table 2.3 Truth table of conjunction (using 1 and 0 symbols)

P	Q	P AND Q
0	0	0
0	1	0
1	0	0
1	1	1

Figure 2.1 is a Venn diagram depicting the behaviour of conjunctions.

Figure 2.1 Venn diagram for the AND operator

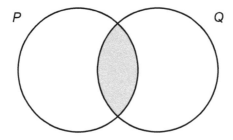

Table 2.4 Truth table of disjunction (logical OR)

P	Q	P OR Q
True	True	True
True	False	True
False	True	True
False	False	False

Table 2.4 shows that it is valid to consider a disjunction true so long as one or more of its propositions are true. That means the intention behind the earlier example – 'A starter can be soup or a salad [but not both]' – doesn't align with this logical meaning of OR (see Figure 2.2).[10]

Table 2.5 Truth table of negation (logical NOT)

P	NOT P
True	False
False	True

Figure 2.2 Venn diagram for the OR operator

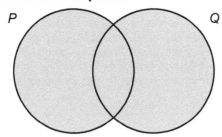

P   Q

Figure 2.3 pictorially represents the difference between a proposition with and without the NOT operator. In other words, whatever is true becomes false, and whatever is false becomes true.

Figure 2.3 Venn diagram for the NOT operator

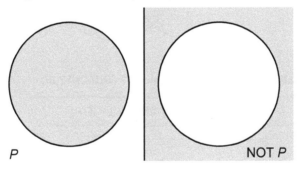

P   NOT P

Table 2.6 Truth table of implication (logical IMPLIES)

P	Q	P IMPLIES Q
True	True	True
True	False	False
False	True	True
False	False	True

The first two lines of Table 2.6 seem sensible. If P being true implies Q is true and both are indeed true, then the implication is valid. Likewise, if P is true, but its consequent is not true, then the implication is invalid. The last two lines, however, seem odd. The implication is valid regardless of the value of P.

Why is it valid for P to imply Q when P is false? In 'P implies Q', P is known as the antecedent and Q as the consequent. The explanation is that no conclusion can be drawn about an implication when the antecedent (i.e. P) is false. Consider the statement 'if it is raining (P), then the grass is wet (Q)'. Saying 'it is not raining' (NOT P) doesn't contradict that the grass is wet. The grass could be wet for another reason, such as because the sprinkler is on. Since there is no contradiction, mathematicians have judged that an implication with a false antecedent is true until proven otherwise (see Figure 2.4).

Figure 2.4 Venn diagram for the IMPLIES operator

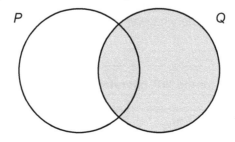

Table 2.7 Truth table of biconditional (logical IF AND ONLY IF)

P	Q	Q IF AND ONLY IF P
True	True	True
True	False	False
False	True	False
False	False	True

Figure 2.5 depicts the IF AND ONLY IF operator. Only when values agree can the statement be considered valid. P and Q can agree when their values overlap, either by being both true or both false.

Figure 2.5 Venn diagram for the IF AND ONLY IF operator

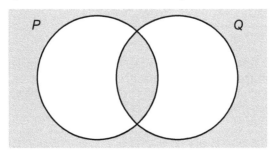

ALGORITHMIC THINKING

We now move from logical thinking on to algorithmic thinking. This section will introduce the basic properties of algorithms (sequence, iteration and selection), as well as the use of state.

In brief: Algorithms

Logic and algorithms are not the same. Rather, algorithms build on logic because, as part of their work, they make logical decisions. The other part of their work is 'stitching' those decisions together.[11]

Logic gives you a set of rules that allow you to reason about some aspect of the world. That world does not have to be static. Logic can deal with things that are dynamic and continually changing. This we saw with the Noughts and Crosses examples. The rules of the game were laid out as logical statements. Sometimes the propositions were true, sometimes false. By working out their truth values, we could come to conclusions about how the game would be in different situations.

But if we want to go further, if we want to build functioning systems based on rules, then logic alone isn't sufficient. We need something that can integrate all these rules and execute actions based on the outcomes of evaluating them. That something is algorithms, and they are the power behind all real-world computational systems.

> **Algorithm**: a sequence of clearly defined steps that describe a process to follow a finite set of unambiguous instructions with clear start and end points.

Algorithms are a way of specifying a multi-step task, and are especially useful when we wish to explain to a third party (be it human or machine) how to carry out steps with extreme precision. As with logic, humans already have an intuitive understanding of algorithms. But, at the same time, a rich and precise science dictates exactly how algorithms work. Gaining a deeper understanding of this will improve your algorithmic thinking. This is important because a correct algorithm is the ultimate basis of any computer-based solution.

Intuition vs precision

Algorithms are tricky things. In a sense, they're intuitive concepts that have been with us for centuries, yet they only received a definition in the last hundred years or so (Knuth, 1997). It's easy to articulate them intuitively, but at the same time computer science's concept of an algorithm is multi-faceted and can take beginners some time to comprehend. Misunderstandings commonly arise (see Pea et al., 1987; Pane et al., 2001), so we'll focus on building a solid understanding.

Before going into the hard details, let's take as our starting point the simple definition in the box above. You've very likely dealt with algorithms in this sense already. Anyone who has followed a recipe while cooking has encountered something like this. Or anyone who went on a treasure hunt as a child. Or anyone who has assembled furniture. An algorithm is a way of making our processes explicit so that you can communicate them to someone else in a way that allows them to carry out those same steps too. These are only analogies however. Strictly speaking, algorithms perform operations on data rather than cake ingredients or coffee tables.

The earliest pioneers of computer science examined what it meant to communicate ideas to a computer. They sought a means for us to take the ideas in our heads and put them into a form that computers can understand and compute on our behalf. They discovered that our existing, intuitive ideas of algorithms were insufficient, so they took those ideas and re-formed them into the kind of clear and unambiguous form that computers require. By doing so, they made algorithms our means for giving computers instructions.

As precise as they became, algorithms were also rendered more complex, so much so that a formal description of them can stretch over several paragraphs. In our case, the best way to approach a definition is to take each property of algorithms, one by one, and explain it. Along the way, we'll use an analogy to one of our intuitive ideas of an algorithm (in this case, following a recipe) to help us understand.

Defining algorithms

The definition of an algorithm is complex and involves several properties. This subsection describes those properties.

Collection of individual steps

The first property to mention just restates something said earlier: an algorithm is a **collection of individual steps**. A recipe fits this analogy quite simply, filled as it is with steps like: 'pre-heat the oven to 180 degrees Celsius' or 'add two tablespoons of sugar to the bowl'.

Definiteness

Following on from that property is **definiteness**, meaning that every step must be precisely defined. Each step in an algorithm can have one and only one meaning, otherwise it is ambiguous. Similarly, chefs have come to the same conclusion, which is why they produce recipes using precise measurements instead of writing things like 'some sugar' or 'cook it for a while'.

Sequential

Algorithms are also **sequential**. The steps that make up the process must be carried out in the order specified. Failing to do this means that the result of executing the algorithm is likely incorrect. Think back to the analogy. Dicing an onion and frying an onion are different steps. Dicing an onion **before** you fry it has a different outcome than the reverse. Similarly, multiplying a number by 2 then adding 5 to it yields a different result from adding 5 first **then** doubling it. Like a recipe, you must respect the sequence when running through an algorithm for it to have any meaningful result.

Detour: State in algorithms

It's worth going on a brief detour here to examine why sequence is so important to algorithms. It's all to do with **state**, by which I simply mean the current values of all the things the algorithm is keeping track of. As a computer progresses through an algorithm, just as you progress through a recipe, the state of things can change. Clearly sequencing the steps of an algorithm ensures the that state always changes in the same way whenever the algorithm is executed.

> **State:** the current configuration of all information kept track of by a program at any one instant in time.

There's an important implication to this: there is **no 'global view'** when it comes to algorithms. This means that, at each instant in time, the environment in which the algorithm is being run exists in some particular state. But by the time the next step is executed, something might have changed. The environment really exists as a series of snapshots, one for each step of the algorithm. The recipe analogy spells this out. At the start you might have butter, flour, milk, eggs and sugar. After each step, you take a photograph of the kitchen. The photos will show that, bit by bit, the state of the ingredients changes. Flour goes into a bowl; then the eggs join it; then the butter goes into the pan; and so on. There is no global view of the ingredients; just a series of snapshots.

For algorithms, this means that individual steps are executed one by one and only a single step can be under consideration at any one time. Once a step has been executed, the computer forgets all about it and moves on to the next.

This means that some way of 'remembering' things that happened in previous steps needs to be provided. If you, the algorithm's author, want the computer to remember the result of a step for later use, you have to explicitly tell the computer to do so. Algorithms provide for this by means of **variables**.

> Despite sharing the same name, variables in programming do not correspond exactly to variables from mathematics. Mathematical variables are used in a function to represent quantities that vary. A variable in an algorithm is more like a scratchpad that's used as a placeholder for important information the computer should keep note of. It can also have its values updated throughout an algorithm's execution (this is called **assignment**). For example, if your algorithm counts the number of times a specific word appears in a news article, it would use a variable to keep track of the number as it reads through the text.

Controlling algorithm execution

In this section we'll look at two ways of controlling the execution of an algorithm.

Iteration

As well as recording information pertinent to a problem, variables can also be used to control the execution of an algorithm. At a basic level, they can be used in two ways. One of those is **iteration**, also known as looping. Iteration allows you to repeat a series of steps over and over, without the need to write out each individual step manually. This can be very useful. Imagine having to write out the lyrics to a song like *99 Bottles of Beer*. If you don't know it, it goes like this:

> 99 bottles of beer on the wall,
> 99 bottles of beer.
> Take one down, pass it around,
> 98 bottles of beer on the wall.
>
> 98 bottles of beer on the wall,
> 98 bottles of beer.
> Take one down, pass it around,
> 97 bottles of beer on the wall.

And keeps repeating until the last verse:

> 1 bottle of beer on the wall,
> 1 bottle of beer.
> Take it down, pass it around,
> No more bottles of beer on the wall.

To save yourself a lot of typing, you could, instead, write just one verse along with instructions on how to repeat all the following verses. Something like:

> X stands for the number of bottles. At the start, X is 99. Sing the verse:
>
> X bottles of beer on the wall,
> X bottles of beer.
> Take one down, pass it around,
> X-1 bottles of beer on the wall.
>
> Subtract 1 from X. Repeat the verse if X is greater than 0, otherwise finish.

This is an example of iteration in action and it shows two things:

1. How a variable is used to control algorithm execution. The thing that changes from one loop to the next is encapsulated in a variable, in this case the number of remaining beer bottles. Everything else stays constant.
2. You must specify under what conditions the loop should terminate.

This last point brings us to the second method used for controlling algorithm execution.

Selection

In a loop, one way to control how many times the steps are repeated is simply to specify it; something like 'repeat the following steps 99 times'. But notice that the example above doesn't do that. Instead, it uses *selection* (aka a conditional), which is a way to test a variable's current value and make a decision based on it. In the '99 Bottles' song, the conditional comes at the end (repeat the verse **if X is greater than 0**). It's telling the computer to do something so long as the condition specified is currently true. So long as a positive number of bottles remain, that condition is true and so the verse is repeated. But we know that the number is steadily decreasing and will eventually reach zero. At this point the condition becomes false (zero is not greater than zero), and so the verse is not repeated again.

Conditions can be used at any stage in an algorithm, not only to control loops. Wherever they are, they all serve the same purpose: creating a point at which the computer has to decide between performing a set of steps or not, and encapsulating the information needed to make that decision.

Example algorithm

This example illustrates some of the ideas just discussed. It is a partial and very simple algorithm for controlling a game of Noughts and Crosses. It's written using **pseudocode**, which is an informal means of writing an algorithm. It's aimed at a human audience rather than a computer, but it nevertheless closely follows the conventions of programming languages. This means you can easily translate your ideas into real program code by first writing them as pseudocode.

```
 1. game is started
 2. begin loop:
    3. prompt player to choose a square
    4. if chosen square is not occupied, then put player's symbol in
       that square
    5. check board to see if a row has been achieved
    6. if a row has been achieved, then game is won
    7. if a row has not been achieved and no squares are available,
       then game is drawn
    8. switch to other player
 9. exit loop if game is won or game is drawn
10. display message 'Game over'
```

Let's examine this algorithm:

- When this algorithm is executed, the computer goes through each line one at a time. (This is an example of **sequence**.)

- Line 1 initialises a variable, **game**, with a particular value, `started` (**state**).

- Line 2 sets up the starting point of a loop (**iteration**). All lines that are 'inside' this loop are indented to make it clearer what's inside and outside.

- Line 3 asks for input from the player. The choice is recorded.

- Line 4 makes a **selection** based on the player's choice. (Incidentally, this is a rather user-unfriendly algorithm. If a player accidentally chooses an occupied square, they get no opportunity to fix their mistake!)

- Lines 6 and 7 both make selections, altering the value of the **game** variable under certain conditions.

- Line 9 is the end of the loop. A choice is made whether or not to go through the loop again depending on the associated condition **at this point**. There are two possibilities:

    1. The **game** variable hasn't been altered yet, meaning it still has the value **started**. In this case, execution moves back to line 3.
    2. At some point, the game was won or drawn. In either case, the loop ends and execution continues onto line 10, whereupon the game finishes with a traditional 'Game over' message.

'GOTCHAS'

When first encountering logic and algorithms, most people tend to make the same mistakes or faulty assumptions. This section will point them out and explain how to avoid them.

The need for clarity and meticulousness

You might have noticed the emphasis on clarity, precision and meticulousness when working with logic and algorithms. Computer programs demand precision in their rules and instructions to such an extent that it might have the appearance of pedantry. But it really isn't. There are good reasons behind the need for clarity, which all boil down to a computer's nature.

A couple of facts about this are worth pointing out:

- A computer will do exactly as it is told. If it is told to do something impossible, it will crash.

- A computer has no innate intelligence of its own. It will not do anything that it has not been instructed to do.

- A computer has no common sense. It will not try to interpret your instructions in different ways. It will not make assumptions or fill in the obvious blanks in an incomplete algorithm.

In short, a computer will do only what you tell it to do. If you don't tell it to do something, it won't do it. If you tell a computer to do something stupid, like divide a number by zero, it will try to do it anyway. If a computer does something you didn't think you told it to do, that's probably because you misunderstood your own instructions to it.

Earlier, I drew an analogy between an algorithm and a recipe. However, the audience for a recipe is another person. Granted, a person can be the audience for an algorithm, but people are used to communicating using natural language. Even when it's very formal, that language can still be ambiguous and sometimes open to interpretation. Furthermore, the author may leave certain things up to a reader's common sense rather than labour a point.

You must be mindful of the (electronic) computer's limitations outlined above. Think of giving a recipe to an exceedingly literal-minded robot from a cheesy sci-fi film. Would it be the robot's fault if it read 'stir the milk, flour and eggs in a bowl', then tried to climb into the bowl itself? Or if it waited forever for the 'dough to rise' because the dough hadn't begun to levitate yet?

The point is, the goal of problem-solving using computational thinking is a solution that a computer can execute. That means an algorithm with precise, unambiguous meaning that requires neither creative intelligence nor common sense to understand fully.

And that often means splitting hairs and spelling things out in seemingly pedantic detail.

Incorrect use of logical operators

Our intuitive understanding of language leads to other 'gotchas'. Something as seemingly straightforward as our use of the words 'and', 'or', 'not' and 'then' can catch us out. For example, the statement:

'Everyone whose surname begins with A and B is assigned to Group 1.'

might seem logical to a human, but to a computer, which strictly follows the logical meaning of AND, it's illogical. That's because, as written, the statement tests two things: does a surname begin with A and does it begin with B? However, no surname can have different first letters at the same time. You can ask a computer to carry out this test as much as you like, but it will always fail.

Furthermore, in everyday language, people sometimes use 'and' as a sequencing term, as in:

'The player took their turn and the game was finished.'

Again, that makes no logical sense to a computer. A logical statement like this describes a state of affairs at an instant in time. A player cannot make a move in a game when the game is finished.

To avoid confusion, never play loose with the phrasing of logic. Always use the correct operators. Truth tables are extremely helpful when in doubt.

> Logic and algorithms treat the 'if–then' form a little differently from each other. Consider 'if X, then Y'. Whereas a logical implication states how the truth values of X and Y are related, the intent of the algorithmic 'if–then' form is to make the execution of step Y dependent on X being true. If X isn't true, step Y isn't executed.

Missing certain eventualities

Another 'gotcha' related to the use of 'if–then' in algorithms is what to do when the condition is false. For example, here's an algorithm used to grade a student's work. It's very simple. A student can earn one of two grades (pass or fail) and the student requires a score over 50 per cent to gain a pass (see Figure 2.6).

Figure 2.6 Grading levels for fail and pass

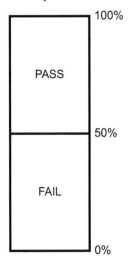

If score is greater than 50 per cent,
then mark student's grade as a pass.

Do you see a problem?

What happens in cases when the student scores 50 per cent or less? Common sense tells a human that the student should get a failing grade, because that's what the problem implies. But remember, computers have no common sense and won't do anything you don't tell them to do. That's why algorithms also include the 'if–then–else' form.[12] Using this, you could amend the algorithm to look like this:

   if score is greater than 50 per cent,
   then mark student's grade as a pass,
   else mark student's grade as a fail.

When the condition in an 'if–then–else' is true, only the part after the 'then' is executed; when the condition is false, only the part after the 'else' is executed.

Complex conditionals

By itself, the NOT operator is simple to understand. For example, the grading algorithm could be rewritten as follows:

   if score is not greater than 50 per cent,
   then mark student's grade as a fail,
   else mark student's grade as a pass.

No surprises there. However, difficulty can arise when a condition becomes more complex. Imagine an additional grade is introduced: students scoring over 80 per cent are awarded a distinguished pass (see Figure 2.7). A pass would only be awarded to scores over 50 and less than 80 per cent.

Figure 2.7 Grading levels for fail, ordinary pass and distinguished pass

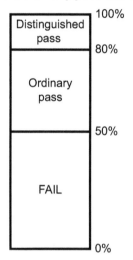

To check for an ordinary passing score, you might begin an 'if–then' that tests two conditions like this:

if score is not less than 51 per cent or greater than 80 per cent,
then mark student's grade as an ordinary pass
...

A deliberate mistake lies in this little algorithm. All will be revealed shortly.

That might seem precise at first glance, but it could be interpreted in at least two different ways. Specifically, does the 'not' apply to both conditions or only to the first? Taking everyday language as a guide suggests it applies to both, just like saying 'the car is not big or red' means the car is neither big nor red. However, the realms of natural language and logic don't always align. This is a case where they don't and we'll see why shortly.

To avoid such confusion, symbolic logic provides very specific rules about how to interpret the various parts of logical statements. These rules are called the **order of precedence**. They dictate in what order each part of a logical expression should be evaluated. It all works just like in mathematics.

Table 2.8 Order of precedence for selected logical operators

Rank	Operator	Name
1	( )	Parentheses
2	¬	Not
3	>	Greater than
	<	Less than
4	∧	Logical AND
5	∨	Logical OR

When evaluating something like

$$9 - 3 \times 4$$

you get different answers depending on the order in which you carry out the subtraction and the multiplication. But strictly speaking, there's only one correct answer. That's because the rules of the order of precedence dictate in which order each part is evaluated; those with higher precedence are carried out first. To make the order explicit, you can put brackets around each expression. If we were to put them in explicitly, it would look like this:

First the multiplication

$$9 - (3 \times 4)$$

then the subtraction

$$(9 - (3 \times 4))$$

Technically, that means exactly the same thing as the original expression. Now we can see clearly that the multiplication must happen first and so the correct answer is -3. If you wanted to perform the subtraction first, that would be fine, but you would need to put your own brackets into the expression.[13] In this case, it would appear so:

$$(9 - 3) \times 4$$

This changes the meaning of the expression and its result (24).

Let's return to our student grading example. Before applying the rules, we should rewrite the expression using correct notation. Taking each condition one by one:

score is not less than 50 per cent
becomes
¬ score < 51

while
    greater than 80 per cent
becomes
    score > 80

Connecting them with the proper OR symbol gives us:

$$\text{if} \neg score < 51 \lor score > 80$$

To help us see the order in which things are evaluated, put the implicit brackets in place. Negation has the highest precedence of the operators here, so it gets brackets first:

$$\text{if} \neg (score < 51) \lor score > 80$$

Comparisons have a higher precedence than disjunctions, so they get their brackets next (the left-hand comparison already has brackets thanks to the negation operator):

$$\text{if} \neg (score < 51) \lor (score > 80)$$

Finally, the disjunction gets its brackets.

$$\text{if} (\neg (score < 51) \lor (score > 80))$$

The expression is ready to be evaluated. To do that, we need to assign a value to 'score'. Let's arbitrarily choose 55.

Now that the brackets are in place, we can go from left to right, evaluating each piece as we go. NOT flips the truth value of the thing to its right, so we need to work out if that thing is true or not. 55 is not less than 51, therefore we substitute 'score < 51' with its truth value:

$$\text{if} \neg (false) \lor (score > 80)$$

In other words:

$$\text{if } true \lor (score > 80)$$

We've worked out the value of OR's left-hand condition. Now we need to evaluate the condition on its right. 55 is not greater than 80, therefore:

$$\text{if } true \lor false$$

Consulting the truth table for OR, we find that when either or both conditions are true, then the whole expression is true. In this case, the student correctly gets an ordinary pass.

Let's try another score to make sure the expression works for distinguished passes too. We'll use 85 as the score. 85 is not less than 51, therefore:

$$\text{if} \neg (false) \lor (score > 80)$$

In other words:

$$\text{if } true \lor (score > 80)$$

And 85 is greater than 80, so:

$$\text{if } true \lor true$$

Again, we've evaluated the expression to find that it is true. But this is not what we wanted. Look again at the expression in the context of the algorithm:

> if score is not less than 51% or greater than 80%,
> then mark student's grade as an ordinary pass,
> ...

We've demonstrated that, according to the algorithm in its present state, the student gets an ordinary pass even though they scored over 80!

The problem is that our natural language way of expressing our intentions doesn't quite agree with the rules of logic. To correct our original algorithm, we would have to put our own explicit brackets into the expression to 'override' the usual orders of precedence, like so:

$$\text{if} \neg (score < 51 \lor score > 80)$$

This time, we evaluate **everything** inside the brackets first before evaluating the negation. Now, for a score of 85, the procedure looks like this:

$$\text{if} \neg (score < 51 \lor score > 80)$$
$$\text{if} \neg (true \lor score > 80)$$
$$\text{if} \neg (true \lor true)$$
$$\text{if} \neg (true)$$
$$\text{if } false$$

The student will therefore not be assigned the wrong grade, which is good because it's always embarrassing when that happens.

> To avoid mistakes like this, it's a good idea to use the correct logical notation from the very start, even when you're just beginning to sketch out your ideas.

SUMMARY

Logic and systematic reasoning are key underpinnings of CT because computer programs are essentially an automation of our reasoning processes. Therefore, writing solutions requires a good understanding of logic and the ability to use proper notation over natural language. This chapter has covered the basics of inductive and deductive reasoning, as well as the importance of Boolean and symbolic forms of logic to computing.

Logic is an essential part of algorithms, which are the among the bedrock of computing. They are the core of any program and thus play a part in every computer-based solution. This chapter introduced the basic building blocks of every algorithm and the notion of state.

It's important in the case of both logic and algorithms to respect the need for a systematic approach. Although both can make intuitive sense on some level, it's also easy to make mistakes when considering them that way. The use of correct logical notation will help you to avoid making common mistakes.

EXERCISES

EXERCISE 1

Mark the following statements as true or false:

    A. An inductive logical argument makes conclusions that are probable rather than certain.

    B. So long as a deductive argument has true premises, then its conclusion is certain.

    C. In Boolean logic, a logical expression can have a maximum of two propositions.

    D. Logical AND has a higher precedence than logical OR.

    E. $x = x + 1$ would be a valid expression in an algorithm.

EXERCISE 2

A recipe database stores the recipes in Table 2.9.

Users can search for recipes by entering search terms, which the database matches to tags and cooking times. Consider the following search terms and decide which recipes will be returned:

    A. cooking time less than 20 minutes and not vegetarian;

    B. includes chicken or turkey but not garlic;

    C. doesn't include nuts.

Table 2.9 Recipes in the database

Name	Tags	Cooking time
Broiled chicken salad	Chicken, lettuce, gorgonzola cheese, lemon juice	15 mins
Holiday turkey	Turkey, rice, onion, walnuts, garlic	60 mins
Three-spice chicken	Chicken, ginger, cinnamon, garlic, green beans	30 mins
Lentil salad	Lentils, onion, peppers, walnuts, lettuce	20 mins
Garlic dip	Garlic, lemon juice, chickpeas, chicken broth	5 mins

EXERCISE 3

Here are some rules of thumb to apply when deciding which supermarket queue to join (assuming you want to spend as little time queuing as possible):

A. People in a queue who are carrying their items by hand take about one minute to be processed.

B. People carrying a basket take about two minutes to be processed.

C. People pushing a trolley take about five minutes to be processed for a half-empty trolley; ten minutes for a full trolley.

D. People in a self-service checkout are processed in about 80 per cent of the time of a normal checkout.

Express these rules of thumb as logical statements. Each statement should make a conclusion about the estimated queuing time.

EXERCISE 4

Take the logical statements from the previous question and incorporate them into an algorithm. The algorithm should take a queue as input, and should output the total estimated queueing time.

EXERCISE 5

Based on the algorithm for singing *99 Bottles of Beer*, write a pseudocode algorithm for singing *The 12 Days of Christmas*.

3 PROBLEM-SOLVING AND DECOMPOSITION

OBJECTIVES

- Explain how to apply a systematic approach to problem-solving.
- Discuss how to create a problem definition.
- Introduce strategies and considerations for the devising of solutions.
- Explain decomposition as a problem-solving strategy.
- Show the benefits of generalising from patterns in problems as well as techniques for creating them.

WHERE TO START

You have your problem. You're ready to start analysing it and coming up with a solution. But not just any solution; one that is specifically formed so that a computer could carry it out. You begin to look at the problem. A question dawns on you.

Where on earth do you start?

It's all very well saying 'come up with a solution'. Real-world problems tend to be big, complex things. Examining any non-trivial problem reveals all manner of hidden details, complex nuances and various facets to consider.

When faced with a complex task, it can be helpful to follow some kind of guide or process, like the instructions for a piece of self-assembly furniture. A step-by-step procedure for problem-solving would be an obvious benefit. Unfortunately, problem-solving is partly a **creative** process. Like painting a landscape or writing a novel, it cannot be totally systematised, but strategies, heuristics and good practices exist to help you during your creative endeavours. These are things that previous generations of problem solvers found useful for attacking a problem's complexity and this chapter will introduce you to them.

A systematic approach

An early example of a systematic approach to general problem-solving was introduced by George Pólya. He was a Hungarian mathematician who in 1945 wrote the first edition of an influential book called *How to Solve It* (Pólya, 1973), which is, impressively, still in print after more than half a century.

Despite its age, Pólya's book still abounds with relevant and helpful tips. Furthermore, it has guided many problem solvers down the years, including various authors who wrote successor books. I will refer to those and Pólya as we examine the various stages of problem-solving.

How to Solve It takes an approach to problem-solving inspired by the best traditions of mathematical and natural sciences.

Whereas the scientific method follows the steps:

- form hypothesis;
- plan experiment;
- execute experiment;
- evaluate results.

Pólya (1973) advocates:

- understand the problem;
- devise a plan;
- execute the plan;
- review and extend.

Computational thinking is compatible with this view of problem-solving. However, this chapter focuses on the first two stages, namely understanding the problem and devising a plan.

Don't panic

Getting started is hard. We all know that. Size, complexity and the sheer number of unknowns can frustrate our attempts to start, but a few rational hints can help us out.

First, **don't be put off by perceived size and complexity**. Big problems are rarely impenetrable monoliths. In fact, you'll usually find that a big problem is really a whole group of smaller, interrelated problems. As we'll see later in the chapter, the trick is to pick them apart and reduce a big problem into smaller, simpler, more manageable ones.

Second, **resist the urge to jump straight into writing a solution**. If you do, the best probable outcome is that you'll solve only a very specific version of the problem. More likely, you'll get partway before finding you're solving the wrong problem altogether.

Now, if you're ready, we can begin by defining the problem.

DEFINING THE PROBLEM

The hardest part of problem solving is characterising the problem.
(Michaelson, 2015)

Problem-solving involves transforming an undesirable state of affairs (the start point) into a desirable state of affairs (the goal). The start point and the goal are intimately linked. By examining the start point, you nail down exactly what is undesirable and why. In doing so, you reveal more about what your goal should be.

You might find things undesirable for any number of reasons.

- Maybe your current process is too slow, in which case your goal will involve making measurable improvements to the process's speed.

- Maybe you regularly need to make certain decisions, but you have too much data to handle. This implies your goal may be to somehow automate your decision-making strategy or filter information before you analyse it.

- Maybe you have missing information about how something behaves. This suggests producing a model or simulation of it.

When trying to understand the problem, Pólya tells us that 'it is foolish to answer a question that you do not understand', and offers the following advice:

- If someone else gave it to you, try **restating the problem in your own words**.

- Try and represent the problem using **pictures and diagrams**. Humans deal better with visual representations.

- There will be knowns and unknowns at the start. You should ensure that enough information is known for you to form a solution. If there isn't, **make the unknowns explicit**.[14]

Whatever the problem, the key thing to remember is that a goal defines what needs to be done and **not** how it should be done. Thinking about details like designs and algorithms at this stage is too early. Focus instead on what your goal looks like.

When considering what the goal looks like, ask yourself: how do you know when the problem is solved? In other words, how will you know when you're done? 'Done' could mean that efficiency has increased 50 per cent. Or that steps 2 to 5 of a process are executable with zero human intervention.

Try describing how a working solution should look. Or perhaps describe how it should work, but only at a **very** broad level (remember, details are no concern yet). If your problem is to plan a conference (allocating slots to all the speakers, scheduling breaks and meals, arranging enough auditoriums, etc.), then the end product would be a time plan in which every event has a time, location and people assigned.

However you specify the goal, make sure that your language is **clear and specific**. For example, if you aim to improve the speed of the current system, don't specify your end goal simply as 'it should be faster'. Give it measurable accuracy.

If the end goal is more complicated, you could describe every desired 'feature' of the solution. In this case, you'd be writing a specification. As you develop your solution, keep comparing it to the specification to make sure you're solving the problem correctly.

Always write your problem definition and goal as though someone else will eventually take what you've produced and verify for themselves that you've solved the problem. This will force you to take a more objective, considered view.

DEVISING A SOLUTION: SOMETHING TO KEEP IN MIND

Once you have a finished problem definition complete with goal, you can consider the strategy for finding a solution.

This chapter will focus on one strategy in particular – decomposition – since it is the problem-solving strategy at the core of computational thinking, but will also look briefly at several others that can be applied. Before looking at strategies however, there are a few things about the problem-solving process you should keep in mind.

Quality

First, notice that I said **a** solution and not **the** solution. For any problem, there are usually multiple solutions: some good, some terrible and others somewhere in-between. You should focus on finding the best solution you can.

For the **overall** problem, there is likely no perfect solution. Trade-offs between competing parts are almost inevitable. On the other hand, individual parts of a problem may be 'perfected', in as much as their role in the overall solution might be optimisable.[15]

Collaboration

Making problem-solving a collaborative effort is often helpful. Something as simple as explaining your current work out loud often helps you to spot mistakes or potential improvements. Seek out the views of others. People's minds work in different ways.

We may not kill an idea stone dead, as you might do when writing fiction, but a fresh perspective might show where you're going wrong and help you improve it. While you have the attention of other people, try brainstorming with them. Brainstorming sessions thrive on spontaneity. All ideas, however radical they seem, should be recorded, and you should reject nothing out of hand. In fact, wild ideas are to be encouraged. In among those crazy ideas may lie the seeds of a creative new approach that you might ordinarily have missed or self-censored.

Iteration

You should accept that your first attempt at a solution will rarely be the best one. Instead of trying to solve everything in one fell swoop, take an iterative approach. Go back and repeat some of the previous steps in an attempt to improve your current solution.

How many steps you repeat depends on the solution's shortcomings. If your model of the problem is mainly correct but contains an inaccuracy, you may need to go back just a couple of steps to correct the model. If you find that your whole understanding of the problem was wrong, you'll have to go back and reappraise the problem from nearer the beginning.

DECOMPOSITION

As well as providing a guide to general problem-solving, George Pólya's book *How to Solve It* also catalogues different problem-solving techniques called heuristics. A **heuristic** is a specific strategy in problem-solving that usually yields a good enough answer, though not necessarily an optimal one. Examples include trial and error, using a rule of thumb or drawing an analogy.

Computational thinking promotes one of these heuristics to a core practice: **decomposition**, which is an approach that seeks to break a complex problem down into simpler parts that are easier to deal with. Its particular importance to CT comes from the experiences of computer science. Programmers and computer scientists usually deal with large, complex problems that feature multiple interrelated parts. While some other heuristics prove useful some of the time, decomposition almost invariably helps in managing a complex problem where a computerised solution is the goal.

Decomposition is a divide-and-conquer strategy, something seen in numerous places outside computing:

- Generals employ it on the battlefield when outnumbered by the enemy. By engaging only part of the enemy forces, they neutralise their opponent's advantage of numbers and defeat them one group at a time.

- Politicians use it to break opposition up into weaker parties who might otherwise unite into a stronger whole.

- When faced with a large, diverse audience, marketers segment their potential customers into different stereotypes and target each one differently.

Within the realm of CT, you use divide and conquer when the problem facing you is too large or complex to deal with all at once. For example, a problem may contain several interrelated parts, or a particular process might be made up of numerous steps that need spelling out. Applying decomposition to a problem requires you to pick all these apart.

Recursion: a technique used to simplify a problem. It defines the solution to a large, complex problem in terms of smaller, simpler problems of the same form as the original problem. This is a very powerful idea and one that is heavily used in CS.

By applying decomposition, you aim to end up with a number of sub-problems that can be understood and solved individually. This may require you to apply the process recursively (see above). That is to say, the problem is re-formed as a series of smaller problems that, while simpler, might be still too complex, in which case they too need breaking down, and so on. Visually this gives the problem definition a **tree structure**.

The conceptual idea of a tree structure is very important to CS and often goes hand in hand with the idea of recursion. A tree represents a collection of entities[16] organised into hierarchical relationships. Each 'parent' entity may have any number of 'child' entities (including none). A tree has a single 'root' entity and all childless entities are called 'leaves'. Visually, it resembles a tree – admittedly an upside-down one, with the 'root' at the top and the leaves along the bottom. Trees can represent a huge range of different structures, including something as rigidly defined as a family tree (see Figure 3.1).

Figure 3.1 Royal family tree

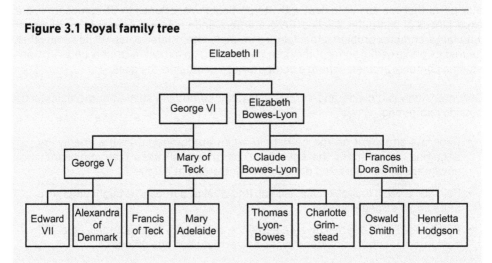

Or something put together arbitrarily like arranging Shakespeare's plays by genre (Figure 3.2).

Figure 3.2 Shakespeare plays arranged by genre into a tree structure

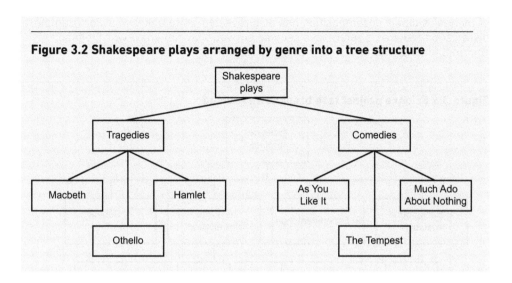

Let's look at an example. One task that many of us encounter during our education is the production of a dissertation. Writing an academic work some tens of thousands of words in length can inspire fear, panic or even despair. By itself, one monolithic task entitled 'write dissertation' is unmanageable, but by decomposing the problem you reduce it into smaller parts, each of which possesses far fewer details. You can then focus your attention on each part and deal with it much more effectively. By solving each sub-problem, you end up solving the overall problem.

The process of writing a typical scientific dissertation can be broken down as in Figure 3.3.

Figure 3.3 Science project task breakdown

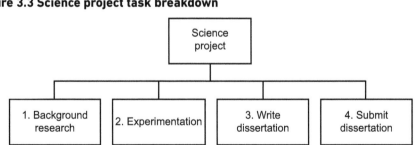

Each of these tasks conceals several sub-tasks. Let's focus on the task 'Write dissertation', which we can break down as in Figure 3.4.

What has this done? First, it has made explicit what constitutes the parent task, making it much clearer what 'write dissertation' actually means. In addition to revealing more of the task's detail, decomposition has also revealed more unknowns. For example, a dissertation requires a references section, but you may not know which citation style your institution demands.

Figure 3.4 Science project task breakdown revised

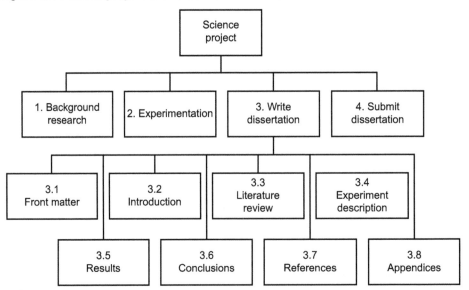

This has decomposed the task somewhat, but some sub-tasks may be still too big. Those tasks should be broken down further by applying the same decomposition process. For example, the front matter of a dissertation is made up of several parts, such as:

- 3.1.1 write title page;
- 3.1.2 write copyright section;
- 3.1.3 write abstract;
- 3.1.4 write contents section;
- 3.1.5 write list of figures section.

This time, all the resulting tasks are now manageable. None of them will contain more than a few hundred words, and some can even be done automatically by the word processor.

At this point, you can go back up the tree and find a different task that requires further decomposition. This process needs to be repeated until all the leaves of the resulting tree are problems you can solve individually.

Avoid getting bogged down in the details of **how** to solve the sub-problems. At this stage, we're still focusing on what to do, not how to do it.

Decomposition won't result in a complete plan of action, but it can give you a starting point for formulating one. For example, a fully decomposed problem definition can show all the individual tasks, but doesn't necessarily show the order in which you should tackle them. However, relationships between individual sub-problems should become apparent. In the dissertation example, writing up the results and conclusions (sections 3.5 and 3.6) can't be done before the experimentation (section 2) is completed. That doesn't mean everything in section 3 has to wait; sections 3.1–3.4 could be written before experimentation begins.

Decomposition aids collaboration. If you decompose a problem well (so that the sub-problems can be solved independently), then different people can work on different tasks, possibly in parallel.

OTHER EFFECTIVE STRATEGIES

Just because decomposition enjoys status as a core idea, that doesn't mean other problem-solving strategies have no a place in CT. While it's out of this book's scope to discuss all strategies, there's space to briefly explain several of the most useful ones. These strategies can complement decomposition by being applied to one or more of the resulting sub-problems. Each one may not useful in every scenario, but it's good to keep them in mind.

Think critically

The purpose of critical thinking is to question ideas and see that they stand up to scrutiny. You should examine the available information and the decisions you've taken **sceptically**, as if justifying to yourself that they are valid. All key decisions should have a good reason behind them.

If, for example, you were to design the layout of a bookshop, you might ask:

Have I chosen the right structure for laying out the books on the shelf?

That's a good starting question, but it's not clear what 'right structure' actually means. A quick look at your goal will help you clarify that. If you want it to be quick and easy for the bookshop owner to add new books to the shelves, then it's probably fine for them to be relatively unordered. The customers will have to browse the books, but that's normally expected in a bookshop. But if the venue is more like a library, where the customer typically looks for a specific book, then that suggests a specific structure. Your question then becomes:

Have I chosen a structure that makes it easy[17] to locate a specific book?

For a bookshop, this usually entails ordering books alphabetically by the author's name. Of course, this also means more work for the bookshop owner, who has to spend some of their time sorting the books.

In addition to validating ideas, you will also expose assumptions in the process. This is very important because assumptions made implicitly could well turn out to be false. Deciding that books need to be sorted assumes that the bookshop owner can afford to put in the time required for it. This raises the question: is that justified? It may turn out that you've exposed the need for further employees or a revised solution.

Perhaps the most common questionable assumption we're all guilty of is that our solutions will work flawlessly. For any system you put in place, **always** ask the question:

What if it goes wrong?

For a bookshop, you might ask: What if a book is not in the correct place on the shelf? If a gap appears on the bookshelf, how do you distinguish between a misplaced book and one that you simply don't have? Your response to such questions can vary. You could either work to improve your solution and eliminate the possibility of the problem occurring, or you could accept the possibility of it going wrong and put a contingency plan in place to be executed when the failure occurs.[18]

Solve a concrete instance

When you're trying to solve a problem, the terms you're dealing with can sometimes feel quite abstract and devoid of detail. While abstraction is certainly useful (see Chapter 4), it can be challenging to solve a problem when things are not defined in detail.

R. G. Dromey, who authored a problem-solving book inspired by Pólya's book (Dromey, 1982), cites this as a common cause of getting stuck early on. Dromey points out that it's easier to deal with problems in concrete terms because the details are more readily manipulated and understood.

As an example, consider automating the drawing of complex shapes and images. The idea of a shape is rather abstract. Just think how many varied types of shapes and patterns exist. To gain a foothold on the problem, you could take one complex shape (let's say a smiley face, see Figure 3.5) and think about how to solve that single example.

Figure 3.5 Smiley face

By combining this strategy with decomposition, we might find we could draw a smiley face by breaking it down into several simpler shapes, which are each easy to draw:

- A circle, to serve as the head.
- Two concentric circles (the smaller one of which is solid) which make eyes.
- A curve, which makes the mouth.

The solution for this one example points the way to a general solution: any complex, unfamiliar shape can be considered as being made up of several simpler, familiar shapes (see Figure 3.6).

Figure 3.6 Breakdown of drawing smiley face

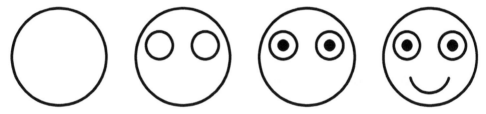

Find a related problem

Another piece of advice from Dromey, useful for gaining a foothold on a problem, advises you to examine the solution to a closely related problem. This helps for reasons that are similar to the previous strategy. A solution to another similar problem (one that's analogous to or a simplified version of your original problem) can point the way to a solution for your own problem.

Think back to the earlier example of writing a dissertation. The approach taken was to break the dissertation down into small tasks that could each be dealt with individually. The solution was tailored towards a science student, but such an approach could be reused by a student of law, economics, politics or whatever.

Just as with the 'solve a concrete instance' strategy, you should use this approach with caution. It is used to give you insight into a problem, not to solve it completely. Any solution you find will need some changes. Reusing it incautiously risks unwittingly moving the goalposts: you will end up solving a different problem without realising it. A law student could reuse the approach, but would need to adapt it – for example, they would have no need for an experimentation stage and so could ditch it.

Work backwards

Working backwards involves starting at the goal state and going backwards stage by stage. At each point, you look at the current stage and deduce what is required to arrive at it. This suggests things about the nature of the preceding stage.

This strategy is especially effective with a well-defined goal state. For example, if your problem is to plan a route somewhere and arrive by a certain time, you begin with a very clear goal state. From there, you can work backwards to the starting point, calculate a route and add up the intervening times.

Example: starting from your house on Main Street, arrive at the Town Hall by 3.00 p.m. What is the departure time?

- 3.00 p.m. Arrive at Town Hall
- 2.55–3.00 p.m. Walk from Town Hall underground station to Town Hall
- 2.45–2.55 p.m. Take underground from City bus station to Town Hall underground station
- 2.30–2.45 p.m. Take bus from Main Street bus station to City bus station
- 2.25–2.30 p.m. Walk from house on Main Street to bus station
- 2.25 p.m. Departure time.

PATTERNS AND GENERALISATION

Effective problem-solving actually involves more than just finding a solution. Once you've found a solution, you should put effort into its improvement by finding ways to make it more powerful. Recognising and exploiting patterns is a crucial early step in this process.

Why look for patterns?

As you analyse a problem and begin work on its solution, you'll probably notice that some elements repeat or are at least very similar to one another. If you don't automatically notice the patterns in a solution, you should make an effort to seek them out because they are the first step to making your solution more manageable and powerful.

In an earlier example, we saw an approach to drawing a simple image of a face. This approach broke the image down into simpler, elemental shapes that could be positioned and drawn easily. An algorithm that draws such an image might therefore look like this:

1. Draw circle with radius 30 at position 50,50 with line thickness 2.
2. Draw circle with radius 6 at position 40,40 with line thickness 1.
3. Draw circle with radius 3 at position 40,40 filled black.
4. Draw circle with radius 6 at position 60,40 with line thickness 1.
5. Draw circle with radius 3 at position 60,40 filled black.
6. Draw red line from position 30,70 to position 70,70 with line thickness 1.

In this example, the patterns across instructions should be fairly simple to spot. The emergence of a pattern provides an opportunity for improvement. Instead of them being disjointed and separated, those parts making up the pattern can usually be brought together and solved using a common approach. In other words, you can take some separate, but similar concepts, and **generalise** them into a single concept. As a result, your solution becomes simpler because it contains fewer distinct concepts, and it becomes more powerful because you can reuse it in other situations and solutions.

Recognising simple patterns

Here's one approach to spotting simple patterns:

- Look for nouns that appear repeatedly. These could correspond to objects that your solution deals with.
- Look for verbs that appear repeatedly. These could be operations that the solution carries out.
- Look for concrete descriptions. These could probably be substituted by placeholders that vary in different situations. For example:
  - adjectives ('red', 'long', 'smooth') which indicate properties of things and could be replaced by the property name (colour, size, texture);
  - actual numbers, which could be replaced with variables.

Let's illustrate all this by examining the algorithm above. What patterns can be seen?

- nouns like circle, radius, position, line, thickness;
- verbs like draw;
- adjectives like red, black, filled;
- numbers in several places.

Looking at the **nouns**, we see that some of them translate into objects (circle and line), while the rest are **properties** of those objects (radius, position, line thickness). Line and circle are specific instances of shapes. Hence, 'shape' is a generalisation of line and circle.

The **verbs** are straightforward – there's only one. Drawing appears to be a fundamental operation in this solution. Operations often need supplying with things to work with. Data given to an operation when it is triggered is called a **parameter**. In this case, drawing doesn't make any sense without having a shape to draw, so the draw operation should be given a shape parameter.

The **adjectives** red and black are specific cases of the more general concept of colour. The word 'filled', being derived from a verb, actually suggests another operation which we could formalise: filling a shape with a colour. Such an operation would then have two parameters.

All the **numbers** match up with object properties. In other words, these properties (position, radius, thickness) have values that can vary.

51

These are the generalisations extracted (if an operation expects parameters, they are listed in parentheses after the operation's name):

- **Draw (Shape)**: an operation that renders a shape.
- **Fill (Shape, Colour)**: an operation that makes the interior of a shape solid with a colour.
- **Shape**: a form with an external boundary. Specific shapes include:
  - **Circle**: a type of shape with a radius, position and a line thickness.
  - **Line**: a type of shape with two positions (aka coordinates) and a line thickness.
- **Colour**: red, blue, green and so on.

To summarise what has been done so far: we took a concrete solution, looked for patterns in it and simplified them. The original solution was a specialisation, capable only of drawing a specific shape. The generalisations taken from it form the core concepts of not only the original solution but any solution that involves breaking down a complex image into simple parts.

The solution is not perfect; it could benefit from improvements. For example, line thickness is not, mathematically speaking, a property of a shape. What's more, in our example, line thickness doesn't vary much between individual shapes. We could improve this by introducing another concept called 'Pen', which is responsible for the appearance of the shapes' boundaries. Line thickness would instead belong to the Pen, and it could be changed in-between drawing each shape, if need be.

More complex patterns

Looking for larger and more complex patterns requires you to expand your scope, because you'll need to consider whole groups of instructions at once. It can be harder and will take some experience getting used to, but it's worth it because you can put those patterns to work in powerful ways.

In brief, the guidelines for some of the more complex patterns are:

- Patterns among a sequence of instructions can be generalised into **loops**.
- Patterns among separate groups of instructions can be generalised into **subroutines**.
- Patterns among conditionals or equations can be generalised into **rules**.

Loops

Chapter 2 introduced us to the concept of looping, that is, executing the same series of steps repeatedly. This is a type of generalisation. In order to roll a sequence of steps up into a loop, you need to look at their specific forms and then derive one general form. A block of instructions that appear very repetitive usually gives the game away.

For example, consider this block:

- Draw circle with radius 6 at position 40,40
- Draw circle with radius 3 at position 40,40 filled black
- Draw circle with radius 6 at position 60,40
- Draw circle with radius 3 at position 60,40 filled black

We see a pattern here. Together, the last two steps essentially repeat the first two, only with a slight difference in positioning. We could therefore put these steps into a loop.

- Let coordinates = (40,40), (60,40)
- For each coordinate x,y do the following:
  - Draw circle with radius 6 at position x,y
  - Draw circle with radius 3 at position x,y filled black

You should remember from Chapter 2 how the execution of loops is often controlled by a variable, which encapsulates the thing that varies from iteration to iteration. In this example, the steps in the loop should be executed for each pair of coordinates. So, we set up a list of coordinates in the first line[19] and use that as the controlling variable of the loop. Put into words, the loop essentially says, 'for each coordinate carry out the following steps, where the coordinate values in the current iteration are represented by x and y'. In the first iteration, x = 40 and y = 40. In the second iteration, x = 60 and y = 40.

This generalisation makes the solution more flexible. If you want to draw more eyes in different places, you simply add more coordinates to the list and the loop takes care of the rest. Alternatively, you could draw a cyclops by lopping off a coordinate.

Subroutines

The next type of generalisation concerns patterns among separate blocks of instructions. The two steps inside the example loop encapsulate our approach to drawing an eye. They were put into a loop because the solution just happens to draw a pair of eyes, one after the other.

Imagine that we're drawing several faces. In this case, those two steps would be repeated in several different places. But then imagine you wished to alter the way you draw eyes, maybe by giving the iris a larger radius. You would have to update the steps in all those different places.

Instead of that, we could apply a generalisation that not only keeps the definition of an eye in one place, but also saves time when first writing the solution.

As a reminder, a concrete example of drawing an eye looks like this:

- Draw circle with radius 6 at position 40,40
- Draw circle with radius 3 at position 40,40 filled black

A generalised version might therefore look like this:

- Draw circle with radius r1 at position x,y
- Draw circle with radius r2 at position x,y filled black

We could then declare that these steps constitute a **subroutine**, that is to say, a sequence of instructions that perform a distinct, often-invoked task and which can therefore be 'packaged' as a unit. It would look something like this:

- 'Draw eye' is a subroutine (r1, r2, x,y):
  - Draw circle with radius r1 at position x,y
  - Draw circle with radius r2 at position x,y filled black

As per convention, any parameters supplied to a subroutine are declared in parentheses after its name. In this case, drawing an eye requires a pair of coordinates (x and y) and two radii (one each for the outer and inner circle of the eye).

As with the loop, the instructions contained inside the subroutine are indented for clarity. Now, whenever you want to draw an eye, you simply call on your subroutine to do the work for you (remembering to fill in the information it needs!):

- Call 'draw eye' with parameters r1 = 6, r2 = 3, x = 40, y = 40
- Call 'draw eye' with parameters r1 = 6, r2 = 3, x = 60, y = 40
- Call 'draw eye' with parameters r1 = 4, r2 = 2, x = 240, y = 40
- Call 'draw eye' with parameters r1 = 4, r2 = 2, x = 250, y = 40

Rules

The drawing routines defined above contain a pattern I've not yet picked out, although you might have spotted it already. When drawing an eye, the radius of the inner circle is always half the radius of the outer circle. If that is indeed the rule, then we can encode it explicitly into the subroutine so it becomes:

- 'Draw eye' is a subroutine (r, x, y):
  - Draw circle with radius r at position x,y
  - Draw circle with radius ½r at position x,y filled black

In addition to equations, conditionals are a good identifier of rules. Rules are normally indicated by words like 'when' and 'unless', as well as patterns like 'if–then'. For example, 'if a circle is not filled with a colour, then it takes on the background colour' – this is a rule that has been implicit in drawing every circle so far.

SUMMARY

Decomposition and generalisation are related. Whereas decomposition involves break-ing the problem down into smaller parts, generalisation involves combining those smaller parts. These actions are not the inverse of one another; when you generalise the individual parts, you're not putting the problem together again in the same way as before.[20]

The point of generalisation is to look at the decomposed parts and find ways to make the solution easier to handle and more widely applicable to similar problems. In the example above, instead of having numerous parts which can each draw only one type of eye, there is one generic part that can draw many different types of eye.

EXERCISES

EXERCISE 1

Mark the following statements as true or false:

    A.   Your goal defines how the problem should be solved, not what needs to be done.

    B.   It is inadvisable to begin writing a solution before the goal is defined.

    C.   For any non-trivial problem, there is likely only one solution.

    D.   Decomposition guarantees an optimal solution.

    E.   A tree structure is hierarchical in nature.

    F.   All nodes in a tree structure have one or more child nodes.

    G.   Patterns among separate groups of instructions can be generalised into subroutines.

EXERCISE 2

You're planning to hold a birthday picnic for a child and her friends. Break down the preparation into a tree structure of tasks. The facts are:

    A.   You need to send out the invitations to the parents of the other children.

    B.   Food you'll provide: sandwiches (ham, chicken, and cheese), homemade cake.

    C.   Fresh ingredients (meat and dairy) need to purchased on the day.

    D.   Other things you need to take: disposable cutlery, blankets, games.

    E.   The park where the picnic is held requires you to reserve a spot.

    F.   All guests will get a goody bag with sweets when they leave.

EXERCISE 3

Update the drawing of the smiley face discussed earlier in the chapter so that the positioning of the features (eyes and mouth) are calculated automatically based on the positioning of the face.

EXERCISE 4

Further update the drawing of the smiley face so that:

      A. All features have colour (for example, skin colour, red lips, brown eyes, etc.).

      B. The cheek has a scar.

      C. A round, red nose that partially obscures the eyes is included.

EXERCISE 5

You can group animals by their shared characteristics into a hierarchical tree structure (like the example with Shakespeare's plays). Consider these animals: bat, crocodile, fox, human, octopus, ostrich, penguin, shark, snake, swan, turtle. Group them into three different tree structures by:

      A. number of legs;

      B. whether they can fly;

      C. their class (mammal, fish, etc.).

Imagine these animals were used in a 'Twenty Questions' style game where your opponent thinks of an animal and you may ask them a limited number of yes/no questions to work out which animal they're thinking of. Use your tree structures to guide your questioning strategy. Which one of the three structures would minimise the number of questions you would have to ask? Try dividing groupings into sub-groupings to see if that helps to reduce the number of questions.

4   ABSTRACTION AND MODELLING

OBJECTIVES

- Introduce the concept of abstraction and explain its importance.
- Show the importance of layering abstractions.
- Discuss the dangers and limitations of abstraction.
- Introduce modelling as part of the problem-solving process.
- Show typical types of models available.
- Explain the difference between static and dynamic modelling.
- Show typical uses of models along with examples.

ABSTRACTION

This section introduces the concept of abstraction, a key concept in CT for devising powerful solutions.

From generalisation to abstraction

The previous chapter showed the decompositional approach to problem-solving, whereby a large, complex problem is divided into smaller, simpler sub-problems. The motivation behind it is that solving a series of simple problems is easier than trying to tackle a big complex one.

Following on from that was generalisation, an activity that identifies patterns among those individual sub-problems and simplifies them. The effect is to make the overall solution more manageable and widely applicable. In an example (drawing a simple face), we went from drawing very basic shapes (lines, circles, etc.), to drawing an eye with specific dimensions, and then ended up able to draw an eye of *any* size.

In a sense, generalisation is about hiding details.[21] Construction of the drawing solution started with a handful of low-level 'atomic' details and ended up at a more conveniently abstract level. In our example, we went from speaking in terms of constituent elements (two concentric circles, the inner of which was filled solid), to simply referring to an eye. The resulting generic eye is an example of an **abstraction**.

> **Abstraction:** a way of expressing an idea in a specific context while at the same time suppressing details irrelevant in that context.

The importance of abstractions

> The essence of abstractions is preserving information that is relevant in a given context, and forgetting information that is irrelevant in that context.
>
> (Guttag, 2013)

Abstraction is a key feature of both computer science and computational thinking. Some have gone so far as to describe computer science as 'the automation of abstraction' (Wing, 2014).

The reasoning behind this goes right to the core of what programmers and computer scientists are trying to do; that is, solve real-world problems using computers. They can't magically transport the real world into the computer; instead, they have to describe the real world to the computer. But the real world is messy, filled with lots of noise and endless details. We can't describe the world in its entirety. There's too much information and sometimes we don't even fully understand the way it works. Instead, we create models of the real world and then reason about the problem via these models. Once we achieve a sufficient level of understanding, we teach the computer how to use these models (i.e. program it).

Perhaps if we were hyper-intelligent superbeings with limitless mental capacity, we wouldn't need abstractions, and we could take into account every minute detail of our solutions. I hate to be the one to break it to you, but we're not superbeings; we're an intelligent species of ape with the ability to keep about seven or so pieces of information in working memory at any one time.[22]

Consequently, we're stuck struggling to understand the world via our own models of it.

Examples of abstractions

In the previous chapter's drawing example, we created a shape as an abstraction. By itself, the idea of a shape tells you some things – such as that we're dealing with a form that has an external boundary or surface – but other things, like the number of its sides and its internal angles, are unknown details.

A shape might seem an elementary and academic example. In fact, we're surrounded by abstractions in everyday life. Many familiar things are abstract representations of a more detailed reality. One example is an underground metro map. Figure 4.1 shows the underground metro system of Rotherham (a hypothetic system, sadly, as the great and historic town of Rotherham has yet to achieve an underground).

Look at this figure and compare it with the more realistic representation in Figure 4.2. You'll notice it doesn't present a completely accurate picture of reality. The tunnels are not all dead straight at 45-degree angles to one other. The stops along the lines are not evenly spaced out. However, you wouldn't know that if the only information you had about the underground came from the map.

Figure 4.1 A metro map of the Rotherham underground

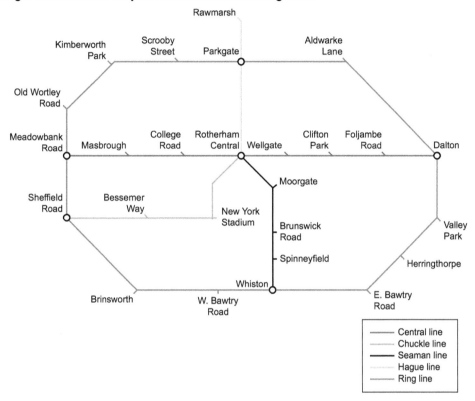

Are the map-makers trying to fool us? No, they're leaving out details you don't need to know. It doesn't matter that they left out the U-shaped bend in the line east of Rotherham Central. It doesn't matter that the distances between stations – consecutive and equidistant on the simplified map – are in fact separated by varying distances. It all makes no difference to how you use the underground. What's important is the ordering of the stations, which lines they're on and where those lines converge as interchanges.

Therefore, a typical metro map is an abstraction. It represents certain details (order of stops on the line, intersections of different lines) and suppresses others. As a result, the map is simpler for commuters to use.

If you ask a computer scientist what's so great about abstractions, they may well give you a more technical example, say, an email. Most of the world knows what an email is: a message written on a computer and transmitted via a network to another user. However, this is an abstraction in the same way that 'letter' is an abstraction for a piece of paper with intelligible ink markings on it. There's a lot more underlying detail to an email. If you imagine an email, you probably think of the text in your mail client.

Figure 4.2 A more realistic map of the Rotherham underground[23]

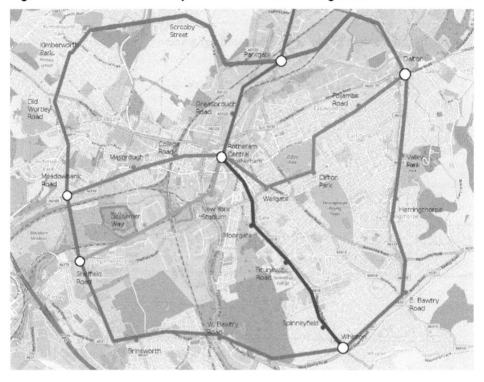

But an email exists as digital information, organised as packets of ones and zeroes in your computer's memory. What's more, when in transit, it exists as a series of electrical impulses travelling through a cable, or as electromagnetic waves hurtling through the atmosphere. If you operated at this level of abstraction, you'd be saying to your friend, 'I'll send you an encoded series of ones and zeroes via electrical impulses over the Internet for you decode into the original human-readable message.'

To which your confused friend might unwittingly reply, 'Why not just send me an email instead?'

Context and layers

That last example of an email hinted towards an important fact about abstractions: context is key. An abstraction of something operates at a certain level of detail and puts a layer over the top to obscure some of the information. You can take any abstraction, peel back the layer and go further 'down' to reveal more information (thus considering it in a more detailed context), or go further 'up', adding more layers to suppress further details about it (a less detailed context). Figure 4.3 can be read as saying 'An email application makes readable the contents of computer memory', as well as 'computer memory stores as digital information the signals from the network'.

Figure 4.3 Layers of abstraction involved in email

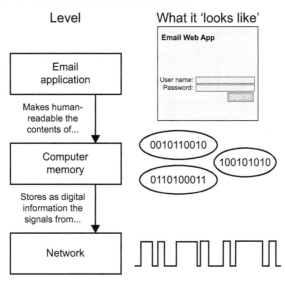

Let's look at a couple of real-world examples to illustrate this. Imagine a vehicle rental company builds a system to manage their inventory. Using the techniques from Chapter 3 (for example, identifying entities, the processes they carry out and the properties they possess), the system designers break down the task and pick out the various concepts. The company has several types of vehicles (cars, vans, motorcycles, etc.) and numerous operations are carried out daily (booking, checking in, checking out, cleaning, road testing, etc.). Once the company identifies all these concepts, it's up to them how to define their abstractions. For example:

- If the company offers a no-frills 'any-old-car-will-do' service, then all the individual cars could be grouped into one abstraction (called, imaginatively, a car).

- Alternatively, if they want to give customers more choice, they could group the cars according to transmission, giving them 'manual cars' and 'automatic cars'.

- All the vans could be classified according to capacity, yielding the abstractions 'small van' or 'large van'.

- When it comes to obtaining a complete listing of everything available at a specific site, no discrimination among all the various types is necessary. In this case, everything – cars, vans, motorcycles – can be dealt with using the single abstraction 'vehicle'.

You can see that each level of abstraction is built up recursively from the levels below.[24] All the Fords and Audis and Nissans, and so on, join to become cars. All the cars join the vans and motorcycles to become vehicles. All the vehicles, spare parts, and tools can be treated collectively as inventory items (see Figure 4.4).

Figure 4.4 Some layers of abstraction in the car rental example

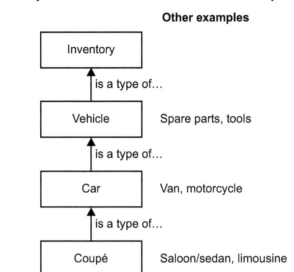

Looking at it this way, the vehicle rental company takes numerous concrete ideas and unifies them into more abstract concepts. However, building abstractions can sometimes go the other way: that is, start with a fairly abstract concept and add more detail as you go along.

Let's take a different example to illustrate this. An online video service like YouTube or Netflix can recommend videos to a user because it has built an abstract model of them. An ideal model of the user would include a perfect replica of their neurons and brain chemistry, so it would know with uncanny accuracy which videos they would like to watch at any moment. Or, failing that, maybe a complete and thorough biography including a run-down of every book, film and TV show they've ever consumed.

However, online video services operate with far less information than that. They know almost nothing about the viewer aside from their video-watching habits (O'Reilly, 2016). This means the video service has to reduce the customer to an abstract video-watching entity. The service knows what kinds of videos the viewer watched in the past and so might push a list of other unseen videos based on that information. It assumes the viewer is most interested in other videos of the same genre.

At the time of writing, online video platforms are in a formative period and such models are constantly changing and rapidly becoming more sophisticated. But, at the moment, however powerful their approaches are, they're still operating by building an abstract model of you, the viewer, based on a tiny subset of information.

Producing better recommendations might mean introducing more detail into their models and taking into account more about the viewer. That would mean having to operate at a lower level of abstraction, which opens up considerations of what is important or meaningful at that level. A service may decide to divide users by geographical region, so that there isn't just a single concept of a viewer; rather, there is an American viewer, a British viewer, a German viewer and so on. Now, the procedure for building a list of recommendations can be extended with additional steps matching a viewer's region to certain types of films. A German viewer's recommendations would widen to also include some German-language films. But the German-language films wouldn't be included in recommendations outside German-speaking regions.

Exercising caution

Abstractions undoubtedly help, but they should also come with a warning label. Perhaps 'Caution: Abstractions may distract from reality.'

The reason you should be cautious is that abstractions are a way of avoiding details, either by suppressing or deferring them. As in life, when you do that carefully and with good foresight, it can be useful and productive. Doing it recklessly may very well come back to bite you later because it can be easy to get lost in the abstractions. A fuzzy marketing message might imply that a product solves more problems than it really does; a philosophical argument that tries to account for everything might be so lacking in detail that it explains nothing.

In the end, the real question is: how does it work? You can't execute an abstraction. The acid test for a solution depends on how well the concrete implementation works.

Putting abstractions to use

Abstractions are fine for doing things like organising your solution, managing its complexity and reasoning about its behaviour in general terms. But when you actually put the solution into use, it has to work with some level of detail. Put another way: you can't tell a computer to draw a shape, but you can tell it to draw a circle.

To put an abstraction to use requires it to be made concrete somehow. In other words, it is **instantiated** and this requires attention to details. For example, the car rental company may need to list all vehicles according to how soon they need servicing. A generalised procedure for doing this needs some concrete detail to work with. Specifically, the date of its next service must be able to be specified for each vehicle. 'Next service date' is therefore a property of every vehicle. Also, another procedure may involve showing all vans above a specified payload.[25] This procedure only makes sense for vans, so only they need to provide this information when instantiated (see Figure 4.5).

Leaking details

Even after sorting out the underlying details, a risk persists with the use of abstractions: you may have unwittingly ignored a detail that affects the way the abstraction behaves.

Sticking with our automotive theme, the way you operate a car can be considered as an abstraction. A car is a very complicated piece of machinery, but operating it is a simple matter because all those details are hidden behind a few relatively simple control mechanisms: steering wheel, pedals and gear lever. But occasionally, details hidden behind this clean interface affect how the driver uses the car. Revving the accelerator pedal too high can cause wear on the engine. Braking distance will increase over time as the brake pads become worn. The engine may not start if the weather is too cold.

Figure 4.5 Layers of abstraction including Vehicle and Van

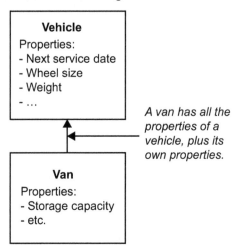

When things like this happen, hidden details have become important to how something works; those details have 'leaked' out of the abstraction. In actuality, no complex abstraction is perfect and all of them will likely leak at some point. But there's no reason to treat this as bad news. The same has been happening in science for centuries.

You may have learned at school (although it might have been phrased differently) that all of science is built on abstractions. Scientists cannot take every single aspect of something into consideration when studying it, so they build simplified models of it: models that ignore friction and air resistance, or models that assume no losses to heat transfer. Technically, such models don't fully reflect reality, but that's not the most important thing. What's important is that they are shown to work.

I know of no general advice to anticipate leaky abstractions ahead of time. However, when yours are shown to leak, you should do as the scientist does: amend your model to take the problem into account. Details that turn out to be important need to be brought explicitly into the model.

MODELLING

'Model'. That word that cropped up quite a lot during the discussion of abstraction. As representations of real-world things that ignore certain details, models are a type of abstraction and an important one in CS. Furthermore, CT has recognised the value of modelling by placing it as one of its fundamental practices. This section explains what models are in the context of computing and how you can put them to use.

Motivation

Abstraction can be a challenging concept to get to grips with. The word itself might be off-putting due to our preconception that abstract things are difficult to understand. Examining specific forms of abstraction can help in understanding it.

In CS, abstraction can take many forms. At its simplest level, abstraction can just mean naming things. For example, a calendar is an abstraction of time; it gives names (day, week, year) to our observations about how long the Earth takes to complete certain movements. Also, the loops and subroutines that we saw in Chapter 3 can be considered abstractions.

By showing a simplified view of things in your problem, models help you to improve your understanding because they allow you to focus only on the relevant parts. This section of the book will explain the fundamentals of modelling in the context of CT. It will show how to use our in-built ability to picture things when developing computer-based solutions.

Basics

There's nothing particularly magical about models. Put simply, a model shows the entities in your solution and the relationships between them.

We all intuitively understand how to model things because we have imaginations. We make models whenever we sit back and try to picture how a complex thing works, or imagine how a thing will behave in the future. People had been modelling things long before computer science showed up. Some models of the solar system date back to the Ancient Greek world.[26] Economists have modelled the workings of societies throughout the modern era. As already mentioned, scientists build models of reality, from the tiniest atoms to galactic clusters.

All models hide some details of the reality they represent. The things judged irrelevant in a model's context are left out of it (see Figure 4.6). The things remaining play one of two roles in the representation:

- **entities**: the core concepts of the system;
- **relationships**: a connection that relates entities in the system.

Figure 4.6 Abstraction as modelling

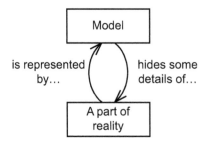

Many types of models exist. The same entities in your solution can be modelled over and over again in different ways by using different types of models. Each one offers a different view of the same system, so it's up to you choose the appropriate model(s) depending on which aspects you want to show.

The variety of relationship types is endless. It all depends on what you want the model to describe about your entities. For example, relationships could say things like:

- A belongs to B;
- C contains D;
- E happens before F;
- G occupies the same space as H.

Sometimes, those relationships are directional. Hence:

- B owns A;
- D is contained by C;
- F happens after E.

Entities and relationships are often labelled with additional information if it's necessary for the model. These include:

- **Properties:** discrete pieces of information about that particular entity or relationship, like a station's name on an underground map.
- **Type:** a classification that the entity belongs to. This can tell you lots of things about that entity implicitly. For example, a line between two underground stations relates them by saying they're on the same line; the colour denotes the line's type (e.g. Bakerloo, Circle, Victoria, etc.).
- **Rules:** statements about an entity that must hold true. An underground station might be labelled with a rule saying 'Closed between 10 and 15 November.'
- **Behaviours:** descriptions of actions which may be expressed in natural language or algorithmic form. For example, one section of a metro line might state that trains travel at a slower pace along it.

Static vs dynamic models

Static models give us a snapshot view of the system. They depict entities and relationships at a single point in time. An underground map is a static model. It's a snapshot of the current state of all the stations and lines. True, its state may change in the future (a station may close, another line may be added), but the layout changes so seldom that a static map serves the public just fine.

However, it may be sometimes important to take into account that the world you're modelling changes over time. **Dynamic** models do this. The goal of a dynamic model is to explain the changes in state as time proceeds. They always involve the following:

- states: descriptions of the entities at specific points in time;
- transitions: a change in state.

Although there are different varieties of dynamic models, they generally include some or all of the following as well:

- events: things that happen to trigger transitions;
- actions: computations that are carried out as part of a transition.

An example of a simple dynamic system is a turnstile – something that transitions through a series of states as people use it. It can be modelled using a state machine diagram, which depicts the progression of a system through various states (see Figure 4.7).

- At the start point (the solid black circle), the turnstile is in a locked state.
- Inserting a coin is an event. It triggers the transition of a locked turnstile into an unlocked one.[27]
- Pushing an unlocked turnstile (another event) transitions it back to the locked state.
- Pushing a locked turnstile has no effect.

Figure 4.7 State machine diagram of a turnstile

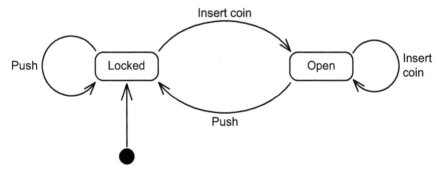

Uses of models

This section shows examples of models assisting in various capacities.

Simplifying and explaining

When faced with a problem in a complex world, modelling a part of that world can greatly clarify both the problem and the way towards a solution. A classic example of this dates back a couple of centuries.

Leonard Euler, a Prussian mathematician living in eighteenth-century Königsberg (modern Kaliningrad), was given a challenge by the city's mayor. Seven bridges in the city crossed the river running through it. The mayor asked Euler whether it was possible to walk across all seven bridges without re-crossing a single one.

To understand the problem, Euler could have studied a map of the city. But the map (see Figure 4.8) was complicated, full of distracting detail. Instead, he reduced it down until only the essential elements remained: the land masses and the bridges. These alone formed the essence of the problem.

Figure 4.8 Map of Königsberg[28]

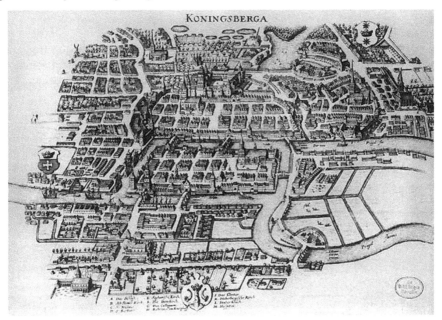

This simplified form, depicted in Figure 4.9, is a type of model called a **graph**. A graph is made up of nodes (which represent entities) and edges (connections between entities that represent relationships). In Euler's model, the nodes represent land masses and the edges represent bridges between land masses.

With this new representation, Euler could focus all his effort on solving the problem. In the process of solving this single concrete question, he came up with some of the fundamental rules of graph theory that can now be applied to any problem when it's represented in graph form.

Just for your interest, the problem has no solution. Euler showed that it's impossible to cross all bridges without re-crossing at least one. His proof was expressed, not in terms of Königsberg, but purely in terms of a graph. So long as every node in the graph has an even number of edges connected to it (with the exception of the start and end node), then the walk is possible. That's because you have to arrive at the node the same

Figure 4.9 Map of Königsberg

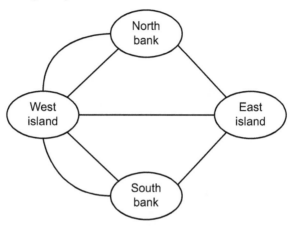

number of times you leave it. In this form, Euler's solution applies not just to Königsberg, but to every city in the world.

A graph is just the generic name for this type of model. Quite a few varieties of graph exist. The one in Figure 4.9 is a simple undirected graph. The state machine in the section 'Static vs dynamic models' (p. 66) is also a graph, but in this case it's a directed graph because each relationship flows in one direction.

Executing a representation

Certain dynamic models, once defined, can actually be executed. If that model is a good enough approximation of reality, then executing a model tells you how reality should pan out in the future.

Taking another example from a long-past era, the orrery is a physical model of the solar system (see Figure 4.10). A large ball representing the Sun sits at the centre, while smaller balls (the planets) are perched on arms of varying length. It is, furthermore, a dynamic model. A complex series of gears control the arms. When the gears are turned (i.e. the model is executed) the smaller balls move relative to one another in a way that exactly mimics the real planets. That means you can configure the orrery to make it represent the Solar System of today and then move the gears to see the configuration of the planets at a future date.

Today, computers mostly perform this type of modelling and it's a key product of the marriage between science and high-performance computing. Modern science uses mathematical models to make predictions of extremely complicated systems where theory and simple experimentation are insufficient. Climate models are one of most powerful examples. They describe the nature of global entities – like atmosphere, ice masses, land surfaces and ultraviolet rays – and the complex interactions between them using mathematical formulae. Executing a model like this means taking measurements, plugging the results into the model and then playing it out to obtain a prediction of the future (see Figure 4.11).

Figure 4.10 An orrery[29]

Figure 4.11 A climate model from NASA

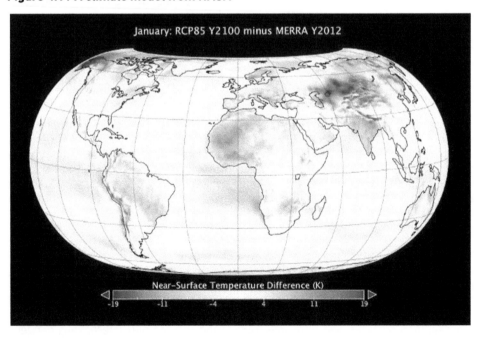

Executable models often need supplying with parameters that represent the starting state. In the case of the orrery, those parameters are the positions of the planets. In the case of the climate model, things like cloud cover, albedo, convection and so on.

Modelling data

Computerised solutions very often have to process and store data as part of their work. The algorithms that make up a solution work with that data, so they must have knowledge about the data's structure if they want to read and store it properly. As the solution's architect, it's up to you incorporate this into the algorithms.

To do this well, you should model the data before you get into the algorithmic details. This way, you'll have a much clearer understanding of the types of data your solution works with as well as the relationships between them.

Figure 4.12 Model of a student record

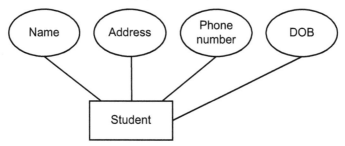

For example, if your task is to design a solution for storing the records of university students, there are plenty of considerations in terms of data. A simple data structure for a student record might look like Figure 4.12. With entities and relationships, this looks very much like previous examples of models. In this case, the entities are specific data fields and the relationships show how one field belongs to another. A student has a name, a date of birth, an address and so on.

So far so good, but then you need to think about how the data will be used in your solution. Perhaps at some point you'll want to distinguish between students who live locally and those from out of town. That tells you the address field needs breaking down into constituent parts to enable the eventual algorithm to find out which city a student lives in.

Furthermore, you might wish to store multiple phone numbers for each student. To model this, you can add **cardinality** to a relationship, which tells you how many instances can be involved. In this example, a student mostly has one instance of each data item – with the exception of phone numbers.

Cardinality: a property describing the number of elements in something.

After taking these considerations into account, the revised data structure looks like Figure 4.13. The address has become a more complex entity, made up of several subfields. The cardinality added to the relationship between student and phone number states that each student record has space for up to three phone numbers.

Figure 4.13 Expanded model of a student record

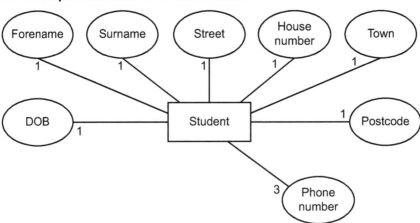

Modelling interaction

If your solution involves some kind of user interaction, then you can (and should) model the interaction as early as you can. There are different ways to do this, including:

- Take the data model and pick out which data the user will see and manipulate. This helps to define the various views available to the user. For example, the data model of the student record system (see p. 261) suggests the following views:

  - personal details (name, address, telephone number);

  - course overview (a table listing each course the student is enrolled on);

  - grade overview (a table of the student's grades).

- Model the navigation. If your system provides a lot of views, the user will need a way to navigate between them all. There are numerous guidelines to follow to achieve a good user navigation. For example, the user shouldn't have to navigate through an excessive number of views to reach the one they want.

- Prototype the user interface. By creating a mock-up of the expected interface layout, you can validate it against usability standards. The process need not be at all sophisticated. In fact (where appropriate), paper prototyping is a recommended approach, wherein you draw the individual parts of the user interface onto little pieces of paper. You can then arrange them at will on one large piece of paper that represents the area of the whole view. What's more, you can show these to potential users to get feedback and collaborate with them in rearranging the pieces to improve layout.[30]

Things to remember

A few general hints and pointers to keep in mind when you carry out your own modelling are covered in this section.

Purpose

Your primary concern should be that the model is useful. The main purpose of a model is to convey an idea. If modelling something genuinely helps you to form your ideas or to communicate them to other people, then it's worthwhile effort.

Formality

Some types of models have very specific rules about how to use them. Certain symbols might have specific meaning; entities might be allowed a maximum number of relationships and so on. These are called formal models.

There's a lot to be said for more informal models, where rules are much looser, especially when you're playing with ideas or chewing things over with colleagues at a whiteboard. But there's also a time and a place for formal models. Their stricter rules are important when validity and correctness are big concerns. Furthermore, standardised formal models are essential for the smooth exchange of information between different parties.

Accuracy

All models are wrong, but some are useful.

(Box, 1987)

All models are, to varying extents, approximations. They're our attempt at taking real-world phenomena and making simplified representations. One question to ask when making a model is: what level of accuracy is acceptable? Any modern map, no matter how detailed, is not totally accurate. Consider the coastlines. The boundary between the land and the sea changes hour to hour as the tides advance and retreat. The shape of the coastline is reflected at something like the kilometre scale. No map depicts the shape of the land right down to the tiny cracks on cliffs or pebbles on the beach, but that doesn't matter for everyday navigation. A model may not be perfectly accurate, but it can be perfectly sufficient.

Precision

Values in the real world can be thought of as continuous. There are an endless number of possible values between a temperature of 24.1 °C and 24.2 °C. No matter how precisely you measure a temperature (for example, 24.134 °C), you could always be more precise (24.1342 °C). However, computers deal with discrete values, that is, values which are distinct and individual. Computers store numbers by turning on or off a small group of transistors. As a result, they have maximum/minimum values and can be precise only to a certain number of decimal places.

When modelling continuous, real-world phenomena, we are usually constraining them, putting them into a more restrictive discrete box. It's up to you to judge how precise your model needs to be. Be mindful of the context and let it guide your judgement.

SUMMARY

This chapter introduced abstraction as a key driver behind helping to understand solutions and make them more powerful. By picking out only the relevant details and suppressing the remainder, you can represent only what it is essential to a problem, leaving you free to concentrate on solving the essence of the problem. By using layers of abstraction, you can consider a problem from multiple points of view, while still benefitting from a reduction of mental load.

Modelling, a type of abstraction, plays an important part in problem-solving by representing the key parts of a solution. This helps you to understand the system you're trying to build, as well as predict its eventual behaviour. Models come in numerous forms, which you can freely choose from.

EXERCISES

EXERCISE 1

Mark the following statements as true or false:

- A. An abstraction leaks when it takes details into account unnecessarily.
- B. An abstraction must be instantiated before it can be executed.
- C. A dynamic model shows the changes in state of something over time.
- D. A directed graph is a dynamic model.
- E. Accuracy describes closeness to the true value; precision describes the level of refinement in a measurement.

EXERCISE 2

Order the following into layers of abstraction, starting with the most general and ending with the most specific.

- A. penguin;
- B. bird;
- C. Tommy the Penguin;
- D. animal;
- E. Emperor penguin.

EXERCISE 3

For renting out a car, which of the following is it necessary for a rental company to know about? For each one, explain your answer:

    A. the car's current mileage;
    B. the customer's height;
    C. number of wheels on the car;
    D. the car's current fuel level;
    E. ID number of the customer's motorcycle licence.

EXERCISE 4

A shopping website allows you make purchases online and have them delivered to you. Here are the facts:

    A. You can create an order and use it to compile a list of items.
    B. When you're happy with an order, you place it with the system.
    C. Eventually, the people running the site look at your order to confirm it can be fulfilled. If it can, it is confirmed and the user is informed by email.
    D. When the goods are packaged and sent, the order is dispatched.
    E. The order can be cancelled at any time prior to confirmation.

Model all the possible stages of an order using a state machine diagram.

EXERCISE 5

Look again at the final diagram in the section 'Modelling data'. Extend the diagram so that the data structure records the student's grades. A student is enrolled on up to eight courses maximum and each course has a predicted and actual grade.

5 ANTICIPATING AND DEALING WITH ERRORS

OBJECTIVES

- Explain techniques for preventing errors being introduced into your solution.
- Discuss how to mitigate the effects of errors that are introduced.
- Introduce a systematic approach to testing via top-down and bottom-up strategies.
- Show how to test individual parts of a solution in isolation.
- Discuss a number of debugging strategies.
- Explain how to manage the bugs found in your solution.

COMING TO TERMS WITH BUGS

> I well remember when ... the realization came over me with full force that a good part of the remainder of my life was going to be spent in finding errors in my own programs.
>
> (Wilkes, 1985)

You should get used to the idea that solutions you create will not work flawlessly. They will contain bugs somewhere, despite your very best efforts. Even the most talented programmers and computer scientists in the world produce software that contains bugs, even if some are loath to admit it. A bug can be as simple as a typo in a formula or as disastrous as a complete misunderstanding of the original problem definition.

Bug: a fault in a solution that can cause erroneous behaviour.

Bugs can be caught and eliminated at any stage in the development process, but the earlier you find and fix them the better. You'll find it much easier to change something when it exists only as an idea rather than after it's been implemented. Think of the effort a writer needs to put into fixing a plot hole when it's found during the planning phase as opposed to in the finished draft. Or think of the cost of recalling and fixing an error in a smartphone after millions have been sold. Therefore, designing out the bugs is a good practice. This chapter will examine such practices.

> **Error:** any behaviour observed when executing a solution that does not match expected behaviour.

Some bugs will only become apparent after your solution (or parts of it) has been put into effect. For those cases, you need different approaches, namely testing and debugging. These will also be discussed in this chapter.

DESIGNING OUT THE BUGS

This section examines the various types of bugs that can cause erroneous behaviour.

Typos

During the early planning phases, your solution exists in various design forms: documents, notes, diagrams, algorithm outlines and so on. The simplest way of preventing errors at this stage is to look for elementary mistakes, in both the problem definition and your solution.

Typos include:

- spelling errors;
- incorrect capitalisations;
- missing words;
- wrong words (for example, 'phase' instead of 'phrase');
- numbered lists with incorrect numbering, and so on.

Such mistakes may often be trivial, but any of them could cause problems.

Poor grammar and ambiguities

Like typos, some types of grammatical error are quite easy to locate and correct. Its easy to find the mistake in this sentence, right?[31] However, some grammatical errors are quite subtle. For example:

After having a coin inserted, the user will be able to push the turnstile.

What or who exactly is having a coin inserted here?[32] Statements like these need rephrasing so they can only be interpreted one way. You should therefore **not** underestimate the usefulness of good writing skills.

Still, ambiguities can appear in sentences that are grammatically fine. For example:

After the login process fails a number of times in a row, the incident should be reported in an email to the security administrator.

The intention behind this statement is fine, but what does 'a number of times' actually mean? Two, five, a hundred? It may be permissible to decide on the exact number at a later stage, but in general you should nail down such details as early as possible.

Another type of ambiguity that can potentially cause problems is when the (apparently) same concept is referred to using different terms. This may seem innocent enough, but the implicit differences might suggest there are several concepts that need distinguishing or that an abstraction can be created. For example, if your solution makes various references to a 'smartphone', 'tablet', and 'handheld device' all in the same context, you should question whether those terms can really be used interchangeably or whether you should treat them differently.[33]

Keep a glossary of key terms used in your solution and stick to it.

Inconsistencies

Eliminating ambiguities helps to counter another source of bugs, namely inconsistencies. An inconsistency arises when parts of a solution separately make statements that make no sense when considered together. These bugs are harder to locate because each part of the inconsistency might appear in very different contexts.

Consider the example of the login process (above) rewritten as follows:

After the login process fails five times in a row, this incident should be reported in an email to the security administrator.

Also imagine that a different part of the solution contains the following statement:

After the login process fails three times in a row, the login screen should automatically lock and refuse further login attempts.

Here we have an inconsistency. If a login attempt fails three times consecutively, then the user is unable to make further login attempts. Consequently, they can never actually perform five login attempts in a row, and so the first statement is redundant.

Logical and mathematical errors

Simple bugs might be found in logical expressions. For example, the following algorithm is supposed to print the maximum value of two numbers, x and y.

```
If x > y, then print y
Otherwise if y > x, then print x
```

This actually contains two bugs. One should be obvious: the algorithm prints the minimum instead of the maximum. The second is slightly more subtle: what happens if both numbers are equal? You would expect a value to be printed, but in fact, nothing is printed at all. This example demonstrates that errors can result from expressions that are valid (that is, they can be evaluated without a problem) but whose semantic meaning is incorrect.

Similarly, mathematical errors can also result from seemingly valid expressions. An in-car computer that evaluates the car's efficiency based on the trip counter might use a formula like this:

$$e = \frac{m}{g}$$

where efficiency (*e*) is the miles travelled (*m*), divided by the gallons of fuel consumed (*g*). This will mostly work fine, except that when the trip counter is reset, the gallons consumed becomes zero and dividing by zero is mathematically invalid. The solution would have to take this special case into account.

Being exhaustive

Chapter 2 pointed out some of the limitations of human–computer interaction. Here's a reminder: computers have no common sense; they will not try to fill in any gaps in your instructions, and they can't conduct a dialogue with you to pin down exactly what you meant to say.

The path that a computer takes through an algorithm varies at different times. It all depends on the parameters passed, as well as other changeable factors in the environment. Therefore, algorithms should be exhaustive and contain instructions for all conceivable outcomes. If you fail to account for any of them, the computer's behaviour becomes unpredictable: it might take an unwanted action or it might do nothing when it should in fact do something.

These kinds of mistakes are easily made and are common with beginners (Pea et al., 1987; Pane et al., 2001). Even the professionals make such mistakes, more than they'd care to admit. Writing a robust algorithm that accounts for all possible pathways (both desired and undesired) takes experience, but you can learn some general principles as well as how to avoid some common errors:

- To reiterate some advice from Chapter 2: think critically. Once you've written a sequence of instructions that you expect to be followed, start to question what might go wrong. Examine each step and ask yourself how it might be possible for things to turn out differently from how you wish. If necessary, add instructions that take action in case of those undesired outcomes.

- Look especially at conditionals:

  - If you have a sequence of instructions in the form 'if X is the case, then do Y', ask yourself what happens if X is **not** the case? Sometimes a contingency is required. Therefore, always be mindful of Z – as in, 'if X is the case, then do Y, else do Z'.

  - Compound conditionals can be troublesome (for example, if A and not B or C...). Think about all the possible combinations and be aware that the number of combinations increases exponentially as a conditional increases in size.

- An old and trusted piece of advice says 'bugs lurk in corners and congregate at boundaries' (Beizer, 1990). Take this example: 'if score < 50, then performance is OK; if score > 50, then performance is good'. What's missing? It doesn't take account of the case when the score is exactly 50. The advice is telling you to take extra care when testing ranges and boundaries.

- Also look especially at loops:

  - If a loop can be exited early, insert an explicit instruction to do so at the correct point.

  - If the rest of a loop iteration can be skipped and the computer can move onto the next iteration, again, insert an explicit instruction to do so at the correct point.

  - Make **absolutely** sure the loop cannot go on endlessly.

General tips

As the author of the solution, you're not an impartial observer. You will find it hard to see any problems that exist, partly because you're too wrapped up in the details of how it **should** work, and partly because you don't want to think of your beloved creation as flawed. You may also, without realising it, have made implicit assumptions that prove unwarranted. It's therefore a good idea to find a friend or colleague who will look over your proposed solution and perform these checks in addition to you.

It was recommended in Chapter 3 that you approach problem-solving iteratively. Now is a good time to reiterate that advice. When designing the solution, do so in small steps. Work on the solution in stages, rounding off each iteration by applying these checks.

Do your utmost to keep different parts of your solution self-contained by minimising the number of relationships between them.[34] This should localise the effects of any errors and help to prevent knock-on effects.

Finally, if the problem definition came to you from someone else, call on that person to verify your solution design. Misunderstandings between the solution designer and the 'client' are a notorious source of problems.

MITIGATING ERRORS

So far, this chapter has examined some **preventative** actions you can take to stop bugs making their way into your solution. The bad news is that your finished solution will very likely contain bugs, despite your best efforts. The good news is that steps exist for you to take against errors. The following sections examine what you can do to **mitigate** their effects.

Getting defensive

One way to minimise the effects of errors is to anticipate where a problem might occur and then put some 'protective barriers' in place. Computer science calls this **defensive programming**. The approach verifies that certain conditions are as expected before carrying out the main business of the solution. A failure to meet those conditions could either indicate anything from a warning to a potential system failure.

As with other practices in CT, we can see this same approach in other disciplines too. Physical systems where safety is an important issue are designed defensively. That is, they are safe by default. The default state of an elevator without power is to have its brakes **on**. To make the elevator move, power must be supplied to the brakes to switch them **off**. If the elevator loses power, it reverts to its default, powerless state with brakes applied. Hence, when something goes wrong, the people inside the elevator are automatically kept safe without any need for action. In essence, the elevator needs explicit 'permission' to carry out its normal business.

You can make your solution behave analogously to the elevator. Before the solution takes a possibly erroneous step, make it verify a set of preconditions before the 'normal business' can proceed. For example, if a step divides two numbers, you know that it will fail if the divisor[35] is zero. Therefore, you can create a precondition that checks this value. If it isn't zero, then normal business may proceed.

Reacting to problems

What to do in the case of a failed precondition depends on the context, and, in particular, on the consequences of an error. If the severity is low, the action taken could be something as minor as displaying a message. If the severity is high and risks causing real damage, the system should enter into some kind of emergency mode or even shut down.

For example, normal business for a drink vending machine is to read the value of inserted money and serve the customer their choice of drink. But several things could go wrong and the programmed responses vary:

- The customer might insert unreadable or foreign money. The machine recovers simply by returning the money (ideally with a helpful message to the customer).

- A particularly smart vending machine might have the ability to detect when a cup has fallen over on the dispensing tray. In this case, the machine should refuse to continue functioning until the cup is righted, after which it returns to normal business.

- A leak in the vending machine's water supply is a severe problem, since it risks water running onto the floor or into the machine's electrics. If a leak is detected, the prudent thing is probably for the machine to shut down.

Other general considerations when reacting to errors include:

- whether the system is interactive or not (which dictates whether or not it can ask the user what to do);

- whether the system is transactional or not. If it is, then it's possible to undo the changes made during a defective step.

Checking user input

In cases where your solution asks for input from a user, a little 'healthy paranoia' goes a long way. Humans make mistakes all the time (and malevolent users do so intentionally), so it's best to assume that your user will enter faulty input at some point. Think of all the ways an input could be wrong:

- If your solution expects a number, check that it really is a number before doing anything with it. Entering '9O' instead of '90' is an easy enough mistake to make.

- Similarly, if your solution requires input within a certain range, check it after it's been entered. Making sure an account number is the expected eight digits in length is quick and easy. All you have to do is count the number of digits in the input and ensure it's the right amount.

- Incorrect formats: phone numbers, website URLs, email addresses, dates and times are all examples of data that **must** match a specific format.

Being proactive and guarding against unwanted behaviour is essential. However, some bugs will slip in despite your efforts.

TESTING

This section describes testing, a method for locating hidden bugs in a fully or partially working system.

Goal

The aim of testing is to use the actual system you've produced in order to verify whether it performs as expected and to identify specific areas where it fails. Therefore, testing has to wait until your solution has reached some kind of working state. It could be fully working, meaning you can test the whole system, or it could be partially working, allowing you to test individual parts.

In order to perform testing effectively, you need to actually know what the solution aims to do. This makes the advice from Chapter 3 – clearly define the goal of your solution – essential. You gain little by verifying that a system performs as expected when you have poorly defined expectations. The solution's goal serves as a guide for testing.

Approach

It's very important in testing to be **systematic**. Ad hoc testing using no particular approach is easy to do, but the only thing you're likely to learn is that something is wrong somewhere. Being systematic will help you to localise the problem and find out exactly what is wrong and where.

You can choose between two approaches to testing, depending on what you want to achieve. The first is **top-down** testing, where you test the solution as a whole to ensure that it works. This is most effective at finding design flaws and verifying that the system hangs together well. The second approach is **bottom-up**, which requires you to begin by testing the smallest parts of the solution individually. This allows you to verify that they correctly fulfil their own obligations within the whole system and to show that your solution is built on solid foundations.

Table 5.1 Advantages and disadvantages of top-down and bottom-up testing

	Advantages	Disadvantages
Top-down	• Effective for finding design flaws. • Can be encouraging to test a full system, even if it is incomplete or contains bugs.	• Difficult to apply when the system is incomplete. • Requires you to use placeholders[36] for the unfinished parts to simulate their behaviour. • Harder to localise bugs when errors occur.
Bottom-up	• Easy to apply in early stages of development. • Effective for localising problems.	• Requires you to simulate the controlling parts of the solution.[37] • Doesn't expose design flaws until much later.

If you can, you should combine these approaches when testing, thereby gaining the best of both worlds. When you begin to implement your solution, you can start by putting together a skeletal structure filled with placeholders. This should be executable, even though it might not actually do anything useful yet. Subsequently, you can start to implement the individual pieces, replacing each placeholder with a functioning part that you can immediately test in isolation (this is bottom-up testing). At the same time, because you have a working skeletal structure, you can test the whole system to make sure it still functions as expected (top-down testing).

Testing individual parts

If you followed the advice in Chapters 3 and 4 so that your solution exists in reasonably independent pieces, testing will be made simpler. By testing only small parts of the solution at once, you make localising the problem easier. Tests that exercise only individual parts are called **unit tests**. However, testing individual parts can be tricky and merits some explanation. The trickiness comes because the individual parts of your solution normally operate as part of a larger whole and so assume that the rest of the system is present and correct. That's not the case when they're being tested in isolation, so you have to simulate whatever things the part is dependent on.

For example, some components expect to be given parameters as part of their normal work, so to test them you'll need to provide some dummy data that simulate normal operation. In the ideal case, you would come up with every conceivable different value that could possibly be provided and then run a test for each one. If you could do that, you would be able to give a solid guarantee that the component works as expected. However, that's often unfeasible because there are too many possible variants.

To illustrate this, I'll use the example of the FizzBuzz game. In this game, players take turns to count upwards from 1, replacing any number divisible by 3 with the word 'Fizz' and any number divisible by 5 with 'Buzz'. Numbers divisible by both 3 and 5 are replaced with 'FizzBuzz'. A player loses if they say a number when they should have said one of the words. The first few numbers in the correct sequence are:

1, 2, Fizz, 4, Buzz, Fizz, 7, 8, Fizz, Buzz, 11, Fizz, 13, 14, FizzBuzz, 16, 17, Fizz, 19, Buzz ...

A computer-based FizzBuzz game requires a subroutine that calculates the correct response for a given number. To test that this subroutine works, you could try it out for the first 20 values. That would tell you for certain whether it works for those values. But does it work for 21? Technically, you don't know for certain. The problem is, no matter what how large the set of test values, more numbers exist that you could include. Furthermore, the larger the set of test values, the longer it takes to carry out all the tests.

Despite this, you can be systematic. A component in a solution usually dictates requirements regarding its input data and you can use this information to make your testing systematic. Each requirement corresponds to a distinct set of inputs called equivalence classes. The thing that relates all inputs in each class is that they elicit the same type of response from the solution. Consequently, you can choose one (or several) pieces of representative test data from each group to stand in for all other values in that class. You can do the same with input data that contradict each requirement.

Figure 5.1 All inputs divided into equivalence classes

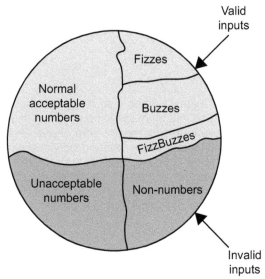

For the FizzBuzz game, we can divide all input into several equivalence classes (Figure 5.1), choose a representative value from each class, give them to the subroutine and then verify that in each case the correct response is returned. The classes include:

- **Normal acceptable numbers (for example, 8):** represents all acceptable numbers not divisible by 3 or 5. The subroutine should return the same number we gave it. If this number works, it implies that all other numbers in this class also work.

- **Fizzes (for example, 3):** represents all numbers divisible by three. Subroutine should return 'Fizz'.

- **Buzzes (for example, 10):** represents all numbers divisible by five. Subroutine should return 'Buzz'.

- **FizzBuzzes (for example, 30):** represents all numbers divisible by both three and five. Subroutine should return 'FizzBuzz'.

- **Unacceptable numbers (for example, -10):** numbers out of range should be rejected.

- **Non-numbers (for example, VII):** Arabic numerals only, please. A computer regards this as a piece of text and should reject it.

And, because 'bugs lurk in corners and congregate at boundaries' (Beizer, 1990):

- **Acceptable boundary (for example, 1):** this should work.

- **Unacceptable boundary (for example, 0):** this should be rejected.

Testing is a great place to benefit from another pair of eyeballs. You should record all your tests in a document (a test plan).[38] Make them clear and easy to understand. Then, give that plan to a third party and have them test your solution. Another perspective will help you to find problems that you, on your own, might miss.

DEBUGGING

> You know my methods. Apply them.
> Sherlock Holmes in *The Sign of Four* (Conan Doyle, 1890)

Inevitably, at some point during testing or real-world use of your solution, a puzzling error will occur. It will be unclear what particular step of the solution caused the problem, but there's no need to panic. Once again, you can be systematic in finding and fixing, that is **debugging**, the error. There are methods you can apply.

Take inspiration from Sherlock Holmes, who treated detection as a science. Your goal is to explain the facts (that is, the specific error(s) that occurred) and reconstruct the chain of events that led up to them. You need to look for clues and use them to make deductions. These will help you to build a hypothesis that might explain the problem. Once you have that, you can put it to the test. If your test is successful, you will have found the error(s) in your solution and can proceed to think about a fix.

That is the approach **in general**. In actuality, there is no single guaranteed method for debugging, but numerous different strategies are available (listed below) for building and testing your hypothesis. You'll need some creativity and imagination to help you. Naturally, you'll get better at debugging the more you do it.

Be ruthless with hunches

If you have a hunch about the problem, try it. You created the system, so you should have a good feel for how it works and how it might go wrong.

However, if your hunch is proved incorrect, **discard it immediately!** Don't get overly attached to your favourite explanation.

Respect Occam's Razor

You may well have several ideas about what could be causing the problem. Some might be simple, others complex. Occam's Razor is a principle in problem-solving that tells us the simpler explanation – the one that requires us to make the fewest assumptions – is most likely the correct one.

In other words, resist the urge to dream up complicated explanations. Try the simple ones first and eliminate those.

Divide and conquer

If you're unsure where the problem lies, make life easier for yourself by reducing the number of places you need to search. If, when designing your solution, you broke down your problem using a divide-and-conquer approach, you can now take advantage of that by using the same approach to debugging.

Divide and conquer allows you to eliminate whole areas of your system as suspects at once. The layout of your system – the components and their relationships – should resemble a tree structure. As your system executes, control is passed from component to component. Consequently, if the problem you're investigating arises **before** control ever passes to a certain component, then you can eliminate that component as a cause of your problem. Furthermore, any component that is **only** invoked by that eliminated component can itself be eliminated also.

Change one thing at a time

Good debugging is like good experimentation. When a scientist carries out an experiment, they're looking for the cause of something. In their case, they vary some factors and analyse the consequences to establish a link between cause and effect. However, a scientist takes extra care to vary only one factor at a time. After all, if they tweak three factors at once and then successfully detect an effect, how can they know which of the three factors was responsible?

Apply that same lesson during your debugging. If you think a change can fix your problem, apply it and then test it. If it didn't work, undo the change and put the system back to its original state before you try anything else.

Logging

At some point you'll likely observe that your solution does something unexpected; either it does something you didn't intend it to or it **doesn't** do something it should have. You need therefore to investigate which instructions in your system are executed at what point. But since execution happens inside the computer, you're not in a position to 'see' it.

However, you can get something of an overview by inserting an additional logging instruction somewhere in your algorithm. When this instruction is executed it will flag it up (for example, by printing out a message). The logging instruction acts like a turnstile; every time the computer 'goes through', this fact is reported. For example, you might expect that the computer goes through a particular loop five times, so you add a log instruction inside the loop that does nothing other than print out the word 'Loop'. If, when you run the system, the final result is:

```
Loop
Loop
Loop
Loop
```

you know that the loop was executed only four times.

You can do similar things if you're suspicious of certain values. You might observe that your solution does something unwanted, making you suspect that an incorrect value is the cause. It's not unusual, for example, that a block of instructions fails to trigger when you expected.

```
if x > 10, then do stuff
```

If, when you run the program, the instructions represented by '**stuff**' are not carried out, what would you suspect causes the problem? A strong possibility is that the variable x is actually less than or equal to 10 when this line is carried out. You could confirm this by adding a log instruction (immediately before the if-statement) that prints out the value of x. Once you have established the actual value, you can then investigate why x ended up with this particular value.

Tracing

Sometimes the only way to diagnose a problem is to go line by line through each instruction and see for yourself what the computer is actually doing.

You can do this yourself by hand, pretending to be the computer. You will need to go through each instruction, execute it, and keep track of the changes to any data the algorithm maintains. Figure 5.2 shows an example algorithm from a Minesweeper game where the game board is divided into squares. Each square may or may not be adjacent to a hidden mine. The game calculates the number of mines in the immediate vicinity of a square by going clockwise through each adjacent square and counting up the number of mines. Figure 5.2 shows someone partway through tracing, having gone through the 'repeat-until' loop six times already. They've executed each line and kept track of each change to the two variables.

Figure 5.2 Partway through tracing a Minesweeper algorithm

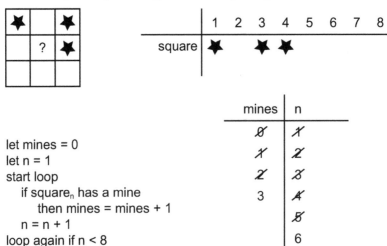

Once your system is implemented for a computer, you can also perform tracing using a **debugger**. This is a computer-aided tool that executes a program under your careful control. Essentially, it reveals to you what's going on in the computer's mind as it runs your solution. You can use a debugger to step through instructions one by one and print out the current state of various data, although many debuggers have many more advanced features. Use of debuggers is explored in more detail in Chapter 12.

Explain the problem aloud

Whenever an unexplained error stumps you, try explaining the problem vocally.[39] Step through what is wrong, what you've already tried and what you haven't tried. You might be surprised by how quickly a new explanation occurs to you after putting the problem into words.

This can be effective even when you do it alone (I won't tell anyone you talk to yourself). But for best results, explain your problem to someone else. It doesn't matter if the other person doesn't fully understand your solution. In fact, it's better if they don't because the other person might unwittingly help you to respect Occam's Razor. The problem might be so simple that it needs a 'silly' question to expose the simple mistake you've made.

YOU CAN'T HAVE EVERYTHING: DECIDING WHICH ERRORS TO FIX

Every piece of non-trivial software in the world has bugs in it. Your solution will be no different. You can keep testing and debugging until the cows come home, but there will always be flaws.

This is an important thing to acknowledge. It forces us to stop embarking on an endless pursuit of perfection, and instead manage the list of problems. If not all flaws can be repaired, then we need a way to choose which ones to fix. Software developers have built up extensive experience in the management of errors. This section examines some of that experience.

The first question to ask about an error is: what is its level of **severity**? This describes how strongly the error prevents proper usage of the system. For example, a bug that causes the system to fail has a high severity; when a logo is coloured slightly incorrectly, that's a low severity. Severity values are typically 'Minor', 'Moderate', 'Major' and 'Critical'.

The next question to ask is: what is its **priority**? This is a slightly more complex question to answer because you have to take several factors into account:

- **Frequency:** the more often the error occurs, the higher priority the bug should get.

- **Feature value:** if the bug affects an unimportant feature, it can get a low priority. If a key feature is broken, the bug should get a high priority.

- **Scheduling:** estimate how long it will take to fix an error and ask if it's worth the time. Is it worth fixing a rarely occurring, minor flaw if it's estimated to take a whole week? On the other hand, almost any amount of effort spent fixing a regularly occurring system failure is time well spent.

Priority values are typically 'Low', 'Medium' and 'High' as shown in Figure 5.3.

Figure 5.3 Priority severity matrix

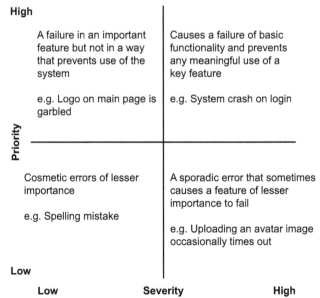

High

| A failure in an important feature but not in a way that prevents use of the system | Causes a failure of basic functionality and prevents any meaningful use of a key feature |

e.g. Logo on main page is garbled | e.g. System crash on login

Priority

Cosmetic errors of lesser importance | A sporadic error that sometimes causes a feature of lesser importance to fail

e.g. Spelling mistake | e.g. Uploading an avatar image occasionally times out

Low

Low   Severity   High

Putting bugs on an axis, as in Figure 5.3, helps us to sort them and choose which ones to fix next. It's clear that bugs that are high-priority/high-severity should be ranked as most important, while low-priority/low-severity should be ranked last. For the two middle categories, I would suggest that high-priority/low-severity problems are tackled earlier.

SUMMARY

Bugs are mistakes that can cause errors in your solution. Numerous techniques exist either to prevent bugs making it into your solution or to deal with them after they've made their way in.

Preventing bugs from getting into your solution means careful design effort. The earlier bugs are found, the cheaper they are to repair.

Mitigating errors means anticipating and controlling their potential consequences. Programming defensively is a great way to prevent bugs causing havoc.

Hunting for bugs and removing them is done by testing and debugging. Testing lets you search for bugs and both top-down and bottom-up strategies offer systematic ways to approach testing. Debugging using logs or tracing helps you track down the ultimate cause of errors.

EXERCISES

EXERCISE 1

Mark the following statements as true or false:

    A. Errors can result from statements that are grammatically valid.
    B. The exit condition of a loop is evaluated after each statement inside the loop is executed.
    C. Defensive programming assumes that code is safe until proven otherwise.
    D. Bottom-up testing is an effective way of finding design flaws.
    E. An equivalence class groups all inputs to an algorithm that elicit the same type of response.

EXERCISE 2

Explain the difference between a bug and an error.

EXERCISE 3

An 'if–then' conditional tells the computer to carry out some instructions if a certain condition is met. How could you modify this form to carry out instructions if the condition is **not** met?

EXERCISE 4

The algorithm in the Minesweeper example (Figure 5.2) contains an error. Find it and fix it.

> The squares as they are configured in the example won't necessarily expose the error. Try debugging with the mines in different positions.

EXERCISE 5

Write an algorithm for the FizzBuzz game that analyses an input number and returns the correct response. If the number isn't in the expected range, the algorithm should return a suitable error message.

6   EVALUATING A SOLUTION

OBJECTIVES

- Discuss key quality measures of a solution's effectiveness, including:
  - correctness using empirical means;
  - efficiency by examining time and space complexities;
  - elegance, specifically the maximisation of effectiveness and simplicity;
  - usability according to industry-standard measures.
- Explain the importance of trade-offs with regard to quality measures.

SOLUTION EVALUATION

You did it. You analysed the problem, broke it down into pieces, came up with a solution design, which you then implemented, tested and debugged. You have something that functions. So, you're finished, right?

Well, not quite.

The work is not over just because you have a solution. Before you can really finish, you have to make sure you've produced a **good** solution. You must evaluate its quality.

There are many aspects to quality. Evaluating a solution involves asking several basic questions, each addressing a specific aspect. Important questions about the solution include:

- Is it correct? Does it actually solve the problem you set out to solve?
- Is it efficient? Does it use resources reasonably?
- Is it elegant? Is it simple yet effective?
- Is it usable? Does it provide a satisfactory way for the target audience to use it?

This chapter explores how to answer these questions for your own solutions.

IS IT CORRECT?

The most important question to ask of your solution is: does it actually solve the original problem you set out to solve? In other words, is it a correct solution? If it's not, then that basically renders every other measure of quality redundant. It doesn't matter how fast, clever or sexy your solution is; if it doesn't solve your problem, then it's incorrect and you need to make changes.

The prudent approach is to assume a program is incorrect until shown to be correct. Practically speaking, this makes sense; after all, a solution is rarely correct before testing and debugging has been done. Philosophically, it's also the right thing to do. Endless possible incorrect solutions exist; there are comparatively few correct ones. It's the same sceptical approach used in fields like science, medicine and law, where the burden of proof lies with those making positive claims, so as to guard against false positives.

Technically speaking, program correctness is a deeply theoretical issue in computer science. In academic circles, talk of proving a program to be correct usually refers to **mathematical** proof. Such a proof, if successful, establishes a program's correctness as incontrovertible fact. However, practitioners outside academia rarely invoke this costly approach when not dealing with critical systems.[40]

Most of the time, showing a program to be correct is done **empirically** by carrying out a series of tests, something covered in Chapter 5. At the beginning of a development process, a problem is specified a certain way. This specification is mirrored in the test plan (see an example plan in Figure 6.1), which rephrases each requirement as a test. The testing runs each aspect of the solution and verifies that the resultant behaviour fulfils the specification.

Figure 6.1 Excerpt from a test plan for a vending machine

Test No.	Test subject	Test description	Expected outcome	Actual outcome
1	Coin slot	Insert an acceptable 50 cent coin	Coin accepted. '0.50' appears on display.	Behaved as expected.
2	Coin slot	Insert an unacceptable foreign coin.	Coin rejected. 'Unrecognised currency' appears on display.	Failed. Coin was rejected but no message appeared.
3	Keypad	Enter valid selection '15'.	'You selected hot chocolate' appears on display.	Behaved as expected.
4	Keypad	Enter invalid selection '99'.	'Invalid selection, please try again' appears on display.	Behaved as expected.

As opposed to the mathematical approach, which aims to prove a solution correct, the aim of an empirical testing approach is to show that the solution is incorrect. This is easier because just one failed test is enough to demonstrate that. It's usually infeasible to test every possible value that could be input to a solution (and every combination thereof), so every test that passes adds one more piece of supporting evidence.

More supporting evidence further strengthens your claims of the solution's correctness. Consequently, showing correctness via testing is not a binary matter of true or false. Rather, testing gives a gradated picture of correctness. This set of levels allows you to grade the correctness of your solution, from least to most convincing:

1. The solution contains no syntax errors or invalid operations that can be automatically detected.
2. The solution yields the correct answer for some set of test data.
3. The solution yields the correct answer for test data that are typical or random.
4. The solution yields the correct answer for test data that are deliberately difficult to process.
5. The solution yields the correct answer for all test data that are possible with respect to the original problem specification.
6. Same as level 5, except a correct (or reasonable) response are given for erroneous test data.
7. For all possible input, the solution gives correct or reasonable responses.

Reducing the number of failing tests doesn't strengthen your claim to a solution's correctness. The presence of even one failing test shows your solution to be incorrect. In other words:

- No passing tests and no failing tests means you have no evidence of correctness.
- Some passing tests and no failing tests means you have some evidence of a correct solution.
- Some passing tests and at least one failing test means you have an incorrect solution.

Correctness shows only that the solution solves the problem. It doesn't matter if it's slow, inefficient, too complicated or someone else simply doesn't like the solution, this doesn't affect correctness.

IS IT EFFICIENT?

Every algorithm requires some amount of resources to do its work. Different algorithms, even ones that solve the same problem, can perform differently in terms of efficiency. This performance is usually measured in terms of time and space.

- **Time:** the duration of an algorithm's running time, from start to end. The duration can be measured as the number of steps taken during execution.
- **Space:** the amount of memory storage required by an algorithm to do its work.

The question of an algorithm's efficiency comes down to its time and space requirements. If, when you analyse an algorithm you find that its use of resources is acceptable, then it may be deemed efficient.

But can its efficiency really be measured reliably in a way that can be fairly compared to that of other algorithms? At first glance it may seem not to be the case. After all, algorithms run on input data and they perform differently depending on the size of input data they get. Imagine an algorithm that totals up a list of numbers: its processing time increases the more numbers are in the list.

Complexity class: a profile that tells you how algorithms belonging to it will behave in general.

This is all true, but CS can measure algorithm efficiency because it examines computation **in general**. It provides general principles about efficiency that you can apply to your specific situation. CS doesn't rank every conceivable, possible algorithm in terms of efficiency.[41] Instead, it provides a relatively small set of complexity classes, into which every algorithm can be placed. It even takes into account that input data size can vary.

Judge your algorithm's efficiency by analysing its behaviour and matching it to one of those categories.

Each category describes how its algorithms perform **in the worst case**. In other words, what the maximum amount of resources an algorithm might use is. Because an algorithm's performance depends on the input data, the resource usage is a function of input data size. Table 6.1 shows some example categories and their efficiency in terms of time.

Table 6.1 Sample of common complexity classes

Name	Running time	Comments
Constant	$O(1)$	Doesn't necessarily take 1 time unit, rather it takes a fixed number of time units. An example is determining if a number is odd or even.
Logarithmic	$O(logN)$	As the input size grows, the running time increases at an ever-smaller rate. Divide-and-conquer approaches often perform like this.
Linear	$O(N)$	This is the best possible performance of any algorithm that must go through the entire input sequentially.
Quadratic	$O(N^2)$	The running time of algorithms in this class quadruples when the input size doubles.
Factorial	$O(N!)$	Algorithms in this class are often brute force and considered too slow for practical use.

In Table 6.1, the running time of each category is expressed in a funny looking notation imaginatively called 'Big-O', thanks to its use of a big letter O. The term inside the parentheses denotes how much time algorithms of this class generally require to process input. N stands for the number of items contained in the input.

Here are some rough examples. An algorithm that carries out one step (or one set of steps) for each item is classed $O(N)$. You can say it takes 1 time unit to process input with just 1 item, or it takes 5 time units to process 5 items. In more general terms, it takes N time units to process N items. As another example, an algorithm that carries out N steps for each item,[42] that is $N \times N$, is classified as $O(N^2)$. It takes 4 time units to process 2 items, or 16 time units to process 4 items. More generally, it takes N^2 time units to process N items.

A more concrete example will explain more about complexity classes.

Example: Linear search

A linear search algorithm takes two input parameters: a list of items of size N, and one additional item we'll call a search item (the items could be numbers, pieces of text or whatever). Its goal is to ascertain whether the list contains the search item or not. The algorithm works by searching through the list from start to end, comparing the search item with each item in the list as it goes. As soon as a list item and the search item are found to be equal, the algorithm returns 'true' and immediately halts. If the algorithm reaches the end of the list without finding a match, it returns 'false'. The question is, which complexity category does the algorithm belong to?

- In the best case, the search item matches with the first item in the list. This is $O(1)$.

- On average (assuming each item is just as likely to be sought as any other), the search item will match somewhere in the middle on the list, meaning its average performance is $O\left(\frac{N}{2}\right)$

- In the worst case, either the search item matches with the last item in the list or it isn't found at all. That gives a performance of $O(N)$.

Someone wanting to use a linear search algorithm now has some knowledge to apply. They should have an idea of what kinds of list sizes their solution will have to process, as well as how long it takes to carry out one comparison. Knowing that their chosen algorithm has a worst-case performance of $O(N)$, they can decide whether this is acceptable for their solution.

As you can see, not all algorithms are created equal in terms of performance. Algorithms with worst-case performances like $O(logN)$, $O(N)$ and $O(N^2)$ are considered efficient because their running times are usually acceptable even when N is very large. Algorithms with worst-case performances like $O(2^N)$, $O(N^N)$ or $O(N!)$ are generally considered inefficient because their running times become unacceptable relatively quickly as N grows larger.

Big-O Cheat Sheet (bigocheatsheet.com) categorises many popular data structures and algorithms.

IS IT ELEGANT?

So far, we've seen that evaluation is an objective endeavour. A software solution is not a piece of art;[43] it's a functional thing, just like a bridge, a scientific theory or a mathematical proof. As such, its correctness and efficiency don't come down to a matter of opinion.

However, some aspects of evaluation cause things to become a little fuzzier in this regard. One of these aspects is elegance, something you might associate more with artistic pursuits. Two different solutions might both solve a problem, but they could be judged apart by the elegance of their respective approaches. This applies not only to software; it's true of other 'functional' disciplines like engineering, science and mathematics.

Roughly speaking, elegance maximises both effectiveness and simplicity at the same time.

To an engineer, something achieves elegance if it performs something very useful with only a few, simple parts. It might also be non-obvious and solve several problems at once. As an example, consider the pipe that drains water away from the sink in your kitchen or bathroom. It's connected to a sewage outlet and so risks leaking foul stenches back up the pipe and into the room. We could prevent this in any number of ways. One would be to attach some kind of pleasant-smelling filter inside the pipe, but that is easily clogged and would require regular cleaning and changing. Or perhaps a check valve that only opens in one direction to allow water to run out? Not bad, but it would require hinges which are at risk of rust. The actual solution is a trap.[44] This allows water to gather (as a side effect of normal usage), which then blocks any air coming back up from the sewage outlet. It's an incredibly simple, non-obvious solution that works automatically and requires little or no maintenance (see Figure 6.2).

To a scientist, an elegant theory explains a lot with very little. Theories like Newton's second law ($F = ma$) or Einstein's mass–energy equivalence ($E = mc^2$) boil hugely complex phenomena down to very simple equations. The same equations can be applied to something as small as atoms or as large as a galaxy. They also serve as the basis for innumerable other theories.

A mathematical proof is elegant if it's a simple, effective solution to a non-trivial problem. An example of mathematical elegance comes from a (possibly apocryphal) story featuring mathematician Carl Friedrich Gauss (Haynes, 2006). One day in his youth, his mathematics teacher gave the students in his class a problem: calculate the sum of the integers from 1 to 100.[45] All the students embarked on the obvious solution; they started a running total and began adding numbers to it one at a time (1 + 2 = 3, 3 + 3 = 6, 6 + 4 = 10 and so on). All students except Gauss that is. He noticed a pattern in the problem:[46] 1 + 100 = 101, 2 + 99 = 101, 3 + 98 = 101 and so on, right up to 50 + 51 = 101. This pattern showed that those 100 numbers could be grouped into 50 pairs, each of which totalled 101. Instead of carrying out 100 sums, Gauss needed only to carry out a single multiplication (50 × 101) to get the same answer.

Figure 6.2 Cross section of a trap

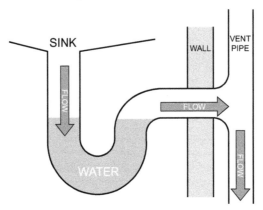

It's the mathematician's idea of elegance that is perhaps closest to a computer scientist's. If a programmer were to encode these two solutions for a computer, they would look something like this.

The obvious solution:

- Let total = 0;
- For each number, *n*, between 1 and 100:
  - Let total = total + *n*.

Gauss's more elegant solution:

- Let total = 50 x 101.

Gauss's solution achieves the same as the obvious solution, but does so using less space (one variable instead of two) and less time (one step instead of roughly 100). In terms of complexity (see above), if you were to write generic versions of both algorithms to work out the sum of the first *N* integers, the obvious solution would be O(*N*) while Gauss's solution would be the much more efficient O(1).

> Simple can be harder than complex: You have to work hard to get your thinking clean to make it simple.
>
> (Jobs, 1998)

It might seem paradoxical, but it's harder to be simple than complicated. Coming up with elegant solutions takes time and effort. It requires you to get to the essence of the problem and see the patterns within it. It also requires you to apply some out-of-the-box thinking. But it is potentially very rewarding effort, because the pay-offs of an elegant result can be huge.

The main drawback of a non-obvious solution is just that: it's non-obvious. If some-one else eventually comes to work on your solution, they need to know how it works. Anyone looking at the obvious solution above can easily figure out it's totalling the numbers 1 to 100. However, looking at Gauss's elegant solution in isolation, it isn't immediately clear what it's trying to achieve. The author may understand it, but what about everyone else? Therefore, you should always make sure non-obvious parts of your solution are accompanied by clear explanations.

When I talk about other people having to understand your solution, that includes you too! You may understand the complexities today, but will you still understand them after leaving your solution and resuming work on it a few weeks or months later? There's a very good chance you will have forgotten how it works. Do yourself a favour: always write clear explanations of how your solution works, **especially** the complex bits.

When coming up with elegant solutions, be on your guard against cleverness for its own sake. Always be ready to justify why you're not taking the obvious approach.[47] If there are no tangible benefits to your non-obvious way, you could be making the solution more complex for no good reason.

IS IT USABLE?

Ultimately, the users of your solution will be people. Your solution must therefore cater to humans and their particular ways. In other words, it must **usable** and ought to give users a positive experience.

Criteria like correctness, efficiency and elegance describe a solution on its own terms. However, usability measures how well something can be used by people in order to achieve their goals. Humans bring additional baggage. We're not machines; we have desires and emotions. We make mistakes and have limited patience. People want solutions that are easy to learn, uncomplicated to use, forgiving of our fallibility, and the less effort required from us the better.

Usability captures these desires. It formalises them into several components that meas-ure how easy and satisfying it is for people to use a solution (Nielsen, 2012). Thankfully, despite involving humans in the equation, these components are somewhat measurable. They are:

- **Learnability:** how easy is it for users to accomplish basic tasks the first time they encounter the solution?

- **Efficiency:** once users have learned the solution, how quickly can they perform tasks?

- **Memorability:** when users return to the solution after a period of not using it, how easily can they re-establish proficiency?

- **Errors:** how many errors do users make, how severe are these errors and how easily can they recover from the errors?

- **Satisfaction:** how pleasant is it to use the design?

Usability heuristics are general principles you can apply when designing a solution. If you apply them carefully, then you will have less reworking to do at the evaluation stage. Jakob Nielsen (1995), a leading expert on usability, lists ten such heuristics here: www.nngroup.com/articles/ten-usability-heuristics/

Evaluating usability is ultimately about the reactions of real people. In the end, you will have to involve people in the evaluation. This is done in part by an observational study. People representative of your audience should be recruited as test subjects, who then use the solution to carry out a set of pre-defined tasks (see Table 6.2). While the subject is busy, the evaluator observes their work, noting where the subject is successful and where they have difficulties.

Table 6.2 Sample of a list of usability tasks

Task No.	Description
1	Log into the system.
2	Add an email address to your user profile.
3	Buy a cookery book for under £10.
4	Show a list of your past purchases.

Encourage the test subject to be very vocal when they're testing the solution. They should think aloud, expressing what they're trying to do and what their current thoughts are. This is all information for your evaluation. The evaluator may speak during a test (for example, to clarify what the subject said), but they should keep their interventions to a minimum and should not give the subject explicit hints on how to use the solution.

After the subject completes the test, the evaluator provides them with a questionnaire. The questions are typically broad and don't focus on specific features. Instead they ask the subject to rate various factors on a scale. Here's an example set:

Rate the following on a scale of 1 (strongly disagree) to 5 (strongly agree):

1. Overall, I enjoyed using this system.
2. I found this system easy to use.
3. It took me too long to get used to this system.
4. I had problems finding the functions in this system.
5. There were too many steps to carry out the functions in this system.
6. The system was forgiving when I made a mistake.

To gain more insight, you should follow up on the responses. Either allow the user to elaborate on each answer in a free-text format, or interview them and ask for the reasoning behind their responses.

Usability testing doesn't necessarily have to be done after the solution is completed. You could create a mock-up of your system as a paper prototype and then let the test subjects use that to give you feedback. The usual rule applies: the earlier you find problems, the easier it is to fix them.

TRADE-OFFS

Various factors conspire to ensure that no solution turns out perfect. Some of those factors are down to mistakes being made or a shortage of hours in the day.

However, another reason is that you can't always optimise every aspect of a solution at once. Improving a solution in one respect can often compromise it in others. Consider solution efficiency. It is expressed in terms of the time the solution takes and the storage space it requires. Although not always the case, sometimes a solution forces you to trade better time performance in return for increased space usage – or, conversely, accept a slower solution as the cost for decreased space requirements. This is called a space–time trade-off.

As an illustrative example, let's look at image compression. Images are stored, sent and rendered by computers constantly every day, on disks, in web pages, via video streaming or wherever. For computers to handle an image, it must be broken down into discrete pieces called **pixels** (picture elements), each of which describes one tiny piece of the image.

Storing all the pixels can add up to a lot of information. A typical 3-megapixel camera (which, even at the time of writing, is pretty run-of-the-mill) produces images with over 3 million pixels.[48] Each pixel needs storing in computer memory. In a simple scheme (which we'll use in this example), the image data is stored as a string of tokens. Each token is stored in 1 byte, the smallest addressable size of memory space. A byte can store a single character or a number between 0 and 255. The colour of a pixel is described by a character token: 'B' means black, 'W' means white.

Consider the 16 × 16 pixel image[49] of a smiley face in Figure 6.3, which has a grid super-imposed over it to show the pixels explicitly:

Figure 6.3 Smiley face image

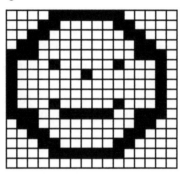

The question here is how to store the image data so the image can be rendered again later. One solution is to store the pixel information in a string of 256 (that is, 16 × 16) tokens, one describing each pixel. Those numbers could be stored on disk or beamed out over the internet for later usage. In this case, rendering means putting the right values (B or W) in the right place (see Figure 6.4).

This would be very fast. To render, the computer needs only go through every pixel from start to finish, grabbing the next value from the string and putting the corresponding pixel in place on the screen. However, this approach is not optimised for space. Notice that most of the image is taken up by a white background. Consequently, the image data contains lots of repeated, contiguous values.

Figure 6.4 Smiley face image with pixel values

Image	Pixel values
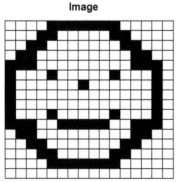	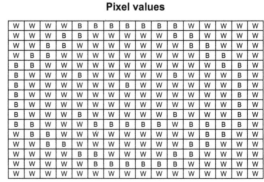

Pixel values:

W	W	W	W	B	B	B	B	B	B	B	B	W	W	W	W
W	W	W	B	B	W	W	W	W	W	W	B	B	W	W	W
W	W	B	B	W	W	W	W	W	W	W	W	B	B	W	W
W	B	B	W	W	W	W	W	W	W	W	W	W	B	B	W
B	B	W	W	W	W	W	W	W	W	W	W	W	B	B	W
B	W	W	W	W	W	W	W	W	W	W	W	W	W	B	W
B	W	W	W	B	W	W	W	W	W	W	B	W	W	B	W
B	W	W	W	B	W	W	B	W	W	W	B	W	W	B	W
B	W	W	W	W	W	W	W	W	W	W	W	W	W	B	W
B	W	W	W	W	W	W	W	W	W	W	W	W	W	B	W
B	W	W	W	B	W	W	W	W	W	B	W	W	W	B	W
B	B	W	W	W	B	B	B	B	B	B	W	B	B	B	W
W	B	B	W	W	W	W	W	W	W	W	B	B	W	W	W
W	W	B	B	W	W	W	W	W	W	B	B	W	W	W	W
W	W	W	W	B	B	W	W	W	W	B	B	W	W	W	W
W	W	W	W	W	B	B	B	B	B	B	W	W	W	W	W
W	W	W	W	W	W	W	W	W	W	W	W	W	W	W	W

Figure 6.5 Smiley face image with compressed pixel values

Image	Pixel values (compressed)

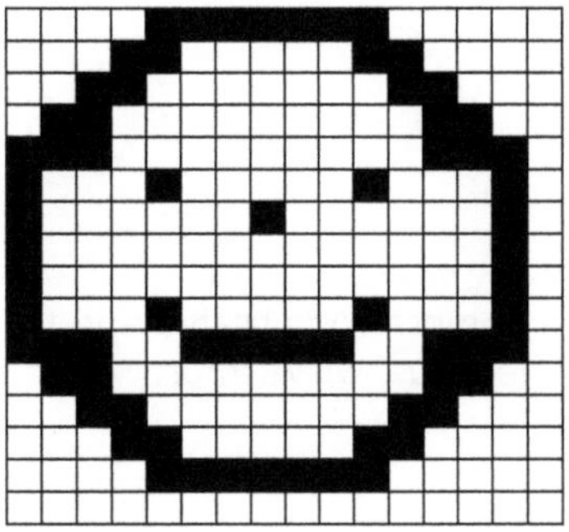

4	W	7	B	5	W										
3	W	2	B	5	W	2	B	4	W						
2	W	2	B	7	W	2	B	3	W						
1	W	2	B	9	W	2	B	2	W						
2	B	11	W	2	B	1	W								
1	B	3	W	1	B	5	W	1	B	3	W	1	B	1	W
1	B	6	W	1	B	6	W	1	B	1	W				
1	B	14	W	1	B	1	W								
1	B	14	W	1	B	1	W								
1	B	3	W	1	B	5	W	1	B	3	W	1	B	1	W
2	B	3	W	5	B	1	W	4	B	1	W				
1	W	2	B	9	W	2	B	2	W						
2	W	2	B	7	W	2	B	2	W						
4	W	2	B	4	W	2	B	4	W						
5	W	6	B	5	W										
16	W														

> When data contains a lot of repetition, it can be compressed to take up less space.

We can optimise the amount of space required to store the image by altering the scheme slightly. Instead of describing each pixel, we describe the **patterns** of pixels. For example, when there are five black pixels in a row, instead of storing that information as 'BBBBB' (which requires 5 bytes), we store it as '5B' (which requires 2 bytes: one for the number and one for the pixel colour – see Figure 6.5). By using this scheme, we reduce space requirements. This helps particularly in a situation like sending images over the internet, where reducing the amount of data to be transmitted is greatly beneficial.

Being 16 x 16 pixels, the image data is always stored using 256 bytes when uncompressed. However, using this compression scheme, we can store the smiley face using just 154 bytes. That means the compressed image data is reduced to about 60 per cent of its original size.

However, there's a cost that balances out this saving of space. The amount of work needed to interpret the uncompressed data is less than that of the compressed data. An algorithm for interpreting the uncompressed data may be something like this:

```
p = 0
for each token, t, in the image data:
    make pixel p the colour t
    p = p + 1
```

Whereas interpreting the compressed image data would need an algorithm more like this:

```
p = 0
n = 0
for each token, t, in the image data:
    if t is a number then
        n = t
    else
        repeat n times:
            make pixel p the colour t
            p = p + 1
```

The process of interpreting compressed image data is more complicated and takes more steps in total, and more steps means more time. Thus, we've improved space usage, but at the expense of time usage when rendering.

You might have spotted other examples of trade-offs in earlier sections of this book. The trade-off between cleverness and comprehensibility for example, where incorporating powerful tricks into your solution can make it harder to understand how it works. Or the compromise between usability and flexibility, where solutions that are made more flexible become less user-friendly.[50]

In summary, your solutions will inevitably involve compromises. A situation will often arise along the lines of 'I want better X, but that will make Y worse.' The question then is: how much of Y should you trade-off for X?

Make sure you know beforehand where it makes sense to optimise for your current solution, otherwise you'll have no guiding principles for what trade-offs to make. For example, if your solution involves sending data over a network, then it usually makes sense to optimise for storage space at the expense of additional compression/decompression time. That's because it takes longer to transmit a piece of data than to decode it.

SUMMARY

Evaluation of a solution encompasses many aspects. The most important aspect of a solution is its correctness, that is, does it actually solve the original problem? Beyond correctness, there are numerous other aspects to the quality of a solution. Which ones are important vary from solution to solution. This chapter examined several.

Efficiency measures the time and space usage of a solution to ensure that it solves a problem with acceptable usage of resources. Elegance determines whether a solution maximises both effectiveness and simplicity. Usability introduces a human aspect to evaluation by examining whether the user finds a solution easy and satisfying to use.

In these aspects and more, a degree of trading off is involved. A solution cannot optimise all quality aspects all the time. An essential part of forming a solution is deciding which quality aspects are more important and so which ones are chosen for optimisation.

EXERCISES

EXERCISE 1

Mark the following statements as true or false:

A. Most real-world software solutions are shown be correct empirically rather than mathematically.

B. Reducing the number of failing tests doesn't strengthen your claim to a solution's correctness.

C. An inefficient solution cannot be considered correct.

D. An elegant solution maximises both effectiveness and simplicity at the same time.

E. A usability evaluation begins by explaining to the test subject how to use the system.

EXERCISE 2

Look back at the two examples in the section 'Is it elegant?' Write generic versions of both the obvious solution and Gauss's solution, both of which sum up numbers from 1 to N.

EXERCISE 3

Look at the answer for the previous question. Which one of these two algorithms is more efficient in terms of time complexity?

EXERCISE 4

Look back at the image compression example in the section 'Trade-offs'. The compressed image data is not as efficient as it could be. Can you see how the data could be made to take up less space?

Hint: try writing out the data in one long line instead of splitting it over several lines.

EXERCISE 5

What are the names of the five components of usability and what do they measure?

PART II
COMPUTATIONAL THINKING IN SOFTWARE DEVELOPMENT

The second part of this book takes the theoretical computational thinking concepts explained in Part I, and walks you through applying them practically in software programming.

Things you see in Part II can be traced directly back to specific concepts in Part I. Notifications like this point out where in Part I to find them.

These practical lessons are applicable to a wide range of different programming languages.[51] However, for the sake of consistency, a single language will be used for demonstrations of executable source code. Python has been chosen because it is a clean, minimalist language that allows you to build simple, understandable programs quickly.

Keep in mind that Part II is not a comprehensive manual on Python or software programming in general. It only relates the specific principles of computational thinking to relevant aspects of programming.

7   TUTORIAL FOR PYTHON BEGINNERS

OBJECTIVES

- Learn how to use the Interpreter Prompt.
- Introduce basic types like numbers, strings, booleans and lists.
- Explain basic arithmetical operators, assignment and comparisons.
- Show how to add comments to code.
- Explain how Python uses indentation to denote structure.
- Demonstrate what a function is, at a basic level.

INTRODUCING PYTHON

This section covers the basic Python knowledge required to understand the examples used throughout Part II of this book. If you are already familiar with Python, feel free to skip over to the next chapter.

We assume you are using Python 3 in this chapter.

In addition to this tutorial, you can find many good online tutorials here: https://wiki. python.org/moin/BeginnersGuide/NonProgrammers

FIRST STEPS

You can run a Python program from the command prompt on your computer.

If you enter the python command, you should see something like this:

```
$ python
python 3.5.2 (default, Nov 17 2016, 17:05:23)
[GCC 5.4.0 20160609] on linux
Type 'help', 'copyright', 'credits' or 'license' for more information.
>>>
```

This brings you into the Interpreter Prompt. Using this, you can enter Python instructions one line at a time and they will be executed immediately. This is useful for experimenting with small ideas. For example:

```
>>> x = 1 + 2
>>> print(x)
3
```

Alternatively, you can write your code into a text file and then have Python execute it all at once. If you were to write those same two instructions into a file called **my_code.py**, you could run it like this:

```
C:\Users\Me> python my_code.py
3
```

The code above uses the built-in **print** command, which causes the program to display the value which is contained in quotes. The traditional first step when learning a new programming language is to write a program that greets the world:

```
print('Hello, World!')
```

Running the program from a source file[52] should look like this:

```
> python hello.py
Hello, World!
```

BASIC TYPES

Python allows you to process data of a variety of types. The most fundamental ones are already built into Python. These include:

- Numbers like 7, 42 or 3.14

- Strings, that is, an arbitrary sequence of characters. A string is denoted by being enclosed in quotes, either single (`'Hello, world'`) or double (`"Hello, world"`). There's no difference between choosing single or double quotes, it's just a matter of choice. However, you **must** be consistent once you've made a choice.

- Boolean values, that is, **True** and **False**.

- Lists, that is, a sequence of items that are logically grouped together, like `[1,2,3]`.

The examples used above are all literal values. A value can be assigned to a variable. The following code causes three different variables to be created:

```
the_number = 3
message = 'Hello, World'
done = True
```

Variables allow you specify one set of steps that can be carried out on different values.

```
total_books = number_of_hardbacks + number_of_paperbacks
```

If you give the **print** command a variable, it will display the value of that variable.

```
>>> print(total_books)
41
```

Sometimes, you need to include the value of a variable inside a message. In Python you can simply do that by typing the variable name next to the string, separating them with a comma. For example:

```
>>> age = 35
>>> print('I am', age, 'years old.')
I am 35 years old.
```

BASIC OPERATIONS

Manipulating data sits at the heart of computation. In a program, operations allow you to manipulate data. Python provides numerous such operations.

For example, you can manipulate numbers using arithmetic operators, like:

- addition (for example, `x = y + 2`);
- subtraction (for example, `x = y - 2`);
- multiplication (for example, `x = y * 2`);
- division (for example, `x = y / 2`);
- exponentiation (for example, `x = y**2`);
- modulo, aka remainder division (for example, `x = y % 2`).

You can also use operations to interrogate values and establish facts about them. Such operations evaluate to **True** or **False**.

For example, the equality operator, ==, tests if two values are equal or not. This would display **True**:

```
x = 3
print(x == 3)
```

Whereas this would display **False**:

```
x = 3
print(x == 4)
```

You can also compare two values to establish if one is larger or smaller, for example, this would display **True**:

```
print(3 < 4)
```

While this would display **False**:

```
print(9 < 4)
```

FUNCTIONS

A subroutine is a sequence of instructions within a program packaged up as a distinct block. They are the basic organisational blocks of a program.

The lines of code in a subroutine are not executed until the programmer explicitly requests them to be. When a subroutine is called on to execute its instructions, the flow of control jumps to that subroutine. When the subroutine has completed, the flow of control then returns to the point where the call took place.

Python supports a particular type of subroutine called a function. It behaves just like a subroutine except that it can also return values back to the calling line of code. In this code, two functions are defined (the keyword **def** is short for 'define'):

```
def output_hello():
    print('Hello, World!')

def double_2():
    num = 2 * 2
    return num
```

The first one doesn't return anything. The second returns the number 4.

You can call a function by typing its name followed by two parentheses:

```
def output_hello():
    print('Hello, World!')

def double_2():
    num = 2 * 2
    return num

output_hello()
result = double_2()
print(result)
```

Notice that the contents of each function are indented. This is how Python denotes that a line of code is part of a block. Any line that immediately follows a colon must be indented to show that it is contained in that block. All following lines that are similarly indented are considered part of the same block. The first line that's **not** indented denotes that the block has ended. In the previous example, that means that the **double_2** function contains the lines **num = 2 * 2** and **return num**, but the three lines that follow are not part of the function.

When you call a function, you can pass an arbitrary number of pieces of data to that function which it can use. These are called parameters. For example:

```python
def output_message(msg):
    print(msg)

def multiply(x, y):
    return x * y

# Print a greeting
output_message('Hello, World!')

# Multiply these numbers (product becomes 6)
product = multiply(2, 3)
```

COMMENTS

The previous example also featured comments (the lines that begin with a # symbol). When your program is being executed, any time the computer encounters a #, it ignores the rest of that line. This gives you the means to add comments that explain how your code works.

```python
# This is a comment. It will be ignored by Python, even if it
# contains valid source code, like x = y + 1
```

SUMMARY

After reading the material in this chapter, you should be able to write short, basic programs using the Python programming language, either at the Interpreter Prompt or in a source file.

EXERCISES

For the following exercises, you need to write a program to answer the questions.

EXERCISE 1

Write a program that creates two variables, **r** and **pi**. Assign **pi** the value of the mathematical constant (or a suitable approximation of it) and give **r** any value you want.

EXERCISE 2

Use the variables from the previous question to create a third variable called **area** that holds the area of a circle with radius **r**.

EXERCISE 3

Write a program that creates two number variables, **a** and **b**. Give each variable a value and then use the **print** command to output **True** or **False** depending on whether or not **a** is greater than **b**.

EXERCISE 4

Take the code from the previous answer and write a function called **bigger**. This function should accept two parameters, **x** and **y**, and return a value denoting whether **x** is bigger than **y**. Add at least three calls to **bigger** with different values.

8 EFFECTIVE BUILDING BLOCKS

OBJECTIVES

- Show how to apply logic in programming languages.
- Demonstrate good practices when using loops and conditionals.
- Discuss the important programming styles available.
- Explain how best to handle state and its effects in your programs.
- Demonstrate advanced constructs that help to make programs easier to manage.

LOGIC

Chapter 2 introduced the basic ideas of logical thinking. This section shows how to incorporate some of those ideas directly in a programming language using Python as a demonstration.

Recap

Proper use of logical operators is discussed in Chapter 2, section called 'Logical Thinking'. Some common mistakes using logical operators are discussed in the same chapter in a section called 'Gotchas'.

Logical propositions are statements in logic that evaluate to true or false. Individual propositions can be combined into a compound proposition that is true or false overall. In this case, they're combined using logical operators that correspond (imperfectly) to those in natural language ('and', 'or', 'not', etc.).

Propositions in Python

Python is a programming language, not a logic language. As such, it doesn't provide a means to write propositions, but it does support something similar in the form of expressions. An expression is a piece of code that you can evaluate to obtain a result. For example, '1 + 2' is an expression because it evaluates to 3.

'x > 42' is also an expression because (depending on the value of **x**) it evaluates either to **True** or **False**. An expression that evaluates to **True** or **False** is the nearest thing to a proposition you'll find in Python.

Expressions typically form parts of Python statements (a statement is a line in a program that performs an action). `if x > 42:` and `my_number = 1 + 2` are both examples of statements containing expressions.

Logical operators in Python

Python provides three logical operators (see Table 8.1), which work in much the same way as their counterparts from pure logic. These operators can combine several expressions into a single, complex expression.

Table 8.1 Logical operators in Python

Operator	Python keyword	Python code example
Logical AND	`and`	`on_vacation and is_sunny`
Logical OR	`or`	`player_has_row or all_ squares_occupied`
Logical NOT	`not`	`not (score < 50 or score > 80)`

Parentheses can be used in expressions, either to improve readability or to override the usual order of precedence for operators. Python borrows the order of precedence from mathematics intact, although it also adds some additional symbols without equivalents in mathematics (such as the assignment operator). See Appendix A for the order of operations in Python.

BASIC ALGORITHMIC CONSTRUCTS

Chapter 2 introduced algorithms as a fundamental means of creating solutions and explained the basic building blocks of every algorithm. Every programming language gives you ways to use those basic building blocks. This section demonstrates them.

Recap

Basic constructs of algorithms were discussed in Chapter 2, in the subsection, 'Defining algorithms'.

Let's recap the basics of algorithms. Despite their enormous applicability, even the most complex of algorithms is essentially made up of the following basic constructs:

- **Sequences:** a series of instructions executed (one after the other).
- **Conditionals:** a branching point where instructions are executed only if a certain condition is met.
- **Iterations:** a sequence that is executed repeatedly so long as a certain condition holds.

Figure 8.1 depicts each construct as a flow chart.

Figure 8.1 Flow charts of the three basic algorithmic constructs

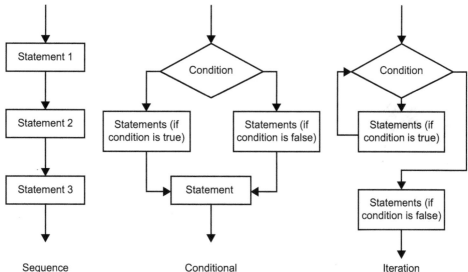

While other more sophisticated constructs exist, all of them boil down to some arrangement of these three constructs.

Sequence

Sequence takes place automatically in Python. Each line is executed one after another.

```
# This program asks you three questions, and then echoes
# back your responses in a sentence.
# input() is a function in Python that allows the user to
# type in some text. That text is assigned to a variable.
name = input('What is your name?')
quest = input('What is your quest?')
colour = input('What is your favourite colour?')
```

```
print('Your name is', name, 'your quest is', quest, \
'and your favourite colour is', colour)

print(response)
```

A couple of ways you might get caught out:

- One statement usually occupies one line in a file, but longer instructions can be split over several lines to improve readability. Any line that ends with a backslash (\) character means that the current instruction continues on the next line.
- Exceptions[53] can cause the expected flow of control to be interrupted in unpredictable ways. Read more about exceptions and how to tame their unpredictability in Chapter 12.

Conditional

Python has one conditional construct: the if-statement, an example of its simplest form being:

```
if number_of_chairs == 0:
    standing = True
```

 Notice the indentation of the second instruction. Python uses indentation to denote structure, so blocks of instructions 'inside' a particular construct are pushed along a few spaces. To make it even clearer, a statement that opens up a new code block (like an if-statement does) ends with a colon.

You must respect this rule, otherwise your code won't run correctly.

Complex conditionals

An if-statement can also include many optional parts. First of all, it can include an optional 'else' block. The instructions in this section will be executed only if all previous conditions were evaluated as false.

```
# This prints a different message depending on whether the
# program is executed during December or not.

if month == 12:
    # The following line will only ever execute during December
    print('It is Christmas time!')
else:
    # If it's not December, this line is executed.
    print('Just another ordinary day...')
```

An if-statement may include any number of **elif** blocks (**elif <condition>:**). **elif** is a short way of saying 'else if'. At most, one **elif** is executed and only if all previous conditions were evaluated as false.

The following example demonstrates **elif**. It calculates a grade based on test scores (80+ gains an A grade, 70–79 a B, 60–69 a C, 50–59 a D, and anything else is an F).

```
if score >= 80:
    grade = 'A'
elif score >= 70:
    grade = 'B'
elif score >= 60:
    grade = 'C'
elif score >= 50:
    grade = 'D'
else:
    grade = 'F'
```

As soon as one condition in an if–statement is evaluated as true, the code in its corresponding block is executed and all following parts of that if-statement are ignored. In other words, only one part of an if-statement at most will be executed.

Be careful with your conditions. If none of the conditions in an if-statement is true, then none of those corresponding blocks will be executed. Also, if more than one condition can be true simultaneously, you will need to order the parts carefully or you risk executing the wrong block. Keep in mind that conditions are evaluated top to bottom.

The previous example works correctly because conditions are tested in descending order of grade value. But what would happen if the conditions were rearranged like this?

```
if score >= 50:
    grade = 'D'
elif score >= 60:
    grade = 'C'
elif score >= 70:
    grade = 'B'
elif score >= 80:
    grade = 'A'
else:
    grade = 'F'
```

A student who scored 56 would be (correctly) awarded a D. However, a student who scored 73 would also be awarded a D, because their score matches the first condition.

As noted in Chapter 2, the behaviour of the 'if-then' form differs somewhat from the similarly named concept in pure logic. An if-statement in a Python program instructs the computer to make a decision regarding whether to execute the code inside the following block. That decision depends on how the associated condition is evaluated at that instant.

Conditional expressions

Python also includes a variation on the if-statement called a **conditional expression**. If the value of something depends on some condition, you might normally write code like this:

```
if a > b:
    # a is higher than b, therefore it's the maximum.
    max = a
else:
    # Return b, either because it's higher than a, or
    # because a and b are the same.
    max = b
```

A more concise way is to use a conditional expression, which has the form: `[value if true] if [condition] else [value if false]`. The previous example could therefore be rewritten like so:

```
max = a if a > b else b
```

Iteration

This construct allows you to execute the same sequence of steps repeatedly. Python provides two constructs for this.

The **while loop** executes a block of instructions repeatedly for as long as some condition evaluates to true. The value of the condition is only checked at the beginning of each iteration. As soon as the condition evaluates to false, the loop ends and execution jumps immediately to the next line following the end of the while block.

```
# This program invites the user to guess a number (set in the
# age variable). As long as they haven't guessed correctly,
# the program keeps asking.

age = 25
guess = 0

while age != guess:
    # Whereas a == b tests whether a and b are equal, a != b tests
    # whether a and b are not equal
    # The int() function turns the user's input (which is
```

```
# text) into an integer.
guess = int(input('Guess how old I am> '))

print('You got it right!')
```

The built-in function **len(x)** calculates the length of its parameter x. For example, if x is a list with 3 items in it, **len(x)** would evaluate to 3.

The **for-loop** sets up a control variable that manages execution of the loop. Execution iterates over the items in a sequence (the value of each item is assigned to the control variable at the beginning of each pass through the loop). That sequence could, for example, be a list. In the following code sample, the variable word is used as a control variable. At the beginning of each iteration of the loop, it is assigned the next value from the list words from beginning to end.

```
# This prints out the length of each word in a list of words

words = ['my', 'big', 'meal', 'comes', 'mostly', 'bearing', 'doubtful',
'garnishes']

for word in words:
    # The following line prints the length of the word
    print(len(word))

# Prints: 2 3 4 5 6 7 8 9
```

The built-in function **range (x, y)** produces a list of numbers from x to y-1.

or, if you know exactly how many iterations to execute, a range:

```
for number in range(1, 13):
    print(number * 42)

# Prints out the 42 times table
```

Exercise caution when using ranges. Remember Beizer's (1990) advice mentioned in Chapter 5: 'bugs lurk in corners and congregate at boundaries'. In a Python range, the first number is inclusive and the second is exclusive. Hence, **range(1, 5)** includes the numbers 1, 2, 3 and 4.

Cutting an iteration short

To prematurely end an iteration and move onto the next, Python provides the **continue** statement. This can be placed anywhere inside a loop. Upon encountering it, execution will immediately skip the rest of the block, jump to the beginning of the loop and start the next iteration.

Figure 8.2 depicts this as a flow chart.

Figure 8.2 Flow chart of the continue statement

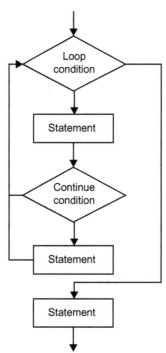

The following program compares each number in a list to see if it is greater than, less than, or equal to a test number. If either of the first two comparisons are successful, all the following comparisons don't need to be carried out, so the computer can jump immediately back to the beginning of the loop and move onto checking the next number in the list.

```
numbers = [3, 8, 1, 9, 5]
test_number = 5

for n in numbers:
If test_number > n:

print('Greater than')
continue
if test_number < n:
```

```
print('Less than')
continue
if test_number == n:
print('Equal to')
```

Prematurely exiting a loop altogether

Sometimes it makes sense to stop execution of a loop immediately and move on. For these situations, Python provides the **break** statement.

Figure 8.3 depicts this as a flow chart.

Figure 8.3 Flow chart of the break statement

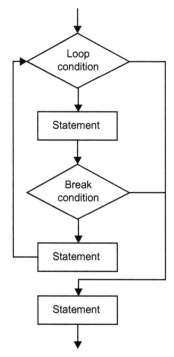

For example, in a number-guessing game, where the computer thinks of a number and the player is allowed several guesses, there's no need to keep asking the player after they've guessed correctly:

```
computers_number = 9
guessed_correct = False
```

```
# Player gets 5 guesses
for guesses in range(1, 6):
    players_number = input('Enter your guess> ')

    if computers_number == players_number:
        guessed_correct = True
        # Break out of the loop immediately because the player guessed
correctly
        print('Try again!, guesses, 'left.')

# At this point, player either guessed correctly or used up all
# guesses without success.
message = 'You win!' if guessed_correct else 'You lose!'
print(message)
```

PROGRAM STATE

> The fundamental nature of state in algorithms is discussed in the Chapter 2, subsection 'Defining algorithms'.

Because a program is executed step by step, you sometimes need to record the results of certain steps for use in later steps. The term 'state' describes the current values of all pieces of information kept track of by a program. But because the values of variables can change from moment to moment during a program's execution, it's essential to **carefully** manage the handling of state.

Using variables

The state you deal with in a computer program takes the form of variables. Because a program is executed one statement at a time, the value of variables can vary from moment to moment, so it's important to be able to track changes in variables.

It can be helpful to think of program variables as you would variables in a mathematical formula. However, because programming languages store variables in computer memory, this raises some important distinctions you must keep in mind.

This first, simple example demonstrating a value changing from one moment to the next highlights one of the differences:

```
x = 42
print(x) # Prints 42

x = x + 1
print(x) # Prints 43

x = x * 2
print(x) # Prints 86
```

Writing a mathematical formula like x = x + 1 would be nonsensical. That's because the formula is stating 'x is the same as x plus one' (which cannot be true), whereas the same statement in a Python program is saying 'compute the value of x plus one, then assign it to x'. This is perfectly fine in a Python program, because of the way it stores variables.

Each programming language stores variables in memory in its own way. Whichever language you choose, you must learn its approach to handling variables. Since this book uses Python, we focus on how Python handles variables.

In Python, a variable[54] can be thought of as a label that's attached to a value. The act of assigning a variable name is like attaching it to a value in memory. Therefore, executing this:

```
x = 42
name = 'Arthur'
```

can be thought of as creating the values 42 and 'Arthur' then attaching to them the labels **x** and **name** respectively (see Figure 8.4).

Figure 8.4 Assigning values

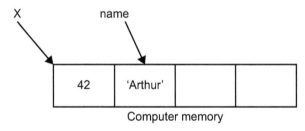

Computer memory

Normally, once a Python creates a value in memory, that value can't subsequently be changed. However, we've already seen examples that show variables can easily be reassigned new values. This is possible because giving a variable a new value is akin to creating the new value in a different place in memory and then moving the existing label to point at it. If we extend the last program like this:

```
x = 42
name = 'Arthur'
x = x + 1
```

then, after execution of the first two lines, the state of the program in memory is represented in Figure 8.4. The state after execution of the third line is represented in Figure 8.5.

Figure 8.5 Reassigning values

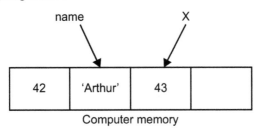

Computer memory

In an assignment, the right-hand side of the equals sign can be a value (like 42) or an expression (like **x** + 1, in which case, the expression is first evaluated before being assigned). Consider this:

```
x = 42
y = x
```

In this example, **x** is not a value, but simply another variable name (a trivial expression). Therefore, the value of **x** is first looked up and that is assigned to **y**.

Mutability

In an ideal world, variables in a programming language would **always** work in the same way. However, that's usually not the case. Programming languages often deal with larger and more complex data differently from simple data due to efficiency concerns, and Python is no exception. The method described in the previous section only applies to simple data (like numbers, Boolean values and strings). This all has effects on how your program behaves, so it's important to know.

Consider what would happen if you execute this program:

```
x = 42
y = x
x = 99
print(y)
```

It should be apparent by now that the statement **x** = 99 doesn't affect the value of **y** and so the program will print '42'. That's because when **x** is reassigned, a new space in memory is created for the value 99 and the **x** label is moved to point to that new space (**y** remains pointing to 42). You probably think that's desirable behaviour – you don't want changes made to one variable inadvertently affecting another. Data that behaves like this (i.e. data that cannot be changed in-place, meaning that assignment means creating new values) is referred to as **immutable**.

Unlike numbers, lists are an example of data that can get large and complex. As a result, managing their state can become complicated. For example, did you know that there are (at least) two ways to add a new item to a list (see Figure 8.6)?

```
names = ['Tom', 'Dick']

# Method 1
names = names + ['Harry']

# Method 2
names.append('Harry')
```

There is a reason for this.

- The approach in method 1 behaves just like the earlier examples that assigned numbers. When it's executed, a new space in memory is created. The computer takes a copy of the existing two names (Tom and Dick), puts them together with Harry and puts the resulting new list into that memory space.

- Method 2 behaves differently. It doesn't create a new memory space. Instead, it changes the list in-place and leaves the **names** label pointing to the existing memory space. This is because lists are **mutable**. Mutable items of data can be changed in-place.

Method 2 works more efficiently, especially on lists that are very large, because the computer doesn't need to go to the trouble of copying the existing list items into a new space in memory. However, efficiency isn't the only consequence to be mindful of.

Using immutable objects can come at an efficiency cost. 'Updating' an immutable object is done by creating a whole new object, and this usually takes more resources. This may or may not be a problem. For example, for a video game, where lots of objects are updated continually, this extra cost might visibly slow the game down.

Consider this program:

```
notes_1 = ['Do', 'Re', 'Me']
notes_2 = notes_1
notes_1.append('Fa')
print(notes_2)
```

When this program executes, we find it prints out "**['Do', 'Re', 'Me', 'Fa']**"! Why? Because, assigning one mutable variable (**notes_1**) to another (**notes_2**) doesn't create a new space in memory. Instead, it makes the label of the assignee point at the existing memory space of the source variable. After line 2 is executed, **notes_1** and **notes_2** both refer to the same memory space (a list containing 'Do', 'Ra' and 'Me'). Altering **notes_1** in-place also alters **notes_2** as a side effect (see Figure 8.7).

Figure 8.6 Executing two different ways of adding to a list

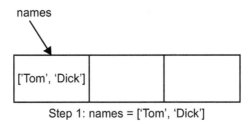

Step 1: names = ['Tom', 'Dick']

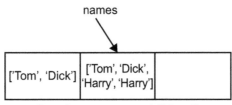

Step 2: names = names + ['Harry']

names

| ['Tom', 'Dick'] | ['Tom', 'Dick', 'Harry', 'Harry'] | |

Step 3: names.append ('Harry')

Such side effects can be quite subtle, especially when functions are involved. The expected behaviour of the function **print_squares** below, is to print the numbers in a list after they've been raised to the power of 2. Its main behaviour matches expectation – **however**, it has a side effect: it also alters the numbers in the original list so their values are lost.

```
def print_squares(nums):
    for n in range(len(nums)):
        nums[n] = nums[n] ** 2
    print(nums)

numbers = [1, 2, 3]
print(numbers) # Prints [1, 2, 3] - Expected
print_squares(numbers) # Prints [1, 4, 9] - Expected
print(numbers) # Prints [1, 4, 9] - Unexpected!
```

Figure 8.7 Altering a single mutable object having multiple names

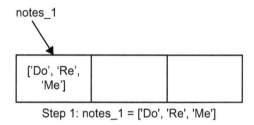

Step 1: notes_1 = ['Do', 'Re', 'Me']

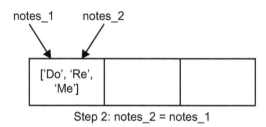

Step 2: notes_2 = notes_1

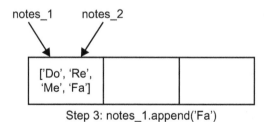

Step 3: notes_1.append('Fa')

If it were important to preserve the original values of **numbers**, this program would be faulty. In general, it is best not to alter the value of parameters given to function. A better alternative would be this:

```
def print_squares(nums):
    # We won't alter nums. Instead, the results will go into
    # a new collection called new_nums.
    new_nums = []
```

```
    for n in nums:
        new_nums.append(n ** 2)
        # Or alternatively: new_nums = new_nums + [n ** 2]

    print(new_nums)

numbers = (1, 2, 3)
print_squares(numbers) # Prints [1, 4, 9] - Expected

# print_squares didn't alter numbers at all, so the original
# data is safely preserved.
print(numbers) # Prints (1, 2, 3) - Expected
```

An object should be immutable unless you have a good reason for it to be mutable.

Alternatively, use equivalent immutable data types like tuples (which forbid changes being made in-place). Make sure you know which data types in Python are mutable and which are immutable. Appendix A contains a list of the most common.

Statement ordering

In addition to ever-changing values, program state also requires you to be mindful of instruction ordering. Problems can arise when things are done in the wrong order. For example, this shows two ways of getting your list of numbers doubled:

```
def get_doubles_wrong(singles):
    doubles = []
    for n in singles:
        doubles.append(n)
        n = n * 2
    return doubles

def get_doubles_right(singles):
    doubles = []
    for n in singles:
        n = n * 2
        doubles.append(n)
    return doubles

print(get_doubles_wrong([1, 2, 3])) # Prints [1, 2, 3]
print(get_doubles_right([1, 2, 3])) # Prints [2, 4, 6]
```

The 'wrong' function works incorrectly because numbers in Python are immutable. When you double **n**, a new value is created that gets the **n** label. The value that **n** used to be attached to remains inside the **doubles** list unchanged.

The 'right' function succeeds because it updates the object's value **before** adding the resultant value to the list.

Python provides the means for avoiding the kinds of errors caused by statement ordering and explicit managing of state. It allows you to rewrite what would be multi-lined blocks as single, atomic statements that yield the exact same results. For example, let's rewrite the previous example using a list comprehension (list comprehensions are explained in more detail in the following section More Advanced Constructs):

```
def get_doubles(singles):
    return [n * 2 for n in singles]

print(get_doubles([1, 2, 3])) # Prints [2, 4, 6]
```

This reduced version of **get_doubles** is just one line in length instead of five. As written, the list comprehension can be read from left to right as **'create a new list where each item, n, is multiplied by 2, sourcing the items from another list called singles'**. A list comprehension manages creation of the list for us. It says only what the resultant list should look like; it says nothing about how to create it.

To read more on list comprehensions go here: https://docs.python.org/3/tutorial/datastructures.html#list-comprehensions

MORE ADVANCED CONSTRUCTS

This section explores some more advanced constructs that allow us to avoid the difficulties presented by statement ordering and the need to continually update values (discussed in the previous section). However, it requires knowledge of the declarative programming style, which we'll discuss next.

Programming styles: declarative vs imperative

Research shows that programmers instinctively express different parts of their solutions using different styles (Pane et al., 2001). It was demonstrated that two styles of programming featured heavily in the results: declarative and imperative.

Declarative style

Use of this style emphasises declaring what is and isn't the case in a solution. It uses logical statements to articulate the initial facts and behaviours, as well as the solution's goals. In other words, it states what the solution does rather than how it does it.

Examples in a Noughts and Crosses game include:

The playing area is a 3 x 3 square.

or:

'High-score' is the greatest score in the list of all scores.

A popular example of the declarative style is functional programming. This emphasises writing programs made up of mathematical-style functions, which explain what a function does instead of how it does it. It also encourages you to avoid using changeable (i.e. mutable) state.

Imperative style

The imperative style stands in contrast to the declarative approach. It focuses on solving a problem by allowing the author to spell out each step in the algorithm explicitly.

For example:

Play intro sound. Display 'Player 1 Get Ready.'

or:

Display player's symbol. Remove arrow pointing at 'Player 1'. Add arrow pointing at 'Player 2'. Message = 'Player 2's turn.' Display Message. Wait 5 seconds. Remove Message.

Comparing the styles

Different styles are better suited to certain types of goals. For example:

- The declarative style works well in setting up the solution scenario and laying out the constraints.
- The imperative style is used when a programmer needs tight control over the execution of steps, particularly when efficiency or the ordering of instructions is critical.

It might come as an unpleasant surprise to learn that programming languages often primarily support only one style. Most popular languages (like Java, C++, Ruby and JavaScript) are mainly imperative. However, this doesn't mean using an imperative language restricts you to a 100 per cent imperative style. Boundaries between styles have recently begun to blur and some languages now include limited support for other styles.

Python stands mainly in the imperative camp, but it also supports some elements of other styles. As a demonstration, we'll consider a program that filters a list of numbers to remove all the odd ones. An imperative solution would look something like this:

```python
old_list = [1, 2, 3, 4, 5]
new_list = []

for number in old_list:
    if (number % 2) == 0:
        new_list.append(number)

print(new_list)
```

whereas a declarative solution would look like this:

```
def is_even(n):
    return (n % 2) == 0

new_list = filter(is_even, [1, 2, 3, 4, 5])

print(new_list)
```

Both solutions have the exact same outcomes, but their styles differ. Instead of telling the computer how to do the filtering (as the former solution does), the latter solution simply asks the in-built **filter** function[55] to do it for us.

Benefits of the declarative style

Using a declarative style brings certain benefits. First, the programmer rarely has to use state to control the program flow, thus reducing the amount of state you need to keep track of. Second, immutable objects are typically the norm. Third, multi-line code blocks can be reduced to very few (sometimes single) lines of code, making it easier to understand a program.

Even though Python stands mainly in the imperative camp, opportunities to use a declarative approach (like replacing multi-line loops with single-line expressions) will present themselves throughout your programming. It's a good idea to pursue them because a declarative approach encourages you to break your program into small, reusable functions possessing no side effects. As a consequence:

- The program will be smaller overall.
- It will be easier to reason about a program's behaviour, because its parts are small and self-contained.
- Testing and debugging become easier.
- Some functions you create will be generic, allowing you to reuse them and exploit the patterns in your solution.

Let's look at ways you can replace long, stateful pieces of code with short, stateless alternatives.

Comprehensions

Programs often work with collections, objects that bunch together a load of items. The usual approach to handling collections in an imperative style is to use a loop, but as we've seen, this can add complications. What's more, loops are unintuitive to programming novices.

In reality, people find that the most natural approach to creating a collection is simply to define them into existence. That is, to describe **what** they should look like, rather than **how** they should be created. Contrast this declarative statement:

Create a list of all even numbers between 1 and 15.

with its imperative equivalent:

> Create a new list, l. Go through each number, n, from 1 to 15. For each n, if n is even, then add it to l.

Python provides a means to apply the more intuitive approach in the form of comprehensions (which we saw a few brief examples of earlier). A comprehension is just a fancy name for a concise way of creating new collections out of existing ones. The following example creates a list of square numbers from a list of numbers:

```
numbers = [1, 2, 3, 4, 5]

# 'n ** 2' = n to the power 2
squares = [n ** 2 for n in numbers]
# squares = [1, 4, 9, 16, 25]
```

You can also filter out unwanted items from the original list by adding an **if** clause. The next example includes in a new list only four-letter names from the old one, and makes sure that the names are properly capitalised:

A set is very much like a list. It collects together a group of items. It differs in a couple of ways, including:

- A set uses curly brackets instead of squares one, i.e. {1, 2, 3} instead of [1, 2, 3]

- A set cannot contain repeated items. For example, adding 3 to the list [1, 2] results in [1, 2, 3] and adding 3 to the set {1, 2} results in {1, 2, 3}. However, adding 3 to the list [1, 2, 3] results in [1, 2, 3, 3], whereas adding 3 to the set {1, 2, 3} results in {1, 2, 3} because 3 is already in the set.

```
# A set of strings
forenames = {'graham', 'john', 'eric', 'terry', 'michael'}

# Set comprehensions work just the same way as list comprehensions
four_letter_pythons = {name.capitalize() for name in forenames if
len(name) == 4}

# Prints {'Eric', 'John'}
print(four_letter_pythons)
```

The last example replaces this imperative version:

```
four_letter_pythons = set() # Create a new empty set
for name in forenames:
    if len(name) == 4:
        four_letter_pythons.add(name.capitalize())

print(four_letter_pythons)
```

Higher-order functions

Chapter 2 drew an analogy between algorithms and recipes. Both describe a series of steps, each of which manipulate objects in various ways.

Like any analogy, it's not perfect. Something that the earlier analogy failed to convey is how the list of instructions can be manipulated as an object itself. (I don't mean by doing something like folding up the paper the recipe is written on and using it as a funnel.) So, let's extend the analogy.

You need to begin by comparing a computer program (made up of lots of functions) to a recipe book (made up of lots of recipes). Some recipes can be combined with others in different ways. For example, a cake recipe might tell you how to bake a generic cake base and give you the choice of fillings to put in it. Instead of that recipe explaining how to make several different fillings, it would simply refer to 'the filling' ('while the cake is baking prepare the filling' or 'spread the filling you made onto the base'). Therefore, the cake recipe is, by itself, incomplete. It only becomes complete when you combine it with another recipe for the filling, which could be blueberry, butterscotch, hot fudge or whatever you fancy.

This way, the filling recipe acts as a parameter to the cake recipe. The cake recipe is generic and (depending on which filling recipe you use) could become a recipe for blueberry cake, butterscotch cake or a hot fudge cake.

Now – assuming your hunger is not distracting you – we'll see how functions can become parameters to other functions in an analogous way. The following example demonstrates this:

```
def is_even(n):
    return n % 2 == 0

def is_positive(n):
    return n > 0

def test_numbers(test_function, numbers):
    return [test_function(n) for n in numbers]

evens = test_numbers(is_even, [1, 2, 3, 4])
positives = test_numbers(is_positive, [-2, -1, 0, 1, 2])

print(evens) # Prints [False, True, False, True]
print(positives) # Prints [False, False, False, True, True]
```

Functions that can be treated as objects, like **is_positive** and **is_even**, are termed higher-order functions. In this example, the functions **is_even** and **is_positive** are the 'filling' functions that are passed to another function. The **test_numbers** function stands in for the generic cake recipe. It tests a series of numbers in a certain way depending on which test function you give it. When you give it the **is_even** function, it becomes a function for testing whether numbers in a list are even or not. When you give it the **is_positive** function, it instead reports on which numbers are greater than zero.

A version without higher-order functions or list comprehensions would look something like this:

```
def test_numbers_even(numbers):
    results = []
    for n in numbers:
        if n % 2 == 0:
            results.append(True)
        else:
            results.append(False)
    return results

def test_numbers_positive(numbers):
    results = []
    for n in numbers:
        if n > 0:
            results.append(True)
        else:
            results.append(False)
    return results

evens = test_numbers_even([1, 2, 3, 4])
positives = test_numbers_positive([-2, -1, 0, 1, 2])

print(evens)
print(positives)
```

The generic solution reduces the size of the program and reduces the amount of state to manage, not only by using list comprehensions, but also by reducing the number of places where tests are carried out. Imagine both versions above having additional functions added to them. The non-generic version would grow in size much quicker than the generic one.

Functional primitives

When using higher-order functions, three operations in particular get carried out so often that they've been given their own names. Together they form the core of a functional programming approach and consequently are sometimes called functional primitives:

- **Map:** applies a function to all the items in a collection and puts the results in a new collection.

- **Filter:** creates a new collection, including only the items that return **True** when a testing function is applied to them.

- **Reduce (aka fold):** performs an operation on each item in a collection and produces a single result.

Python provides the functional primitives built-in. The following code rewrites an earlier example to use a **map**.

```
words = ['my', 'big', 'meal', 'comes', 'mostly', 'bearing', 'doubtful',
'garnishes']

lengths = list(map(len, words))
print(lengths) # Prints [2, 3, 4, 5, 6, 7, 8, 9]
```

We've already seen an example of **filter** in the section 'Comparing the styles' earlier in the chapter.

Finally, an example of the reduce function is producing the sum of a list of numbers:[56]

```
# The reduce function requires importing
from functools import reduce

def add(x, y):
    return x + y

sum = reduce(add, [1, 2, 3, 4, 5])
print(sum) # Prints 15
```

reduce works by taking a function (like **add**) and applying it repeatedly to build up a cumulative value. The function it takes must have two parameters. To the first parameter (**x** in this example), reduce assigns the cumulative value. To the second (**y** in this example), it assigns the next value from the list. These assignments happen automatically. The function is then executed and the result becomes the updated cumulative value.

In the example above, the cumulative value is a running total. At the start this is 0 and the next value from the list is 1. Executing **add(0, 1)** yields a running total of 1. Next, **add(1, 2)** yields 3. Then, **add(3, 3)**, followed by **add(6, 4)**, and finally **add(10, 5)**. The final result of 15 gets assigned to **sum**.

SUMMARY

All programs, even very large and complex ones, can be built from a relatively small number of distinct building blocks. This chapter discussed the most important fundamental building blocks.

You can make logical decisions in programs, using logical expressions, and even chain them together using logical operators. Logical decisions are incorporated into some of the basic algorithmic constructs (such as if-statements and loops).

In addition to logic, algorithms also allow you to keep track of data that are important to your solution (that is, the state). State in programs must be carefully managed, because mismanagement can easily lead to bugs. The data can be structured in various ways using the different data types available.

Finally, this chapter introduced a few advanced programming styles and constructs that can help you create programs that are less error prone and more easily constructed and maintained.

EXERCISES

EXERCISE 1

Mark the following statements as true or false:

    A.   You cannot assign the value of an immutable variable to another variable.

    B.   The **continue** keyword forces a loop to end immediately and continue executing with the code that follows the loop.

    C.   Declarative programming is useful when you need careful control over the step-by-step behaviour of a program.

    D.   Only one part of a multi-part if-statement can be executed at the most.

    E.   An expression is a piece of code that evaluates to a result.

EXERCISE 2

Look again at the example in section 'Mutability', where the value of **notes_1** is assigned to the variable **notes_2**. Rewrite the code so that **notes_1** can be updated without simultaneously altering the value of **notes_2**.

EXERCISE 3

Take your solution to Chapter 2, Exercise 5 (write an algorithm for singing *The 12 Days of Christmas*). Convert the algorithm into a Python program.

EXERCISE 4

Write a program that takes a list of Fahrenheit measurements and converts it into a list of Celsius measurements.

 HINT: Converting Fahrenheit to Celsius is done using the following formula: $C = F - 32 \times 59$.

EXERCISE 5

Using the **filter** function, write a program to filter out annoying words from a list of words, specifically words that are in all upper-case characters and words that end with multiple exclamation marks.

9 ORGANISING YOUR CODE

OBJECTIVES

- Introduce the concept of separation of concerns.
- Discuss how scope can control access to information.
- Show how modules can:
  - form the main organisational unit of a complex program;
  - facilitate reuse;
  - provide interfaces and achieve information hiding.
- Show how packages can add additional levels of organisation.
- Explore good practices for your solution's structure.

RECAP

> People who design aircraft carriers understand how to build modular systems...
> when the toilet on an aircraft carrier gets clogged, it doesn't start firing missiles.
> That's because the toilet system and the missile system are separated very much.
> (Tanenbaum, 2010)

Chapter 3 examined decomposition, a method that breaks a problem down into smaller pieces that can each be solved individually. It was pointed out that a number of patterns appear time and again in solutions, so often in fact that those patterns form the building blocks of any typical programming language, Python included. You should by now be familiar with some of the basic types of building blocks, including:

- instructions (that is, statements and expressions);
- conditionals;
- loops;
- subroutines (that is, functions).

For very small programs – a few dozen lines at the most – these building blocks serve sufficiently well. However, as programs increase in size, you need better ways of organising your code. Just as you can't use the same techniques required to build a kennel as you would to build a skyscraper, you need additional techniques to build large programs. Complex solutions require you to organise your smaller pieces into larger, more manageable parts.

This chapter shows you the techniques on offer and how to apply them in Python. In each case, we'll use the example from Chapter 3 (which showed how to build a complex image out of a collection of simple shapes) to demonstrate the technique.

The image drawing example was introduced in Chapter 3; see 'Patterns and generalisation'.

INTRODUCING TKINTER

So far, our programs have been exclusively text-based. Such programs are easy to write because you only need to use the print statement to make your program display things. However, making your programs display graphics adds a whole new level of complexity. Thankfully, other people have created solutions that you can use to make drawing graphics easier.

The solution we will use in this chapter to draw things is called tkinter. This is a standard, built-in module you can use to draw graphics as part of your program. It provides a collection of functions that allow you to draw various objects onto a canvas.

To use tkinter yourself, here's some of the basics. First, we need to get access to the functions in tkinter by importing the module. (Importing modules is discussed in detail later in this chapter.) This code achieves that:

```
import tkinter
```

Then, we need to create a main window where our graphics will be displayed:

```
window = tkinter.Tk()
```

Next, we need to add a canvas to our window, onto which we can draw things:

```
c = tkinter.Canvas(window)
```

Finally, we then command the window to display what we've done. This is done by telling the canvas to put all the objects we created in place (via a function called pack) and telling the window to display itself (via a function called mainloop):

```
c.pack()
window.mainloop()
```

And that's it. This is essentially startup code. Running it will display a window like this:

Of course, the window is empty because we didn't actually add anything yet, but we'll get to that shortly. After creating the window and canvas (but before making them display themselves), we then need to draw all our objects.

In summary, every code sample in this chapter assumes that you have already added the startup code like this:

```
import tkinter

window = tkinter.Tk()
c = tkinter.Canvas(window)

# Code for drawing objects goes here…

c.pack()
window.mainloop()
```

SEPARATING CONCERNS

This section introduces the idea of separating out the various different concerns of your program into sensible parts.

Concern: a single aspect of carrying out a solution. In a spreadsheet, for example, calculating the contents of a cell and displaying a cell on the screen are two different concerns.

Example (part 1)

Let's start by breaking down the image of a face into a series of simple shapes. We'll use:

- one large circle for the face outline;
- a pair of concentric circles (the inner one filled) for each eye;
- a line for a mouth.

We'll also distinguish between drawing and rendering.

- **Rendering** describes a multi-step process involved in progressively building up a representation.
- **Drawing** describes the action of actually making something appear on the screen.

Chapter 3 demonstrated a way to construct an algorithm for drawing a simple face, an example of which looks like this:

1. Draw circle with radius 30 at position 50,50.
2. Draw circle with radius 10 at position 70,70.
3. Draw circle with radius 5 at position 70,70 filled black.
4. Draw circle with radius 10 at position 100,70.
5. Draw circle with radius 5 at position 100,70 filled black.
6. Draw line from 70,110 to 100,100.

Here's our first attempt at turning that algorithm into a Python program that renders a face. Let's just look at the first step for a moment:

```
# Function: create_oval(x1, y1, x2, y2)
# Tells the canvas to draw an oval whose left
# is at position x1, top is at position y1,
# right is at position x2, and bottom is at y2.
c.create_oval(50, 50, 120, 120)
```

This raises the issue of a coordinate system. A canvas is divided up into pieces like a piece of graph paper. Each resultant square has a position (i.e. a coordinate) of the form (x, y). The top left-most coordinate is (0, 0). As you move right, the x-coordinate increases, so jumping five steps to the right lands you at coordinate (5, 0). As you move down, the y-coordinates increase, so jumping ten steps down from the top left would land you at (0, 10).

Since the example above draws an oval whose width and height are equal, the result is a circle. This will serve as the outline of the face.

Drawing the eyes works much the same. They're simply smaller and positioned inside the larger circle.

```
c.create_oval(60, 60, 80, 80)
c.create_oval(90, 60, 110, 80)
```

We've just created the outline of the eyes, so now let's add some black pupils. The **create_oval** function allows you to optionally fill in the oval you create with a colour like so:

```
c.create_oval(65, 65, 75, 75, fill='black')
c.create_oval(95, 65, 105, 75, fill='black')
```

Finally, let's give our face a flat, neutral mouth by drawing a line.

```
# Function: create_line(x1, y1, x2, y2)
# Draws a line from position (x1,y1) to (x2,y2)
c.create_line(70, 110, 100, 110)
```

Let's put it all together inside a function which we can call whenever we want to draw a face.

```
def render_neutral_face():
    # Draw face
    c.create_oval(50, 50, 120, 120)

    # Draw eyes
    c.create_oval(60, 60, 80, 80)
    c.create_oval(90, 60, 110, 80)

    # Draw pupils
    c.create_oval(65, 65, 75, 75, fill='black')
    c.create_oval(95, 65, 105, 75, fill='black')

    # Draw mouth
    c.create_line(70, 110, 100, 110)
```

Running this function (don't forget to include the startup code we wrote earlier!) results in a window looking something like this:

Let's extend our solution so it can also draw a smiley face.

```
def render_smiley_face():
    c.create_oval(50, 50, 120, 120)

    c.create_oval(60, 60, 80, 80)
    c.create_oval(90, 60, 110, 80)
```

```
c.create_oval(65, 65, 75, 75, fill='black')
c.create_oval(95, 65, 105, 75, fill='black')

# Draw smiley mouth
c.create_arc(60, 110, 110, 80, start=0, extent=-180)
```

The principle behind separation of concerns

All the steps in the previous example could have been put into just one function called **render_faces**. However, that would have resulted in mixing up concerns, meaning it wouldn't have been possible to separate the idea of rendering a neutral face from the idea of rendering a smiley face. Instead the solution follows the principle of **separation of concerns**. It has a pair of functions that each have a single concern – rendering one image – allowing you to choose between them.

Separating pieces of functionality into independent units increases the flexibility of your solution. It's a way of implementing all those patterns you discovered after having broken down the original problem. A function is Python's most basic means of allowing you to create an independent block of code that carries out (ideally) a single, well-defined task within your solution. When functions have just one concern each, it's easier to take advantage of patterns and combine them in creative ways.

A function that performs several tasks is also harder to both reuse and test. By making each function focus on a single, well-defined task:

- Each function becomes more reusable – in the above example, someone using these functions can choose between a smiley face or a neutral face.
- Each function is more testable – it's easier to localise a problem in the solution because you can test smaller pieces.

Example (part 2)

Strictly speaking each function in the example still has, not one, but two concerns: rendering images (that is, breaking down the complex image into steps) and drawing shapes. You might question the latter concern. Surely, **tkinter** is the one doing the drawing? Yes and no. It's true that **tkinter** does the drawing work, but the rendering functions are overly (and needlessly) concerned with how those shapes are drawn.

To see the problem, imagine that at some point in the future you're asked to replace the **tkinter** with a sexy, new-and-improved drawing module (**ultra_draw**). That would mean making a lot of changes to the existing code: every single line that referred to **tkinter** would need altering.

To cut down on the potential work, we could separate these concerns strictly: the rendering functions should focus only on rendering (which was described as a multi-step process that progressively builds up a representation) and we should move the drawing work into new separate functions:

```python
def draw_oval(x1, y1, x2, y2, colour):
    if colour == None:
        c.create_oval(x1, y1, x2, y2)
    else:
        c.create_oval(x1, y1, x2, y2, fill=colour)

def draw_line(x1, y1, x2, y2):
    c.create_line(x1, y1, x2, y2)

def render_neutral_face():
    # Draw face outline
    draw_oval(50, 50, 120, 120)

    # Draw left eye
    draw_oval(60, 60, 80, 80)
    draw_oval(65, 65, 75, 75, 'black')

    # Draw right eye
    draw_oval(90, 60, 110, 80)
    draw_oval(95, 65, 105, 75, 'black')

    # Draw neutral mouth
    draw_line(70, 110, 100, 110)
```

The rendering functions now know a lot less about how the drawing is done, and that's **good**. Instead of controlling the drawing work themselves directly, the rendering functions delegate the work to the new functions, **draw_line** and **draw_oval**.

Of course, the new functions need some information to work with, namely the positions and dimensions of the shapes being drawn. The rendering functions pass these to the drawing functions via parameters.

DEFINING INFORMATION SCOPE

As well as separation of concerns, the previous example also teaches us something about scope. When you look at the code, you'll notice that each rendering function calls a drawing function several times. Each time it does so, it passes some values to the drawing function, which in turn, creates some new variables for those values (like **x1** or **y1**). After a drawing function completes its work, it destroys those variables before passing control back to a rendering function.

Technically this means that variables are being created and destroyed continually throughout execution of this solution. Phrased like this, it sounds as though a lot of extraneous work is being carried out. Why not just create each variable once and allow all functions to refer to them or update them whenever they wish?

Technically, that is possible. Variables that behave like that are called global variables and are created by defining them at the top level of the program. A variant of the previous solution that uses global variables would look like this:

```
# These are global variables (initialised using a neat trick
# for assigning multiple values at once).
x1, y1, x2, y2 = 0, 0, 0, 0
colour = None


def draw_oval():
    if colour == None:
        c.create_oval(x1, y1, x2, y2)
    else:
        c.create_oval(x1, y1, x2, y2, fill=colour)

def draw_line():
    c.create_line(x1, y1, x2, y2)

def render_neutral_face():
    # The global keyword denotes that these variables are
    # global and were defined at the top level. This stops
    # Python from creating new variables with the same name
    # (more on this later).
    global x1, y1, x2, y2, colour

    # Draw face
    x1, y1, x2, y2 = 50, 50, 120, 120
    draw_oval()

    # Draw left eye
    x1, y1, x2, y2 = 60, 60, 80, 80
    draw_oval()

    x1, y1, x2, y2 = 65, 65, 75, 75
    colour = 'black'
    draw_oval()

    # Draw right eye
    x1, y1, x2, y2 = 90, 60, 110, 80
    draw_oval()
```

```
x1, y1, x2, y2 = 95, 65, 105, 75
colour = 'black'
draw_oval()

# Draw mouth
x1, y1, x2, y2 = 70, 110, 100, 110
draw_line()
```

However, global variables are a notorious source of errors because their values are subject to being changed at any time in any number of ways. In fact, there's a deliberate mistake in this example - can you spot it before running the program?

When you run the program, the image looks like this:

What went wrong? After drawing the left eye, the **colour** variable kept its old value of 'black'. That meant, when drawing the outside of the right eye, the program drew a black circle. To fix this mistake, you would need to add the instruction **colour = None** after drawing the left eye but before calling **draw_oval()** for the right eye.

This means a global variable's state must be tracked across a potentially huge number of lines of code. The bigger your program, the harder it becomes.

Experience shows that the availability of information should be strictly limited. By ensuring that functions have access only to objects that they must have, we can avoid the kinds of problems just described. Scoping helps us to achieve this.

Principles behind scope

An object's scope refers to the 'area' of a program in which that object may be referenced. When you create an object in a certain area of a program, that object can only be referred to by instructions within the same area. That area is the object's scope.

For a simple linear program without any functions, this means that an object can be used anywhere in the same program.

```
# file1.py

# Executing print(my_number) before the following line
# would result in an error.
my_number = 1

# Now my_number exists and you can use it.
print(my_number)
```

However, if you then wrote a second program in another file that referred to **my_number**, like this:

```
# file2.py

print(my_number)
```

an error would occur. That's because the scope of **my_number** is limited to the first program and the second program can't see it.

Whenever you create an object, you're implicitly giving it a scope. By default, an object's scope is limited to the area in which it is defined. This results in several levels of scope. For the moment, we'll discuss just two of them: global and local:

- Global objects are defined at the 'top level' of a program and can be accessed from anywhere in the same module. **my_number** was a global object.

- Local objects are defined inside of a function and can only be referenced from within the same function.

In this example:

```
def f():
    print (x)

x = 42
f() # This prints '42'
```

x is a global object.

In this example:

```
def create_message():
    msg = 'Don't panic!'
    print(msg) # This prints 'Don't panic!'

create_message()
print(msg) # This causes an error.
```

msg is a local object and its scope is limited to the **create_message** function. That's why you can refer to it from inside the function, but not from outside. As seen in an earlier example, it's possible for functions to reference globally scoped objects, so long as you identify them using the **global** keyword (for example, by adding the line **global msg** at the beginning of **create_message**).

Scoping variables lets you avoid the headaches that come with the use of global variables. When collaborating functions need to share information, they should do so via parameter passing, as shown in the next section.

Example (part 3)

The full version of our solution using locally scoped variables looks like this:

```
def draw_oval(x1, y1, x2, y2, colour=None):
    if colour == None:
        c.create_oval(x1, y1, x2, y2)
    else:
        c.create_oval(x1, y1, x2, y2, fill=colour)

def draw_line(x1, y1, x2, y2):
    c.create_line(x1, y1, x2, y2)

def draw_arc(x1, y1, x2, y2, s, e):
    c.create_arc(x1, y1, x2, y2, start=s, extent=e)

def render_neutral_face():
    draw_oval(50, 50, 120, 120)

    draw_oval(60, 60, 80, 80)
    draw_oval(65, 65, 75, 75, 'black')
    draw_oval(90, 60, 110, 80)
    draw_oval(95, 65, 105, 75, 'black')

    draw_line(70, 110, 100, 110)

def render_smiley_face():
    draw_oval(50, 50, 120, 120)

    draw_oval(60, 60, 80, 80)
    draw_oval(65, 65, 75, 75, 'black')

    draw_oval(90, 60, 110, 80)
    draw_oval(95, 65, 105, 75, 'black')

    draw_arc(60, 110, 110, 80, 0, -180)
```

USING MODULES

Plans are afoot for the image rendering solution. It is to become a full-blown library of subroutines for drawing emojis. Eventually it will be full of functions that draw a diverse range of little images – not just faces, but weather icons, vehicles, emotional symbols and lots more.

How could we expand the current solution to realise this? We could keep adding a new rendering function for each additional image. However, dozens of new images are planned and that would mean dozens of functions being added to our current module. As a result, it would become **very** long and unwieldy.

Instead, we'll break up our solution into modules.

Principle behind modules

Decomposition was discussed in Chapter 3.

After problem decomposition, your solution will be arranged into a hierarchy of pieces. The broadly phrased goal of the solution sits at the top of the hierarchy. Along the bottom will be a collection of small pieces that each focus on solving one tiny sub-problem. These pieces at the lowest level are ideal candidates for becoming functions in your program, because a function should also be small and focus on doing just one small task (see Figure 9.1).

Figure 9.1 Example partial hierarchy of the emoji drawing problem

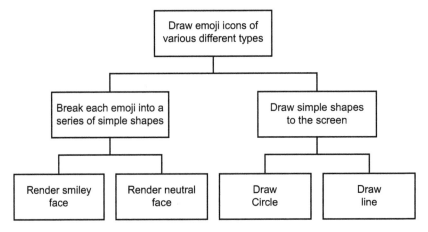

In between the goal at the top and the tasks at the bottom lie a number of organisational layers. Each lowest-level task will be one of several that belong to a parent, which represents a logical grouping of tasks. In a program, this corresponds to a collection of related functions that are organised into one place. That place is termed a **module**.

In Python, a module is a file on the computer's file system. Each module takes its name from the file it's contained within (for example the **tkinter** module has that name because it's stored in a file called **tkinter.py**).

Importing modules

> **Server/client module**: when a module uses something provided by another module, the using module can be called the client, whilst the used module can be called the server.

The earlier section on scoping suggested that code in one module couldn't make use of objects defined in another module. Well, that's not the whole truth. The client module (see the definition box above) can refer to things in the server module, it just has to **import** the server module first. We've already seen this in earlier examples when importing the **tkinter** module.

You import modules in several ways. The recommended form to use is the one we've already seen (for example, **import tkinter**). That's because different modules may contain objects with the same name, so, to avoid ambiguity, a reference to something in a separate module should be prefixed with that module's name. That's why, back at the beginning, we created a canvas by typing **c = tkinter.Canvas()** instead of just **c = Canvas()**.

Python also provides the **from module import name** form, for example:

```
from tkinter import Canvas.
```

Referring to a name imported this way doesn't require you to add a prefix when referencing objects from the server module. Because of this, you should use this form in client modules that are small and use very few other modules (see the box below).

> The **from module import name** form may cut down on typing a little, but it can potentially catch you out. Importing just **function_a** from a module called **module_x** is done like this: **from module_x import function_a**, meaning you can refer to **function_a** without a module prefix. However, if you were subsequently to add your own **function_a** to your module, then all its existing references to **function_a** would suddenly point to the one in your module, not the one in **module_x**.

A variation on the last form is this:

```
from tkinter import *
```

This is the 'wildcard' form and imports everything from a module automatically. This should generally be avoided because it can pollute your client module with lots of unnecessary names.

Reusable modules

Many modules provide functionality for other modules to use (usually termed **library modules**), such as the `datetime` module mentioned in the previous chapter. In such cases, you should organise your module to promote reusability:

- Provide functions that are small, focused on one concern, and have a clear purpose.

- The purpose ought to be recognisable from the function's signature (see the box definition below), but definitely bolster it with documentation.

- A function should always behave in the exact same way when given the same input values. To this end:

  - Avoid using global variables in a module. Favour local variables.

  - If a function requires data to work with, provide it via parameters in a function call.

  - If a function's behaviour can differ between invocations even when given the same input data (for example, it changes depending on the time of day), document this clearly.

Function signature: a description of a function made up of its name and an ordered list of the parameters it accepts.

Executable modules

When you import a Python module, the functions it contains are set up ready to execute on request. However, if a module also contains code at the top level (that is, code that is not indented), those instructions are executed immediately.

As opposed to library modules, some modules are intended to be executed as stand-alone programs. These are also called **scripts**. You should avoid importing executable modules into other modules because the act of importing a module shouldn't cause visible effects.

Here's an example script:

```
import datetime

def print_duration(birthdate):
    today = datetime.date.today()
    difference = today - birthdate
    print('You have been alive for', difference.days, 'days.')
```

```
def get_birthdate():
    year = int(input('What year were you born? '))
    month = int(input('What month were you born? '))
    day = int(input('What day were you born? '))

    return datetime.date(year, month, day)

birthdate = get_birthdate()
print_duration(birthdate)
```

This program is intended to be run on the command line only. If you import this as a library module into your own program, then your program will start asking the user for their birthdate the instant it runs because the instructions at the top level (**birthdate = get_birthdate()** and **print_duration(birthdate)**) are executed immediately.

A module can be made to function as either a library or a script. To do this, you must make the module find out which context it's being used in: if it recognises it's being executed as a script, it **should** execute the top-level code. If it's being imported as a library, it **shouldn't** execute the top-level code.

To achieve this affect, encapsulate the top-level code like so:

```
if __name__ == '__main__':
    birthdate = get_birthdate()
    print_duration(birthdate)
```

The internal variable **__name__** is automatically set to '**__main__**' only when the program is being run from the command line. Thus, the **main** function will be called only when you use the program as a script.

Example (part 4)

Returning to our example, since the module we've written already contains functions for rendering faces, we'll turn that into the **faces** module. Definitions for new face images can be added there.

For each new type of image, we'll add a new module: a **vehicles** module will draw vehicles, a **weather** module will draw weather symbols and so on. For example:

```
# weather.py
def draw_oval(x1, y1, x2, y2, colour=None):
    if colour == None:
        c.create_oval(x1, y1, x2, y2)
    else:
        c.create_oval(x1, y1, x2, y2, fill=colour)
```

```
def draw_line(x1, y1, x2, y2):
    c.create_line(x1, y1, x2, y2)

def draw_sun():
    draw_oval(50, 50, 30, 'yellow')

# More weather emojis follow...
```

Our solution now exists as several modules. However, having broken up the solution like this, we've exposed ourselves to the same problem we had earlier. At the moment, every module we introduce would have to include the same drawing functions for the rendering functions to use, like these (for example, the weather module uses ovals and lines and so has to include a copy of **draw_oval** and **draw_line**).

It's the separation of concerns problem all over again. However, it's not functions that are mixing up rendering and drawing concerns this time, but **modules**. The rendering modules have to duplicate those exact same drawing functions in every module.

Fortunately, the same solution applies here: split those concerns off and isolate them in one place. Since each module focuses on rendering, we'll split off the drawing functions and put them in their own library module called **core_draw**.

```
# core_draw.py
import tkinter

window = tkinter.Tk()
c = tkinter.Canvas(window)

# We want to show the canvas only when our image
# is ready. Calling this function signals the
# image is ready to be displayed.
def show_canvas():
    c.pack()
    window.mainloop()

def draw_oval(x1, y1, x2, y2, colour=None):
    if colour == None:
        c.create_oval(x1, y1, x2, y2)
    else:
        c.create_oval(x1, y1, x2, y2, fill=colour)

def draw_line(x1, y1, x2, y2):
    c.create_line(x1, y1, x2, y2)

def draw_arc(x1, y1, x2, y2, s, e):
    c.create_arc(x1, y1, x2, y2, start=s, extent=e)
```

That will leave us with a collection of rendering modules that each import the core drawing functionality, like this:

```
# faces.py

import core_draw

def render_neutral_face():
    # Draw face outline
    core_draw.draw_oval(50, 50, 120, 120)

    # Draw left eye
    core_draw.draw_oval(60, 60, 80, 80)
    core_draw.draw_oval(65, 65, 75, 75, "black")

    # Draw right eye
    core_draw.draw_oval(90, 60, 110, 80)
    core_draw.draw_oval(95, 65, 105, 75, "black")

    # Draw neutral mouth
    core_draw.draw_line(70, 110, 100, 110)

def render_smiley_face():
    # Draw face outline
    core_draw.draw_oval(50, 50, 120, 120)

    # Draw left eye
    core_draw.draw_oval(60, 60, 80, 80)
    core_draw.draw_oval(65, 65, 75, 75, "black")

    # Draw right eye
    core_draw.draw_oval(90, 60, 110, 80)
    core_draw.draw_oval(95, 65, 105, 75, "black")

    # Draw smiling mouth
    core_draw.draw_arc(30, 70, 40, 10, 0, -180)
```

Modules as interfaces

When you import a module, you may not know how it works internally, especially if you didn't author that module. And that's fine. You shouldn't need to know such details in order to use it. The only thing that should concern you is the **interface** of the server. The interface is essentially a list of all function signatures in a server module (plus any documentation).

Think of a good interface as an old-fashioned switchboard (see Figure 9.2). From the outside, all you see are a collection of sockets, each with a label telling you where that socket connects to. You have no idea what's going on behind the switchboard's front panel, but that doesn't impede your ability to use it in the slightest.

The benefit of implementing to an interface is that those internals can be changed without affecting a system's behaviour. Just as an electrician could tinker with the innards of the switchboard, a programmer could alter the internals of a server module and (so

Figure 9.2 US Air Force (1967). An old-fashioned switchboard[58]

long as they made no mistakes) the switchboard operator/client module wouldn't notice the difference.

More specifically, when programming strictly to an interface:

- Updating a solution requires fewer changes, thus reducing the risk of introducing new errors.
- The risk of causing unanticipated knock-on effects is reduced.
- Modules are more easily reusable.
- When defined purely in terms of their inputs and outputs:
  - Modules are more easily testable.
  - Modules are swappable, meaning you could replace a server module entirely.
- It helps you, as the program author, when trying comprehend the behaviour of individual modules and functions.

Information hiding in modules

We've already seen how separation of concerns is partly achieved by different parts of a solution knowing little (preferably nothing) about the internals of one another. This principle is called **information hiding** and this section explores it in more detail.

In one sense, information hiding conceals the structure of information. This means a server module uses it to store its data and ensure that it's kept secret from the client. As a practical consequence, should that structure change in future, those changes only need to be made in the server module – the client module can remain unchanged.

To illustrate this, let's say that we replace tkinter with the (fictional) ultra_draw, and that ultra_draw works a little differently. Specifically, some of the function signatures differ. For example, instead of this function:

```
create_oval(x1, y1, x2, x2, fill)
```

which tkinter has, ultra_draw has this:

```
make_oval(x1, x2, y1, y2, fill)
```

Thankfully, this change will have little impact on the overall solution because we've structured it according to good principles of information hiding. We've hidden the workings of the drawing functions behind the interface of the **core_draw** module. Only its unseen internals require updating.

A function in **core_draw** can change from something this:

```
def draw_oval(x1, y1, x2, y2, colour=None):
    if colour == None:
        c.create_oval(x1, y1, x2, y2)
    else:
        c.create_oval(x1, y1, x2, y2, fill=colour)
```

to this:

```
def draw_oval(x1, y1, x2, y2, colour=None):
    if colour == None:
        ultra_draw.make_oval(x1, x2, y1, y2)
    else:
        ultra_draw.make_oval(x1, x2, y1, y2, fill=colour)
```

Because the interface of **core_draw** remains the same, the clients will still function correctly untouched.

PACKAGES

As a solution grows and its expanding capabilities become more diverse, the need for larger organisational units emerges. Enter packages.

Mechanics of packages

Since expanding to multiple types of images, our example solution has developed a deeper hierarchy. The number of modules has grown and they've begun to form logical groupings.

In Python, a group of logically related modules forms a package. For example, drawing and rendering can be considered as two logically distinct concerns. Therefore, the solution could be reorganised to group drawing modules into one package and rendering modules into another.

Like modules, packages take their structure from the way they're organised on the file system. One possible structure would be as follows:

```
- emoji/
    - drawing/
        - core_draw.py
    - rendering/
        - faces.py
        - weather.py
        - vehicles.py
```

This structure shows a top-level directory called **emoji** and two subdirectories: **drawing** and **rendering**. However, something is missing. At the moment, Python would consider these as directories and nothing more. Each directory and subdirectory needs to contain an extra (empty) file called **__init__.py**.[57] These files notify Python that the containing directories are in fact Python packages and so can be imported by other code. Hence, the complete file structure would look like this:

```
- emoji/
    - __init__.py
    - drawing/
        - __init__.py
        - core_draw.py
    - rendering/
        - __init__.py
        - faces.py
        - weather.py
        - vehicles.py
```

When importing modules from package hierarchies, you'll need to use **dot notation**. We've already encountered dot notation, such as when adding something to a list (**list.append()**) or calling a function in another module (**core_draw.draw_line()**). This simply denotes that the thing on the right of the dot belongs to the thing on the left. Similarly, if you write a module that includes this line:

```
import emoji.drawing.core_draw
```

this denotes that **emoji** contains a subpackage called **drawing**, which contains a module called **core_draw**. Your module then gets access to all the things defined in the file **emoji/rendering/core_draw.py**.

Typical package layout

Python grants the programmer quite some flexibility in the overall structure of their project. Files and folders can be laid out mostly as you wish. One popular layout looks something like this:

```
- Projectname/
    - docs/
```

```
          - install.txt
          - tutorial.txt
      - projectname/
          - package1/
              - __init__.py
              - module1_1.py
              - module1_2.py
          - package2/
              - __init__.py
              - module2_1.py
      - README.txt
```

Applying this to the emoji example would result in this:

```
- Emoji/
    - docs/
        - install.txt
        - tutorial.txt
    - emoji/
        - __init__.py
        - drawing/
            - __init__.py
            - core_draw.py
        - rendering/
            - __init__.py
            - faces.py
            - weather.py
            - vehicles.py
    - LICENCE.txt
    - README.txt
```

All materials are stored in the top-level **Emoji** folder. Its bare-minimum contents would be a subfolder called **emoji** (note the lower case 'e') that contains all executable source code. Additional materials like a documentation folder and a README can also go into the **Emoji** folder.

SUMMARY

All but the very tiniest programs require careful structuring. Without it, a program becomes an unmaintainable, error-prone mess. This chapter introduced several principles to guide the structuring of programs.

The separation of concerns tells you to divide your program cleanly into pieces, each of which is concerned with one aspect of the program. Reducing the strength of the coupling between those pieces means having them communicate via parameters and using variables with reduced scope.

Modular programming enables you to create large programs made of discrete, reusable components. Python's module system makes modular programming relatively straightforward. Information hiding encourages you to hide the details of modules behind sensible interfaces.

Finally, Python's package system allows you to build programs made of multiple modules that form logical groupings.

EXERCISES

EXERCISE 1

Mark the following statements as true or false:

A. Global variables are the preferred way to pass information between functions.
B. When functions know too much about other functions' workings, altering them risks causing side effects.
C. Objects defined inside a function cannot be referenced outside that function.
D. A module takes its name from the file it's defined in.
E. Files in a Python package may only have names made up of letters or numbers.

EXERCISE 2

What is the output of the following program?

```python
def my_function():
    s = 'No, print this!'
    print(s)

s = 'Print this message.'
my_function()
print(s)
```

EXERCISE 3

Try running this program, and explain why it results in an error:

```python
def my_function():
    print(s)
    s = 'No, print this!'

s = 'Print this message.'
my_function()
```

EXERCISE 4

Look back at the example program in section 'Executable modules', which calculates how many days the user has been alive. Extend the program so that it also tells the user the following (organise the program so that it could be used as stand-alone or as a library module so each function could be called in isolation):

A.   roughly how many days of their life they've spent asleep (assuming 8 hours of sleep per day);

B.   roughly how many times they've been to the loo (assuming six visits per day);

C.   roughly how many meals they've eaten (assuming three per day).

10 USING ABSTRACTIONS AND PATTERNS

OBJECTIVES

- Learn simple principles for finding patterns in programs.
- Discuss how abstraction applies in the context of programming.
- Show built-in types available for use in your solution.
- Introduce classes as a means of creating your own types and abstractions.
- Examine an array of ready-made patterns.

FINDING PATTERNS IN PROGRAMS

Finding patterns during problem decomposition was first mentioned in Chapter 3, in 'Patterns and generalisation'.

It's very important to look for patterns in a problem. During problem decomposition, when the problem is being broken down into a series of sub-problems, you'll find concepts that share numerous similarities. These could be procedures that carry out near-identical work to each other. Or they could be entities that together form a single abstraction, a concept that allows you deal with them collectively by ignoring certain details.

This pattern-seeking work begins during early design work, but it doesn't stop when a solution starts to be implemented as software. As you write the code, it continues to reveal further patterns you can take advantage of.

> Each significant piece of functionality in a program should be implemented in just one place in the source code. Where similar functions are carried out by distinct pieces of code, it is generally beneficial to combine them into one by abstracting out the varying parts.
>
> (Pierce, 2002)

This key piece of advice can be boiled down to two oft-quoted principles:

- Don't repeat yourself.
- Find what varies and encapsulate it.

Let's apply these in an example: the shape-drawing program discussed in earlier chapters. Chapter 3 pointed out that patterns among very similar, consecutive instructions can be replaced by a loop. The implementation of the shape-drawing solution in Chapter 9 stopped short of doing this, so let's do it now.

For example, **render_neutral_face** looked like this:

```
def render_neutral_face():
    core_draw.draw_oval(50, 50, 120, 120) # Face
    core_draw.draw_oval(60, 60, 80, 80) # Left eye
    core_draw.draw_oval(65, 65, 75, 75)
    core_draw.draw_oval(90, 60, 110, 80) # Right eye
    core_draw.draw_oval(95, 65, 105, 75)
    core_draw.draw_line(70, 110, 100, 110) # Mouth
```

This function calls **draw_circle** multiple times in a row. However, calls are not identical; the parameters vary. So, let's follow the earlier advice.

First, don't repeat yourself:

```
def render_neutral_face():
    for something in collection_of_somethings:
        core_draw.draw_circle(something)
    core_draw.draw_line(70, 110, 100, 110)
```

Then, find what varies and encapsulate it. The circle parameters vary, so we'll capture those and encapsulate them in their own collection:[59]

```
def render_neutral_face():
    circle_dimensions = [
    (50, 50, 120, 120), (60, 60, 80, 80), (65, 65, 75, 75)
    (90, 60, 110, 80), (95, 65, 105, 75)
    ]
    for d in circle_dimensions:
        core_draw.draw_circle(d[0], d[1], d[2], d[3])

    core_draw.draw_line(70, 110, 100, 110)
```

Recall that the solution draws several faces that differ by the shape of their mouths, so we can move the loop into its own reusable function.

```
def render_mouthless_face(circle_params):
    for param in circle_params:
        core_draw.draw_circle(param[0], param[1], param[2], param[3])

def render_neutral_face():
    circle_params = [
    (50, 50, 120, 120),
    (60, 60, 80, 80), (65, 65, 75, 75),
    (90, 60, 110, 80), (95, 65, 105, 75)
    ]
    render_mouthless_face(circle_dimensions)
    core_draw.draw_line(70, 110, 100, 110)
```

```
def render_smiley_face():
    circle_dimensions = [
    (50, 50, 120, 120),
    (60, 60, 80, 80), (65, 65, 75, 75),
    (90, 60, 110, 80), (95, 65, 105, 75)
    ]
    render_mouthless_face(circle_dimensions)
    core_draw.draw_arc(30, 70, 40, 10, 0, -180)
```

ABSTRACTIONS IN PROGRAMMING

The concepts behind abstraction were discussed in Chapter 4.

Finding patterns helps you to form abstractions. Recall that an abstraction is a means of expressing an idea in a certain context and one that suppresses some details deemed irrelevant in that context. Since Chapter 4, we've seen numerous examples of abstractions. The first part of this book discussed them at a conceptual level. So far in Part II we've seen more concrete abstractions in programming. They might not have struck you as abstractions, but indeed they are.

Take something fundamental: a variable. When you see **x** = **42**, you can think of **x** conceptually as an integer variable. In reality, **x** refers to piece of computer memory, which includes all sorts of details you never need to worry about (its location in random access memory (RAM), the amount of memory it occupies, the maximum value it can store and so on). These details are hidden by the abstraction that is a Python variable.

Most other programming constructs we've covered are abstractions too: list comprehensions, loops, conditionals. The details of how they actually work 'under the bonnet' can be quite complex, but the creators of Python have made using them relatively simple by hiding those details (see the box below). After reading Chapter 9, you'll probably appreciate that functions and modules are abstractions too. That goes for anything that organises blocks of code into single units and hides the details within.

For an example of the extent to which a typical Python abstraction hides detail, consider something like creating a new list. To you, it's as simple as doing **my_list** = **[ ]**, but Python is doing a lot of work behind the scenes. The procedure for creating a new list requires dozens of lines of code in C, the language used to implement Python (Python.org, 2016).

In fact, a programming language is itself an abstraction. The computer doesn't actually understand the code you type. Instead, your code gets transformed into machine language (a string of ones and zeroes) before the computer executes it. This means programming doesn't involve writing out a tedious amount of binary digits but lets you focus on writing your solution instead.

While all this is important to know, this chapter focuses on another type of abstraction: the custom ones that you will be building as part of your solution. It discusses how you can best create your own abstractions using Python, as well as how to apply certain ready-made patterns to your own solution.

BUILT-IN TYPES

As part of a solution's work, it will need to store various pieces of information. Some of the time, the nature of that information will line up with certain data types built into your programming language. For example, when you want to store a number, you'll use an integer variable; when you want to store a piece of text, you can use a string.

Certain types of information are used in programs so often that every useful programming language provides them out of the box. Python is no exception (see Table 10.1).

Table 10.1 List of some of the most commonly used types in Python

Type	Example	Comments
int	answer = 42	Integer. Stores whole numbers.
float	half = 0.5	Floating point numbers. In other words, it stores real numbers (see the box below).
bool	is_ready = True	Stores Boolean values, i.e. True or False.
list	ages = [32, 31, 27, 31, 39]	Traditionally (though not necessarily) used as a variable-sized sequence of data where all the items have the same type.
tuple	profile = ('Palin', 1943, 'Sheffield')	Traditionally (though not necessarily) used as a fixed-sized sequence of data where the items have mixed types.
set	evens = {2, 4, 6, 8}	An unordered collection of items. No item can appear more than once in a set.
dict	num_chapters = {'bible': 929, 'hobbit': 19}	Dictionary. Stores a collection of items (similarly to a list), but gives each item a unique, meaningful identifier to facilitate later retrieval.
str	name = 'Spock'	String. Holds a piece of text.

Exercise caution with the **float** type. Real numbers are theoretically capable of going on infinitely (like ⅓ being 0.33333...), but computers have limited space to store numbers. This means that some decimal calculations will be imprecise in surprising ways (for example, try evaluating **1.1 + 2.2** in Python and see what happens).

See this page for more details: https://docs.python.org/3/tutorial/floatingpoint.html

To avoid these kinds of troubles, consider the **decimal** type, https://docs.python.org/3/library/decimal.html, which behaves more like the arithmetic you learn at school.

As well as storing data, these in-built types provide many of their own functions for manipulating their contents. For example:

```
capulets = ['Juliet', 'Tybalt', 'Nurse'] # list
capulets.append('Rosaline') # Adds a new item

pi = 3.142 # float
pi.is_integer() # Evaluates to False

sentence = 'It was the best of times, it was the worst of times'
sentence.split(' ') # Evaluates to: ['It', 'was', 'the',
# 'best', 'of', 'times,', 'it', 'was', 'the', 'worst', 'of', 'times']
```

Such functions represent very commonly used operations. Taking advantage of them helps to reduce the amount of work you have to do, so spend some time getting to know the functions available (see the Python language online reference: https://docs.python.org/3/library/stdtypes.html). Reusing them means you don't have to do the work yourself, plus they're heavily tried, tested and optimised.

CREATING YOUR OWN TYPES

The car rental example was introduced in Chapter 4; see the section 'Context and layers'.

Sometimes, a structure will emerge from your solution that no built-in type can satisfy. For example, in the vehicle rental scenario of Chapter 4, several patterns emerged, including 'car', 'van' and 'motorcycle'. Furthermore, these were all versions of the more general concept 'vehicle'. Each type turned out to support particular properties (such as fuel amount, capacity) and operations (for example, check in, report mileage).

Python provides no vehicular types to help you here. In a case like this, when no built-in types meet your requirements, you can create your own. In Python, that means getting familiar with **object-oriented programming** (OOP), a subject with a wealth of material behind it. Covering all of OOP, even briefly, is out of scope for this book. Instead, we'll examine only the material of immediate relevance to the creation of abstractions in Python. To illustrate this process, we'll use the car rental scenario.

Whether built-in or not, a type is like a blueprint or template. An object is an instance of a type, put together from this blueprint. As such, there's only one definitive blueprint for each type, but you can manufacture as many objects from it as you like. When you want to create your own type, you must write a 'blueprint' that tells the computer how to create objects of your custom type.

First steps

In Python, types are called classes. The starting point to creating a new type in Python is to define a new class:

```
class Car:
    pass
```

The **pass** keyword in Python effectively says 'I'm purposefully leaving the definition of this thing empty.' It's useful when you want to lay out the structure of a program but need to defer adding details.

Those two lines alone create a new class. You can prove it by entering these lines below:

```
x = Car()
print(type(x)) # Prints: <class 'Car'>
```

The line **x = Car()** creates a new object of the Car class (that is, **instantiates** a Car object). Creating a new object this way is something you can do with any type, even the built-in ones:

```
my_integer = int() # Equivalent to my_integer = 0
print(my_integer) # Prints 0
print(type(my_integer)) # Prints <class 'int'>

my_list = list() # Equivalent to my_list = []
print(my_list) # Prints []
print(type(my_list)) # Prints <class 'list'>
```

Admittedly, **Car** is pretty useless as written. It can't store relevant information and it has no operations to manipulate data.[60] Before it can become useful, we must flesh out its definition. Now we can start to build the abstractions we discovered when planning the vehicle rental scenario.

When you build abstractions, remember that you're operating in a certain context that tells you at what level to operate. For example, a vehicle can be understood at different levels of detail. Someone modelling highway traffic can treat a vehicle as a single object, whereas someone working with car safety has to consider a car as made up of many components, each with their own behaviours.

For each abstraction, you will have identified:

1. properties that belong to each abstraction;
2. operations that can be applied to each abstraction.

These correspond with two things that classes in Python provide:

1. **data attributes**: variables that belong to a particular object.
2. **methods**: functions that belong to a particular object.

Let's add an attribute to our class – the regulatory vehicle category that identifies this type of car (that is, 'B'):[61]

```
class Car:
    category = 'B'
```

category has now become an attribute of every Car object we will create. This makes it a **class variable**, because the value is the same for each instance of this class:

```
fiat = Car() # Creates a new instance of the Car class
ford = Car() # Creates another new instance of the Car class

print(fiat.category) # Prints 'B'
print(ford.category) # Prints 'B'
```

Some attributes vary among different instances of the same class. Every car may be category B by definition, but each car has its own model name. Python treats such attributes (**instance variables**) a little differently:

```
class Car:
    category = 'B'

    def __init__(self, model):
        self.model = model
```

Some remarks about this:

- We've added a new, oddly named method to the Car class: **__init__**. This is a special method called an **initialiser**, which is automatically executed whenever a new instance of a class is created. Its purpose is to provide a place for the programmer to add instructions that every object must execute when first created. It's often used to specify the initial values of an object's attributes.

- The **__init__** method name begins and ends with a pair of underscores. This is a convention applied to all the special methods that objects can have (see the box below).

- An **__init__** method **always** has at least one parameter. By convention it is named **self**. You don't pass this parameter yourself – it just magically appears and is always the first parameter.

  - **self** represents the object itself. It's a way of allowing an object to be introspective and able to manipulate its own properties.

- In addition to the **self** parameter, an initialiser may have an arbitrary number of additional parameters following it.

A Python special method can be called using a specific syntax rather than by calling the method. For example, `__init__` is a special method because you don't instantiate, say, a car by calling `Car.__init__()`, rather you just call `Car()` and that in turn calls `__init__()`.

Now, we can create objects with initial values and access those attributes later:

```python
cars = [Car('Ford Anglia'), Car('Morris Minor')]

for car in cars:
    print(car.model)
```

Let's add another attribute of cars that's very important to a rental agency: the mileage. We'll have each car record its own mileage and also provide an operation to update it.

```python
class Car:
    category = 'B'

    def __init__(self, model, mileage):
        self.model = model
        self.mileage = mileage # New attribute

    # New method
    def update_mileage(self, new_mileage):
        if new_mileage < self.mileage:
            print('Error: New mileage cannot be lower than current
mileage!')
        else:
            self.mileage = new_mileage

my_car = Car('Jaguar Mk III', 123678)
my_car.update_mileage(123789)

print(my_car.mileage) # Prints 123789

my_car.update_mileage(123456) # Prints error message
print(my_car.mileage) # Prints 123789
```

As with the model, the mileage is an instance variable of the Car class. The other addition is the **update_mileage** method. Some remarks on that:

- We could have just written **my_car.mileage = 123789**, but since the process is more complicated than that (we first have to check that the odometer hasn't been tampered with), we put the whole updating procedure into a class method and call that instead. By putting it in one place, this allows us follow the advice from earlier (that is, 'don't repeat yourself').

- Once again, the **self** parameter appears. It has to be included because the method works with instance variables and so needs access to the particular object being dealt with (remember, many **Car** objects might exist and updating a car's mileage applies only to one of them at a time). Again, it is passed automatically. Essentially, the value of **my_car** gets assigned to **self** without you needing to do anything.

Inheritance

Let's take our example further by adding the other classes in the vehicle rental system: van and motorcycle.

```
class Van:
    category = 'C'

    def __init__(self, model, mileage):
        self.model = model
        self.mileage = mileage

    def update_mileage(self, new_mileage):
        if new_mileage < self.mileage:
            print('Error: New mileage cannot be lower than current
mileage!')
        else:
            self.mileage = new_mileage

class Motorcycle:
    category = 'A'

    def __init__(self, model, mileage):
        self.model = model
        self.mileage = mileage

    def update_mileage(self, new_mileage):
        if new_mileage < self.mileage:
            print('Error: New mileage cannot be lower than current
mileage!')
        else:
            self.mileage = new_mileage
```

You should see a problem similar to one observed in Chapter 9. The process for updating the mileage is exactly the same for cars, vans and motorcycles, so we have repetitions of the same code. However, object-oriented programming provides ways to deal with this.

Cars, vans and motorcycles are all types of **vehicle**. So, what we're really saying is that we follow the same process to update the mileage of every vehicle. OOP allows us to model this relationship using **inheritance**. When one class inherits from a parent class, it gains access to all the attributes and methods of the parent.

In terms of our example, we can say that **Car**, **Van** and **Motorcycle** are all subclasses of **Vehicle**. In other words: **Car**, **Van** and **Motorcycle** **inherit** from **Vehicle**. The subclasses take all the attributes and methods of **Vehicle** without you having to add them to each class explicitly:

```
class Vehicle:

    def __init__(self, model, mileage):
        self.model = model
        self.mileage = mileage

    def update_mileage(self, new_mileage):
        if new_mileage < self.mileage:
            print('Error: New mileage cannot be lower than current
mileage!')
        else:
            self.mileage = new_mileage

# class A(B) means that A is a subclass of B
class Car(Vehicle):
    category = 'B'

class Van(Vehicle):
    category = 'C'

class Motorcycle(Vehicle):
    category = 'A'
```

The contents of the Car, Van and Motorcycle classes have (where identical) been moved into the Vehicle class, but they're still implicitly in those subclasses because the subclasses inherit them from **Vehicle**. That means you can still execute the **update_mileage** method for a **Car**, **Van** or **Motorcycle**.

The only place those classes differed was their categories. Since this property varies among the subclasses, it needs to be specified in each subclass:

```
car = Car('Aston Martin DB5', 32890)
van = Van('Ford Transit', 67232)
motorcycle = Motorcycle('Triumph 900', 3221)

print(car.category) # Prints 'B'
print(van.category) # Prints 'C'
print(motorcycle.category) # Prints 'A'
```

Chapter 4, section 'Putting abstractions to use' first mentioned the instantiation of abstractions.

Chapter 4 raised the problem of instantiating an abstraction. It may provide many conveniences but if it's missing certain details, can it actually be made to work? Some details are necessary before you can instantiate an abstraction and put it to concrete use.

The last example instantiated not vehicles but specific types of vehicle. Instantiating a more abstract class might or might not be a valid thing to do – it depends on the context of your problem. Let's say an exciting new vehicle comes along that's like nothing else in the firm's inventory. It's certainly a vehicle, but it's not a car, a van, nor or a motorcycle. So, should we just instantiate it as a **Vehicle**?

```
c5 = Vehicle('Sinclair C5', 10)
c5.update_mileage(20) # Works fine
```

So far, no problem. But what about when you try to access the vehicle's category?

```
print(c5.category) # Error: 'Vehicle' object has no attribute 'category'
```

Because the Vehicle class has no attribute called 'category', objects of that type have no such attribute. There are ways around this problem, ranging from simple to advanced:

- Add the **category** attribute to **Vehicle**. Give it a default value, like <undefined>.

- Create a new subclass for this new type of vehicle.

- **Advanced:** use a **@property** decorator to control access to **category**. Add a method to **Vehicle** like this:

```
@property
def category(self): raise NotImplementedError
```

For more information see: https://docs.python.org/3/library/functions.html#property.

Polymorphism

A feature request for the vehicle rental system asks that a new function be added for printing out the model names of all vehicles in a list. It's our job to write it.

Our new function could look something like this:

```
def print_models(vehicles):
    for v in vehicles:
        print(v.model)
```

In this example, the function is given a list of objects named **vehicles**. All it knows[62] is that the list contains a collection of vehicles, but not which specific types of vehicles. Fortunately, it doesn't need to know in order to do its job. This is possible because of **polymorphism**, a fancy term that describes the ability to deal with different types of objects using the same interface.

The **Vehicle** class provides an interface (that is, its attributes and methods) through which to manipulate any type of vehicle. Thanks to inheritance, we know that whatever attributes and methods the **Vehicle** class has, **every** subclass shares them. That means we can manipulate classes without knowing their exact type. We only require that all those classes support the expected interface. As a result, our code can be more concise and flexible.

It doesn't matter that the underlying implementations might differ. For example, when a customer returns a vehicle, it must be found a parking bay. However, the method for finding a bay differs for each type of vehicle (vehicles are grouped into different parking sections by type).

```python
class Vehicle:
    # ... other methods and attributes hidden for brevity

    def find_parking_bay(self):
        pass

class Car(Vehicle):

    def find_parking_bay(self):
        print('Looking for a bay in the car section...')

class Van(Vehicle):

    def find_parking_bay(self):
        print('Looking for a bay in the van section...')

class Motorcycle(Vehicle):

    def find_parking_bay(self):
        print('Looking for a bay in the motorcycle section...')
```

Just like in the previous example, you can take a list of incoming vehicles of indeterminate type and make them each find an available parking bay in their respective section:

```python
def find_bays(vehicles):
    for v in vehicles:
        print(v.find_parking_bay())
```

Polymorphism has its limits. If a subclass has its own attribute that the parent class doesn't, then you can't access it via the parent class. For example, vans have a payload, which cars and motorcycles don't, so the Vehicle class can't therefore have payload as an attribute. Therefore, we have to treat this attribute a little differently when initialising a **Van**, which means a **Van** has to have a different initialiser.

```
class Van(Vehicle):

    def __init__(self, model, mileage, payload):
        super().__init__(model, mileage)
        self.payload = payload

car = Car('Aston Martin DB5', 32890)
van = Van('Ford Transit', 67232, 700)

print(van.payload) # Prints 700
print(car.payload) # AttributeError: 'Car' object has no attribute
'payload'
```

By giving the **Van** its own initialiser, we're replacing the initialiser inherited from the **Vehicle**.

Initialising the common attributes (model and mileage) can still be done in the Vehicle class. We can just pass those to the initialiser of the parent class (aka the superclass, hence why it's accessed via a method called **super**). Then, we can initialise any attributes that belong solely to the **Van**.

Even when classes have their own particular methods and attributes, we can still take a polymorphic approach. If we have a list of vehicles and want to access payload information (which some vehicles don't have), we can use Python's built-in **hasattr** method, which tells us whether or not an object has a specific attribute or method:

```
def print_all_payloads(vehicles):
    for v in vehicles:
        if hasattr(v, 'payload'):
            print(v.model, ':', v.payload)
```

In this example, the **print** statement is only executed if an object has a payload attribute.

Object composition

Let's look closer at the parking bay feature, because it reveals an alternative way to structure related types that work together. A parking section is a type. It's made up of several parking bays, which are another type. The question is: how can that relationship be modelled in a program?

Using inheritance to relate a vehicle and its subtypes made sense because a car (or a van or a motorcycle) is a particular type of vehicle. This can't be said in the case of parking. A parking bay is not a type of parking section, nor vice versa. Instead, a parking section is made up of several parking bays.

When objects share this '**has a**' relationship, you can implement this in a Python program by using object composition. Instead of one class inheriting another, one class is composed of others, like so:

```
class ParkingBay:

    def __init__(self):
        # None is a special type in Python to denote the
        # absence of value. In this case, an unoccupied
        # bay has no contents.
        self.contents = None

    def put_vehicle(vehicle):
        self.contents = vehicle

    def is_occupied():
        return self.contents == None

class ParkingSection:

    def __init__():
        # This section has three parking bays
        self.parking_bays = [ParkingBay(), ParkingBay(), ParkingBay()]

    def is_bay_occupied(bay_number):
        # A ParkingBay has a method called is_occupied,
        # which returns True or False.
        return self.parking_bays[bay_number].is_occupied()
```

> Inheritance and composition are both often referred to as 'is a' and 'has a' relationships respectively. For example, a car **is** a vehicle, whereas a parking section **has** a parking bay.

Composition and inheritance solve similar problems, but among programming professionals there is often a preference for composition over inheritance. One reason for this is that composition proves to be more flexible than inheritance because it's often easier to compose classes together than to try and put them into some kind of family tree structure. Nevertheless, inheritance is helpful when a family of classes do happen to fit such a structure.

READY-MADE PATTERNS

We've seen already how to spot patterns in your solution. We've also seen how to work those patterns and turn them into your own generalisations.

As you gain more experience in writing programs, you'll notice that some patterns crop up repeatedly. Some details may differ a little in each case (for example, the variable names will differ), but some underlying structure is always the same.

Many useful patterns have already been found and catalogued over the years, lots of them described in books and websites. Becoming familiar with these patterns and applying them in your own solutions brings several key advantages:

- they're tried and tested solutions to common problems.
- they reduce the amount of effort you have to put into your programs.
- being named, they provide a common 'vocabulary' for understanding the ideas in a solution.
- they hide certain details, enabling you to discuss solutions at a higher level. Instead of talking in terms of individual lines of code, you can refer to whole sections of a program using just one or two words.

Patterns range from very simple (realisable in just a few lines of code) to more complicated ones involving several objects acting in concert.

Simple patterns

In a sense, some of the built-in constructs of Python are simple patterns, for example building a list using a comprehension:

```python
def get_doubles(singles):
    return [n * 2 for n in singles]
```

or prematurely exiting from a loop:

```python
for d in droids:
    if d == droid_you_are_looking_for:
        print('Found droid.')
        break
```

These are goals that Python's authors thought were so useful and so common, they decided to build features into Python to support them.

 Patterns have some dependence on programming language. A language might support a pattern directly, and others not. Some patterns might not even make sense in a particular language.

Some other simple patterns don't have direct language support in Python and you must implement them completely yourself. Perhaps the simplest example is the **temporary variable swap**. It's often the case in a solution that two objects need to swap their values with each other. This is a need that occurs so often, it has a standard solution:

```python
my_ticket_number = 133
your_ticket_number = 4

temp = your_ticket_number
your_ticket_number = my_ticket_number
```

```
my_ticket_number = temp

print('Customer number 4 please!')
```

This can be considered a pattern. The names and types of the variables may differ from case to case, but the underlying pattern is always the same.

Another simple pattern is **lazy initialisation**. Sometimes, it makes more sense to delay initialising an object's attribute, but at the same time you might want to make sure that the attribute has a value when needed. Lazy initialisation combines the checking of an attribute's value with the returning of it.

```
class Vehicle:

    def __init__(self):
        # When the vehicle is created, it has no parking bay
        self.current_parking_bay = None

    def get_parking_bay(self):
        # Getting the parking bay this way, ensures it has
        # a parking bay.
        if self.current_parking_bay == None:
            self.current_parking_bay = find_parking_bay()

        return self.current_parking_bay
```

Lots of small patterns like these exist, but they're often harder to spot than the built-in patterns. Despite this, you'll build up familiarity by researching them and, more importantly, getting some practical experience.

Design patterns

Among programming professionals, talk of patterns in software has recently been dominated by object-oriented design patterns. Consequently, a web search for 'software patterns' will almost invariably bring up design patterns.

A design pattern typically involves several collaborating classes. Each pattern has a name and a reference to a specific design problem it solves. While they don't directly correspond to executable code (you can't just instantiate a design pattern), they have an archetypal structure that you can adapt and apply in your own situations.

Let's illustrate this with a simple example: the **facade** pattern. Like an architectural facade, this pattern solves the problem of covering up some complexity by hiding it behind a simpler layer. Specifically, it conceals a complicated interface – probably involving several different classes – behind a simpler, unified interface.

In the following partial program, several objects model the ignition system of a car, which involves a complex chain of events among several components:

```
class IgnitionSwitch:
    def activate_battery():
        # ...

class Battery:
    def draw_power_to_coil(coil):
        # ...

class Coil:
    def send_power_to_dist_cap(dc):
        # ...

class DistributorCap:
    def spin_rotor(rotor):
        # ...

class Rotor:
    def trigger_spark(spark_plugs):
        # ...

class SparkPlug:
    def spark():
        # ...
```

The ignition switch causes the battery to draw power to the coil, which transforms the power and sends it to the distributor cap, which causes the rotor to spin and trigger sparks in a series of spark plugs.

To make the process simpler, you can hide all the complexity behind a new facade class, in this case **IgnitionSystem**:

```
class IgnitionSystem

    def __init__(self):
        self.battery = Battery()
        self.coil = Coil()
        self.dist_cap = DistributorCap()
        self.rotor = Rotor()
        self.spark_plugs = [SparkPlug(), SparkPlug(), SparkPlug(),
SparkPlug()]

    def start_car(self):
        self.battery.draw_power_to_coil(self.coil)
        self.coil.send_power_to_dist_cap(self.dist_cap)
        self.dist_cap.spin_rotor(self.rotor)
        self.rotor.trigger_spark(self.spark_plugs)
```

The **IgnitionSystem** wraps all those components together. As a result, it can behave more like a real ignition system. After all, a real car is not activated by manually carrying out each step – you simply turn a key. This facade provides a **start_car** method, the programmatic equivalent of turning the key.

The facade is an example of a structural pattern, in that the problem it addresses concerns how various objects interact with each other. Design patterns normally come in one of three flavours: creational, behavioural and structural. Let's look at examples from those other two categories.

Creational patterns: suitable ways to create objects in different circumstances.

Behavioural patterns: common communication patterns and assignment of responsibilities among objects.

Structural patterns: simple ways to design relationships between objects.

In the current **IgnitionSystem**, the act of creating each object is very simple: a parameterless initialiser is called. However, creating objects in real solutions often gets complicated because they can be initialised in different ways depending on the circumstances. For example, batteries vary by how many amps they output; spark plugs depend on the size of the engine's spark plug gap and so on. So, if you want your ignition system to be a standardised part able to work with different engines,[63] it's going to have to work out what types of parts are in the engine and react accordingly. This means extra instructions will need adding to each instantiation. You could add them to the **IgnitionSystem**'s initialiser, but it would become a very large and unwieldy method.

The **factory** pattern can help out here. It's a creational pattern that helps when the act of creating a new object is complicated. The solution is to add a new class that encapsulates the instantiation process. An object no longer composes its own objects. Instead, it asks a factory to make them on its behalf.

So, instead of the **IgnitionSystem** making all those decisions, it entrusts them to a factory:

```python
class EngineFactory:

    def get_new_battery():
        # The following step finds out what type of engine
        # the system is currently running on.
        engine_type = lookup_engine()

        if engine_type == 'SuperEngine Mk I':
            # Needs a battery with 300 cranking amps
            return Battery(300)
        elif engine_type == 'SuperEngine Mk II':
            # Needs a battery with 600 cranking amps
            return Battery(600)
        elif engine_type == 'SuperEngine Mk III':
```

```
            # Needs a battery with 900 cranking amps
            return Battery(900)

    def get_new_coil():
        # ...

    def get_new_dist_cap():
        # ...

# etc...
```

And so the initialiser of the **IgnitionSystem** looks like this:

```
class IgnitionSystem

    def __init__(self):
        self.battery = EngineFactory.get_new_battery()
        self.coil = EngineFactory.get_new_coil()
        self.dist_cap = EngineFactory.get_new_dist_cap()
        self.rotor = EngineFactory.get_new_rotor()
        self.spark_plugs = EngineFactory.get_new_spark_plugs()

    def start_car(self):
        self.battery.draw_power_to_coil(self.coil)
        self.coil.send_power_to_dist_cap(self.dist_cap)
        self.dist_cap.spin_rotor(self.rotor)
        self.rotor.trigger_spark(self.spark_plugs)
```

Notice how we can use multiple patterns together. After adding a factory pattern, the existing facade pattern is still in place.

Finally, let's examine a behavioural pattern: **method chaining**. When a process carries multiple steps, it can sometimes involve the creation of many objects. These have to be stored as local variables or instance attributes (as is the case with the **IgnitionSwitch**). Method chaining removes the need for the storing of so many objects.

To see method chaining at a simple level, consider this example:

```
x = 'hello'
y = x.capitalize().replace('e', 'a')

print(y) # Prints 'Hallo'
```

Because Python's strings are immutable, a string method doesn't alter the original string, rather it returns a new string. Therefore, adding a string method to the end of another string method means that the second method in the chain applies to the result of the first method's execution, like this:

```
'hello'.capitalize().replace('e', 'a')
'Hello'.replace('e', 'a')
'Hallo'
```

We can achieve a similar effect with our **IgnitionSwitch**. Each method in the ignition sequence can be made to return the object it was passed, so the next method in the sequence can be tacked onto the end. For example, if the **draw_power_to_coil** method worked like this:

```
class Battery:

    def draw_power_to_coil(coil):
        # Logic of method goes here...

        # Finally, return the coil.
        return coil

# etc...
```

and all other engine parts worked along similar lines, the **IgnitionSwitch** could be simplified to look like this:

```
class IgnitionSystem

    def __init__(self):
        # Initialistion of parts no longer necessary.

    def start_car(self):
    EngineFactory.get_new_battery() \
    .draw_power_to_coil(EngineFactory.get_new_coil()) \
    .send_power_to_dist_cap(EngineFactory.get_new_dist_cap()) \
    .spin_rotor(EngineFactory.get_new_rotor()) \
    .trigger_spark(EngineFactory.get_new_spark_plugs())
```

Many good books have been written on design patterns. Just a couple of them are:

Design Patterns (Gamma et al., 1995), the earliest book on the subject, although written in a rather advanced, cataloging style.

Design Patterns Explained (Shalloway and Trott, 2005), a more beginner-friendly text focused on explaining the concept in easily understandable stages.

Many design patterns exist and many good books describe them in detail. Each pattern may solve a different problem, but collectively their goals are the same: provide a reusable set of solutions to common design problems, simplify your programs, speed up development and give you a common terminology.

SUMMARY

The key pieces of advice when finding patterns in your program are: 'Don't repeat yourself' and 'find what varies and encapsulate it'. Programming languages like Python provide numerous built-in abstractions for encapsulating things (variables, functions, loops, etc.). Part of programming is to match parts of your solution to those built-in parts.

Another part of programming is using the language to build your own abstractions that your solution requires. In a language like Python, this is often done by creating your own types, each of which encapsulate some data and a set of operations and correspond to some part of your solution.

Patterns are found throughout all programs. Some that are not part of a language (but nevertheless often used) have been recognised and catalogued by many programmers over the years, providing you with a rich source of ready-made patterns.

EXERCISES

EXERCISE 1

Mark the following statements as true or false:

  A. All items in a Python list must have the same type.
  B. Creating a new object of a certain class is called instantiation.
  C. A subclass must override all the methods it inherits from the parent class.
  D. Reusing patterns helps to reduce effort when coming up with solutions.
  E. Design patterns are typically categorised into the following three categories: creational, structural and atypical.

EXERCISE 2

Write a Python program that prints out all the unique words in any arbitrary sentence. To keep things simple, it is assumed the sentence contains only letters and spaces (that is, no punctuation).

Hint: take advantage of a built-in type that automatically removes duplicates.

EXERCISE 3

In English, adjectives are expected to come in a certain order depending on type. The order is: opinion, size, quantity, quality, age, shape, colour, proper adjective (such as nationality), purpose. That's why 'the big, old, red, Italian racing car' and 'the pretty, little, old, red racing car' sound right, but 'the racing, red, old, big, pretty car' sounds wrong. Using this rule, write an insult generator in Python that picks a random assortment of adjectives and orders them correctly in an insulting sentence (e.g. 'disgusting, oversized, old, yellow handbag').

EXERCISE 4

In the remaining questions, we'll build a Rock-Paper-Scissors game. First, define a class for each of the three shapes: **Rock**, **Paper**, **Scissors**. Give each a method called **beats**, which takes another shape and returns whether it wins against the other shape or not.

EXERCISE 5

Add a class to act as a computer player. It should need only one method called **choose**, which returns one of the three random shapes.

Hint: if you import the package called **random**, you can access the **random.choice()** method, which returns a random item from a list.

EXERCISE 6

Add code to play one round of the game:

      A.   The computer player should make a choice.
      B.   The program should ask the player to choose a shape (ensuring that the input is valid).
      C.   It should print out the computer's choice.
      D.   It should determine who won and print out the result.

11 EFFECTIVE MODELLING

OBJECTIVES

- Introduce Unified Modelling Language (UML).
- Discuss how various things can be modelled, specifically:
  - entities like classes, packages, nodes and components;
  - relationships like dependencies and associations;
  - processes like state changes and workflows;
  - user interaction.
- Give general advice on creating and using models.
- Explain how software professionals use modelling.

RECAP

Modelling was first introduced in Chapter 4.

As Chapter 4 explained, abstractions – while useful for representing parts of a solution – can be difficult to get to grips with. Models offer a more concrete and manageable means of working with abstractions.

This chapter shows the various types of models you can create using Unified Modelling Language (UML) as an example.

A model represents the entities in a solution (or, more often, in part of a solution) and relationships between them. They typically include only details relevant in a certain context.

Models come in two types:

- Static models depict a system at a particular point in time.
- Dynamic models show how a system changes over time.

Use of models brings several advantages:

- They reduce the mental effort required to comprehend a solution.
- Some models are formal models and help to validate ideas by seeing if any rules are broken.
- Some models are executable models and predict how a solution will behave.

Different disciplines find particular types of model more helpful than others. Engineers focus on physical models that depict working systems. Scientists often favour mathematical models that reduce phenomena down to variables.

Software developers tend to use conceptual models that describe ideas, and they have many different modelling languages to choose from. Conceptual models are often specialised towards a particular sub-domain of computing, like modelling business processes, data structures or network layouts. While they can be very powerful in their place, this limits each language's applicability.

Conversely, a **general-purpose modelling language** can be used to describe any part of a software-intensive system. Today's pre-eminent general-purpose modelling language is UML, an industry standard for describing software systems. Since this chapter discusses modelling in general, it uses UML as an example of how to approach modelling in software solutions.

UML provides a dozen or so different types of diagrams. A complete description of them all lies outside the scope of this book. Instead, more in keeping with this book's focus, this chapter describes each major computational aspect of a solution and how it can be modelled. Specifically, it shows how UML can be used to model:

- entities;
- relationships;
- processes;
- usage.

Each aspect is illustrated with examples, along with corresponding source code listings that implement each example model.

If you wish to buy a book on UML, make sure it covers UML 2, the latest version. There is a wealth of books on UML, including:

UML Distilled (Fowler, 2004) and *UML 2 For Dummies* (Chonoles and Schardt, 2003).

ENTITIES

Static models were introduced in the Chapter 4, section 'Static vs dynamic models'.

Entities are the focus of static diagrams (aka structural diagrams in UML), which depict components in a solution.

Classes

A **class diagram** shows a solution decomposed into classes. It's one of the most important types of diagrams when developing an object-oriented solution.

The building block of a class diagram is a box representing the class itself. This can be as simple as shown in Figure 11.1.

Figure 11.1 Simple class diagram

While this is a valid diagram, it's not awfully helpful. After all, it corresponds to the following code:

```
class Vehicle:
    pass
```

A depiction of a class showing only the name is perfectly fine, but we can add more detail to make it more informative. A class in a class diagram can have three sections:

- The **top** section contains the class's name.
- The **middle** section lists the attributes of the class.
- The **bottom** section lists the operations of the class.

Inspired by the vehicle rental solution from the previous chapter, let's fill in some of those details (see Figure 11.2).

Figure 11.2 Class diagram with attributes and operations

Vehicle
model mileage category
update_mileage(new_mileage)

The diagram now tells us more about the class: we know it has several attributes and one operation called **update_mileage** (which takes one parameter called **new_mileage**). Again, the model can be transformed directly into source code:

```python
class Vehicle:
    def __init__(self):
        self.model = None
        self.mileage = None
        self.category = None

    def update_mileage(self, new_mileage):
        pass
```

Clearly, the model doesn't correspond to a fully working solution, but it's a valid piece of code that can serve as the starting point for complete implementation.

You can also include type information in a class diagram, like Figure 11.3.

Figure 11.3 Class diagram with types included

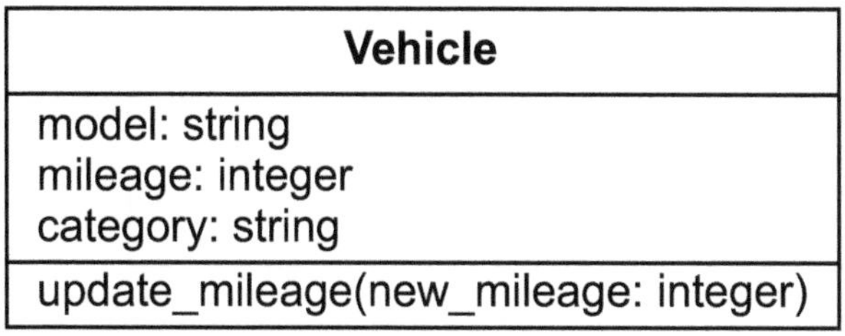

Vehicle
model: string mileage: integer category: string
update_mileage(new_mileage: integer)

Although Python is **dynamically typed** (see the definition box below), it's still advisable to include type information in models for the sake of clarity.

> **Dynamic typing**: a dynamically typed programming language doesn't require the programmer to specify the type of an object. Instead, the computer determines the object's type when it is assigned a value. For example, seeing **name** = **'Keith'** tells the computer that **name** is a string. This stands in contrast to statically typed languages, where objects **must** have their types declared in the source code.

Packages

Recall that Python programs can be organised into modules and packages. UML provides a way to model these too. In UML, a package looks like Figure 11.4.

It holds a collection of related objects, serving as a convenient way to organise your solution into sections. A package diagram depicts its contents like Figure 11.5.

Figure 11.4 An empty package

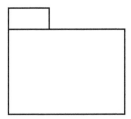

Figure 11.5 A non-empty package

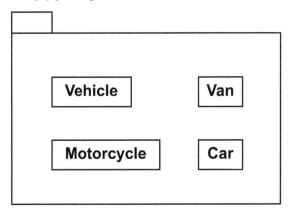

Thus, it can represent a Python module. It can also represent a Python package if the corresponding UML package contains other packages.

Components

A component is a complete, self-contained and replaceable piece of software that performs a function. An example of a component is an executable (like a .EXE file on Windows).

UML depicts a component like that seen in Figure 11.6.

Figure 11.6 A component

Nodes

When physical location is relevant in a solution, you might want to make that clear in a model. UML provides a way to do this via deployment diagrams. These model parts of a solution as **nodes**, where a node corresponds to a physical location.

As an example, let's say the vehicle rental system identifies vehicles in its fleet by a means of bar code. The user takes a handheld scanner and uses it to scan the bar code that is attached somewhere inside the vehicle. The scanner then relays this information back to the main system housed on a server somewhere. Thus, the overall system is necessarily divided between two locations. Figure 11.7 shows this.

Figure 11.7 Examples of nodes

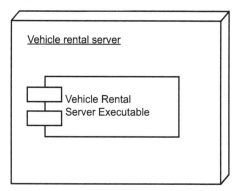
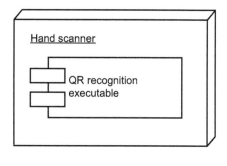

RELATIONSHIPS

Entities in a solution share various connections. UML provides ways of modelling relationships that attempt to capture all different possibilities. The most common relationships can be organised into two categories:

1. dependencies;
2. associations.

The various relationships in each category can be sorted in order of how much information they reveal.

Dependencies

Let's take **dependencies** first. Saying that entity B depends on entity A reveals little. It merely states that B requires A to provide some functionality in some way. It doesn't specify exactly how, but a dependency does imply that B is sensitive to changes in A.

As an example, look back at the **EngineFactory** in the previous chapter ('Design patterns' section). The **EngineFactory** has responsibility for creating objects found in a car engine, therefore it must know some things about how to create them. The **EngineFactory** therefore requires, for instance, a **Battery** type to exist and provide an initialiser. In other words, the **EngineFactory** depends on the **Battery** type and is sensitive to alterations.[64]

A dependency is depicted using a dashed arrow with an open arrowhead (see Figure 11.8).

Figure 11.8 EngineFactory depends on Battery

Next, let's look at a more specific type of dependency: inheritance (first discussed in Chapter 10). Inheritance creates a specific sort of dependency between a type and its subtype, so that they share an 'is a' relationship. In our vehicle rental example, we said that a Ford Transit **is a** van, and that a van **is a** vehicle. In each case, the former is a specialisation of the latter[65] and inherits the attributes and capabilities of its parent (possibly overriding some of them in the process). Therefore, it says not only that the Van type depends on the Vehicle type, but it also specifies the nature of that dependency.

UML allows you to model this relationship. A unidirectional line with a solid white arrowhead depicts an inheritance (the parent class is the one being pointed at).

Figure 11.9 Examples of inheritance

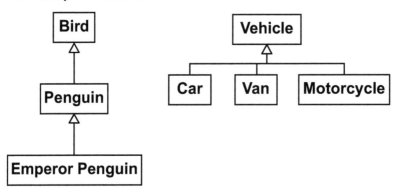

The examples in Figure 11.9 correspond to the following code:

```
class Bird:
    pass

class Penguin(Bird):
    pass

class EmperorPenguin(Penguin):
    pass

class Vehicle:
    pass

class Car(Vehicle):
    pass

class Van(Vehicle):
    pass

class Motorcycle(Vehicle):
    pass
```

Associations

Associations describe a relationship where either:

- entities share a link; or
- one entity aggregates other entities.

You can choose from a range of UML associations, depending on how much information you want the relationship to imply.

Figure 11.10 An association between customers and addresses

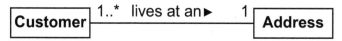

A simple association would look like something the arrangement in Figure 11.10. This models the relationship between customers and their addresses. It states that for each address the system contains, one or more customers are registered as living there, but says nothing more about the relationship.

Another example would be the link between two nodes. We might want to extend Figure 11.7 and include the communication between the hand scanner and central server. The model in Figure 11.11 makes this link explicit. Although the line might look like a cable between the two, it implies any sort of communication (hence we annotate the link to clarify what kind of interface is intended).

Figure 11.11 A link between two nodes in a deployment diagram

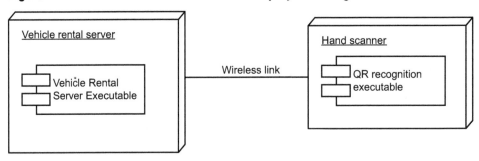

A simple association between classes reveals little about how that link might be implemented in source code. That's fine if you wish to leave that particular question open. However, should you wish to model associations in more detail, you can choose from more detailed versions.

An **aggregation** is an association that implies a loose relationship between two types. One may make use of the other, but their existences are independent of each other. For example, a garage may contain vehicles, but if you were to get rid of the garage, the vehicles would remain. The reverse is also true.

A UML aggregation is depicted like an association, except that the end of the line linking to the aggregating type has a clear diamond shape.

Figure 11.12 An aggregation between a garage and vehicles

The model in Figure 11.12 implies a relationship like this:

```
class Garage:
    def __init__(self):
        self.cars = []

class Car:
    pass

garage = Garage()
garage.cars.append(Car())
```

A **composition** is another sort of association, but a stronger one than an aggregation. It implies that an instance of one type is composed of instances of another and that the existence of the latter depends on the existence of the former. Getting rid of a composite object implicitly means getting rid of all its constituent objects. This means that the composite object has responsibility for creating its constituents (see Figure 11.13).

Figure 11.13 A chessboard is composed of squares

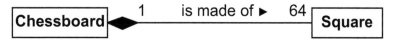

One way we could choose to implement this model in Python is like so:

```python
class Square:
    def __init__(self, column, row):
        self.column = column
        self.row = row

    # The __repr__ function allows you to specify what an
    # object looks like when you print it.
    def __repr__(self):
        return '{}-{}'.format(self.column, self.row)

class Chessboard:
    def __init__(self):
        self.columns = ['A', 'B', 'C', 'D', 'E', 'F', 'G', 'H']

        # A nested list comprehension. This goes through
# every item in self.columns for each number 1 to 8. In
# other words, it goes through all 8 items of self.columns
# 8 times. Thus, it creates 64 Squares in a list.
        self.board = [Square(c, r) for r in range(1,9) for c in self. \
columns]

    # When using a Chessboard, there's no need for you to create
    # Squares because they're created automatically by the
    # Chessboard.
    c = Chessboard()
    print(c.board)
```

The format method provided by a string allows you to put the current values of variables into that string. It goes through a string from left to right and adds the values of the corresponding parameters from left to right. In the preceding example, if a square was at column 3 and row 4, the __repr__ method would return "3-4".

A couple of things to note at this point:

- The code sample represents just one way to implement the model. A model rarely corresponds with only a single implementation, so once a model exists you still have implementation decisions to make.

- The difference between aggregation and composition varies in importance between programming languages. In a language where the creation and destruction of objects are managed by the computer (as it is in Python), it's not such an important distinction.

PROCESSES

The modelling techniques seen so far deal with the static configuration of a system. That is, they don't take into account how things change over time. During execution of a program, things are constantly changing in complex ways, so it's important to be able to model that as well. This section shows how you can model dynamic behaviour in UML.

State changes

Over time, certain elements of a system go through state changes: counters increase or get reset, switches open and close, messages are made to appear and then disappear. By carefully modelling these changes, you can predict how states change and under what circumstances, allowing you to verify that a system cannot enter an unexpected state (which is a key source of errors).

State machine diagrams were first mentioned in Chapter 4. See the section 'Static vs dynamic models'.

We've already seen an example of the standard method for modelling state changes in Chapter 4: the state machine diagram. Let's revisit the original diagram and examine exactly how it works.

The diagram in Figure 11.14 models the changes in state of a turnstile. It demonstrates the following elements of a state machine:

- **Initial state**: the black circle represents the starting point of the system. When the system is first activated, the transition from this point is executed.

- **Transitions**: an arrow depicts the movement of the system from one state to another. It can be labelled with the action that causes the transition (for example, inserting a coin causes the turnstile to become open, pushing a locked turnstile causes no change in state).

- **States**: a box with rounded edges depicts a state.

Figure 11.14 State machine diagram of a coin-operated turnstile

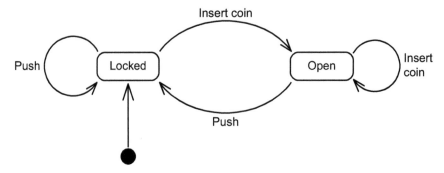

This shows a minimal amount of detail, but state machine diagrams offer additional elements.

One thing that can be added is an **end state**, which represents a point from which no further changes in state are possible (usually meaning the system has shut down). An end state is depicted as a solid black circle surrounded by a larger empty circle.

But the main place where detail can be added is inside the states. A state box may display additional activities relating to that state in an optional bottom section. Each activity is prefixed by a term explaining what kind of activity it is:

- 'entry/' happens when the system enters this state;
- 'exit/' happens when the system leaves this state;
- 'do/': happens while the system is in this state.

To demonstrate these, let's change our turnstile from coin-operated to card-operated. See Figure 11.15.

Figure 11.15 State machine diagram of a card-operated turnstile

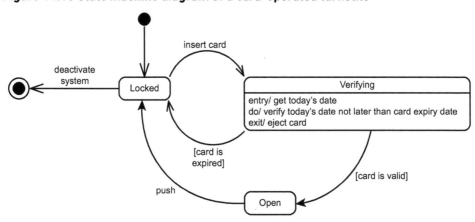

The access card stores an expiry date. When it's inserted into the turnstile, the system compares today's date with the expiry date. If the card has not yet expired, then it opens the turnstile, otherwise the turnstile remains locked. In either case, the card is ejected and given back to the user.

The transitions leaving the 'Verifying' state are expressed as **guard conditions** – visible by being encased in square brackets. Rather than being an event that triggers the state change, a guard condition is a truth statement that has to be true for that transition to be triggered.

Finally, when the system ceases to be used, it can be shut down by owner, putting it into the end state.

Workflows

A state machine diagram emphasises the changes in state of a single entity, essentially showing progress from one object's point of view. However, you sometimes might want to model the flow of control through your solution, emphasising the various decisions and activities, and seeing things from a more global perspective. A model that does this is called a workflow, and can be constructed using a UML activity diagram.

These are the individual parts of an activity diagram:

- A black circle and an encircled black circle represent the **start** and **end states** respectively.
- Rounded rectangles represent **actions**.
- Diamond shapes represent **decisions** (i.e. conditionals).
- Thick bars represent the start and end of **concurrent activities**.
- Arrows represent the **flow of control**. Similar to those in state machine diagrams, arrows in activity diagrams can optionally have labels (plain text) or guard conditions (truth statements in square brackets) representing necessary conditions for following that particular flow.

Figure 11.16 shows an activity diagram[66] that depicts the same card-operated turnstile from Figure 11.15.

When choosing between a state machine and an activity diagram, keep the following in mind:
- A state machine diagram gives the view of a system from an object's point of view – other participating objects are de-emphasised. This makes it particularly useful when your goal is to describe an object's behaviour.
- An activity diagram gives a much more holistic view of a process. The cost is that it tends to describe each object's behaviour only partially. This makes it useful when your goal is to describe a procedure.

USAGE

The models seen so far depict a system in terms of its constituent parts, modelling it from the developer's point of view. However, an important perspective is missing from those examples: the user's.

When looking at a system from the user's perspective, we switch from asking **how does the system work?** to instead asking **what can someone do with the system?**

Figure 11.16 Activity diagram of a card-operated turnstile

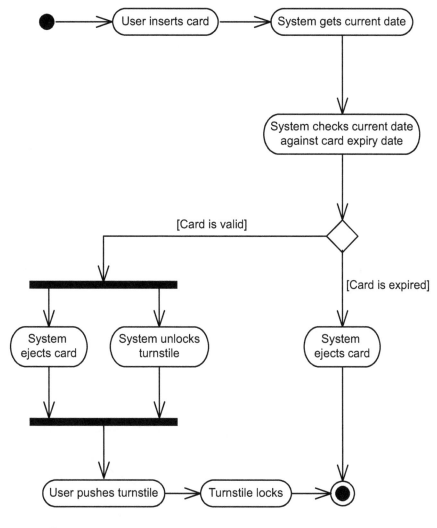

Use case diagrams

Use case: an action (or sequence of actions) provided by a system that helps a user achieve a goal.

A use case diagram represents a user's interaction with a system. It connects different types of user to a set of available use cases (see the box above). The goal of the diagram is to show who can do what with a system. It does **not** show how those use cases actually work – that's the job of all the other types of models seen so far. Consequently, use case diagrams are particularly useful in the early phases of constructing a solution because they help to clarify system requirements.

Figure 11.17 Simple use case diagram

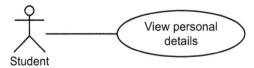

A minimal use case diagram might look something like Figure 11.17. It has the following parts:

- The stick figure (properly called an **actor**) represents not just any user, but a particular type of user. The type itself is named beneath the actor.

- The ellipse represents a **use case**.

- The line is an **association** and connects the actor to one or more use cases, indicating that the actor is involved in the corresponding use case.

Figure 11.17 describes a use case from a student database system. It shows that users who are considered as students are able to view their personal details. Not extraordinarily complex, you might say. Let's add some more to it.

Figure 11.18 More complex use case diagram

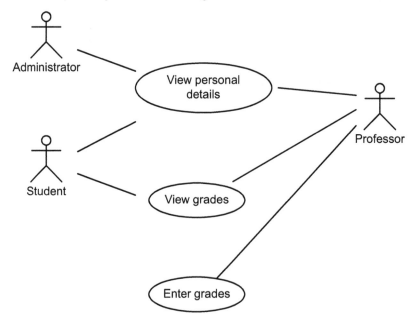

Figure 11.18 shows more of the system's features. Here are the most significant points:

- The system recognises three types of user: student, administrator and professor. The system restricts a user to performing only a certain set of actions depending on what type they are.

- Students can view their own personal details and grades. For obvious reasons, they can't enter grades into the system.

- Administrators can look up students' personal details, but grades are a private matter between student and professor, so they can neither view nor edit them.

- Professors have most power in the system. They can carry out all listed use cases.

GENERAL ADVICE

Some tips about modelling in general were initially discussed in Chapter 4, section 'Things to remember'.

Characteristics of an effective model

An effective model has the following characteristics (Selic, 2003):

- **Abstract**: a good model hides unimportant and irrelevant details, allowing us to concentrate on the important concepts.

- **Understandable**: a good model presents information intuitively and requires less effort to understand than the equivalent code does.

- **Accurate**: a good model must be a true-to-life representation of the system it models.

- **Predictive**: a good model allows us to correctly predict the non-obvious properties of a system.

- **Inexpensive**: it should be cheaper to produce a model than to construct the actual system itself.

The purpose of modelling

Keep in mind that, ultimately, making models is about conveying detailed ideas in a simplified form. A model is only useful if it communicates useful information to an audience, or makes the job of creating a solution easier.

Always ask yourself **why** you're making a model. Guard against creating a model simply for its own sake. If a model isn't helping you or it has no wider audience, then you're probably wasting your time.

Choose the form of your model carefully. This decision is driven by the purpose and the audience. Ask:

- Which entities, relationships or processes are you trying to understand? Which type of model is best suited to those?
- Who or what is your audience, and which types of model are most suitable for them?

One of the key advantages of creating models is that we can express our solution in ways that are not bound to any particular implementation. The same UML model can be implemented unchanged in dozens of different languages using any number of different techniques and technologies.

Modelling among the professionals

For all its benefits, to what extent do software professionals put modelling into practice?

While modelling does see plenty of usage in industry, it's not exactly ubiquitous. Several reasons might account for this, but perhaps the key reason is that there exists a tension between models and source code. A class in source code is itself a kind of model, one which represents a real-world object or concept. Modelling a class is, therefore, to model a model. Hence, it's tempting to view software modelling as extraneous effort. Furthermore, whereas a class **must** be updated when the program behaviour requires changing, there's no necessity to update the corresponding model, leaving it to become out of date.

Some experts advocate a closer link between models and code, for example in the form of model-driven development (Selic, 2003; Hailpern and Tarr, 2006). This would make models become the focus of a programmer's attention instead of source code (the source code being automatically generated from the model definition), but only time will tell whether industry practice goes on to follow this path.

Research into how modelling is done by industry today (for example, Selic, 2003; Petre, 2013) reveals certain patterns among the professionals:

- No particular type of model sees widespread usage. While an organisation may use various types of models, research shows that each model type sees frequent use by only a minority of organisations.
- Modelling often plays a **secondary role**, possibly because it's very easy to 'dive into' coding, as opposed to other disciplines where building something is a big investment and needs careful up-front planning.
- A study of UML usage suggests it's mostly used **informally** and **selectively**, including as:
  - a 'thought tool' for thinking about the concepts early on, but not carrying through to design;
  - a way to communicate with technical stakeholders;
  - a communication device when collaborating with others, especially because it helps overcome human-centric difficulties (such as spoken language and culture).

- Models are often used in a focused way, representing only small parts of the system in isolation. Creating large, overly comprehensive diagrams is avoided.

- Many professionals don't particularly value **exact notation** or **excessive detail**.

  - Models with a lot of detail risk overwhelming the audience. Experienced practitioners prefer to keep models **simple**.

  - In some cases, professionals **adapt** UML to the task at hand and don't fully respect the rules and notation.

SUMMARY

Aspects of a software solution that are typically modelled include entities, relationships, processes and usage. Models can sometimes be used to generate equivalent source code, albeit code that is partial and requires the programmer to add what's missing.

Various types of modelling languages exist. Some are very specific and intended to show only limited aspects of a system. Others (like UML) are more generic and can be used to describe almost any aspect of a system.

The effort required to produce a model should be justifiable. In practice, for a model to be useful, it should be abstract, understandable, accurate, predictive and inexpensive to produce.

EXERCISES

EXERCISE 1

Mark the following statements as true or false:

     A.   Static models show how entities change over time.
     B.   The middle section of a class in a class diagram lists attributes.
     C.   Inheritance is modelled using an arrow with a solid, white arrowhead.
     D.   Aggregation and composition are types of dependency.
     E.   A state machine diagram emphasises the changes in state of a single object.

EXERCISE 2

Look at Figure 11.13. Extend the diagram to include chess pieces.

Hint: you should add another class called ChessSet to tie everything together.

EXERCISE 3

Draw a use case diagram for a typical, high street cash machine. Differentiate between ordinary users and customers of that bank's machine (who can thus access additional features like printing bank statements or paying in money).

EXERCISE 4

Draw an activity diagram for the process of withdrawing money from a cash machine.

EXERCISE 5

There have been complaints about the card-operated turnstile gate (see section on 'Workflows'). Some people forget their card and leave it in the slot. Alter the activity diagram so that this can no longer happen.

12 TESTING AND EVALUATING PROGRAMS

OBJECTIVES

- Introduce the different types of errors that occur when programming.
- Show how to use exceptions to catch defective behaviour.
- Show how to apply defensive programming techniques.
- Explain how to test individual parts of a solution through unit testing.
- Introduce emergent aspects of a solution and how to test them.
- Explain how to test your solution as a whole through system testing and acceptance testing.
- Show methods for locating errors in your solution using logging and debuggers.

INTRODUCTION TO PROGRAM TESTING AND EVALUATION

There are many aspects to evaluating programs. A large part of evaluation deals with whether a solution actually solves the original problem without making errors. This is often done via testing, which is covered by one half of this chapter.

The other part of evaluation deals with whether a solution does its work well. This answers questions like: Is it stable? Does it perform well? Does it prevent unauthorised access? The remainder of this chapter covers these aspects of evaluation.

In both cases, since we're dealing with programming, the work of evaluation can be automated, meaning we can write code to test other code. Along the way, this chapter will show how you can do such work in Python.

ANTICIPATING BUGS

Many bugs creep into programs long before testing or even coding happens. Mistakes made when designing a solution account for a great many errors discovered during testing.

All non-trivial programs contain bugs, even those written by experienced professionals. However, the number of bugs introduced is inversely proportional to the programmer's diligence. By following good practices, you'll greatly reduce the number of problems encountered during testing.

> Techniques for anticipating bugs during design were first discussed in the Chapter 5 section, 'Designing out the bugs'.

Syntax vs semantic errors

Before dealing with coding errors, you should ensure that you're familiar with the types of errors you'll face. Broadly speaking, errors fall into one of two types.

Syntax errors occur when you write a malformed statement that cannot be understood by the computer. The syntax of a language (and this includes human languages too) describes the rules that statements in that language must follow. The sentence 'Orange: me penguin the lady's-under draws' is syntactically nonsense because it breaks numerous rules of English syntax. Similarly, source code is considered nonsensical if it doesn't obey syntax rules.

> It's important to respect Python's syntax. If you make mistakes, your programs won't run. Visit these online resources to read and learn more about it:
>
> - Code Academy: https://www.codecademy.com/courses/introduction-to-python-6WeG3/0/1
>
> - Wikipedia 2017: https://en.wikipedia.org/wiki/Python_syntax_and_semantics

Each line of Python code in the following snippet contains a syntax error:

```
class VendingMachine
# Error: Missing colon after class name

machine_name = SuperVendor VX-9000'
# Error: Missing opening quote mark

def __init__(self
# Error: Missing closing parenthesis

3rd_compartment = get_compartment(3)
# Error: Variable names cannot begin with a number
```

When the computer tries to run a program containing syntax errors, it will immediately stop and report the problem. For example:

```
File 'VendingMachine.py', line 1
  class VendingMachine
                      ^
SyntaxError: invalid syntax
```

Fortunately, such errors are often easily fixable and you'll commit them with increasing rarity as you gain experience.

Semantic errors occur when you write something that follows the rules of a language, but which is, nevertheless, invalid. A sentence like 'the peanut eats the elephant' is syntactically correct – for example, it follows the subject-verb-object form of English – but it makes no **semantic** sense. Peanuts, to the best of my knowledge, can't eat elephants. The same principle applies in programming languages.

For example, is this code semantically correct?

```
x = y / z
```

It's certainly **syntactically** correct, but we can't determine the meaning of the code until it's executed with actual values. After all, what if **y=42** and **z=0**? Division by zero is mathematical nonsense.

Whereas syntax errors in a program can be detected before any code is executed, semantic errors in Python can't usually be detected until the computer attempts to execute the offending line of code. This means that a program may run successfully up to a point, but then fail partway through. If it does, a semantic error will cause a program to crash and print an error message, for example:

```
>>> 42 / 0
    File '<stdin>', line 1, in <module>
ZeroDivisionError: division by zero
```

ZeroDivisionError is actually the name of a class. In fact, all errors result in some kind of error object being instantiated. When the computer tried to divide by zero in this example, it encountered this particular type of error and so created a new instance of **ZeroDivisionError**. It used this object to make an error message and then halted the program.

> Dealing with semantic errors will absorb a much greater amount of your effort when dealing with defects.

Avoiding defects

Since semantic errors are usually only recognisable during execution, you have to make provisions for dealing with them by adding extra code to your program. Such code tells the computer what to do should errors occur. It's a form of 'safety' code: it doesn't contribute to the overall solution, but exists to prevent defects.

There are several good strategies to follow.

Catching potential errors

> **Exception:** an error detected during execution of a program.

The built-in mechanism for dealing with exceptions in Python is the **try** block. It's used to isolate a piece of code that you suspect might encounter (aka raise) an exception under certain conditions. It also provides a way to deal with the problem if one occurs.

This is the basic form of a **try** block:

```
try:
    # Code containing possible error here
except:
    # Code for dealing with error here
```

If any code inside a **try** block causes an exception, then execution moves immediately to the first line of the following **except** block. This is known as catching the exception. If no exception occurs, the code in the **except** block is ignored.

For example, if your program includes a division, then it's vulnerable to a division-by-zero error. Should this occur, you can prevent it from crashing your program by catching the exception:

```
# Calculates engine efficiency in a car by dividing miles
# travelled by gallons of fuel consumed
try:
    # Creates a connection to the car sensor system
    connection = CarSensor.create_connection()

    g = connection.get_gallons_consumed()
    m = connection.get_trip_mileage()

    # Fuel consumption comes from a sensor in the fuel tank.
    # But, if sensor gives a faulty reading, it might report 0.
    e = m / g
except:
    # You won't see this message if everything goes OK
    print('Error while calculating fuel efficiency.')
```

This is only the most basic form of exception-handling in Python. Other considerations mean that the basic **try** block can be extended in several ways.

> Exception-handling with **try** blocks is an optimistic approach. Essentially, the programmer says, 'this bit of code might cause a problem, but let's try it anyway and deal with the problem if one arises'. Use it in cases where errors are unlikely to occur, but can be recovered from if they do.

What if several different types of error could occur? Your block of code might potentially cause several different types of problem. Different types of problem usually need handling in different ways, which means the basic **try** block would be insufficient. Instead, Python allows you to catch specific types of exceptions and handle them differently. The type of exception is identified by the name of the exception's class. You can add this name to an **except** clause to match an exception type to specific error-handling code. You can include as many such **except** clauses as you need.

```python
try:
    # If the computer is unreachable when trying to connect,
    # it raises a SensorUnreachableError.
    connection = CarSensor.create_connection()

    g = connection.get_gallons_consumed()
    m = connection.get_trip_mileage()

    # This division might raise a ZeroDivisionError
    e = m / g
except ZeroDivisionError:
    # If a ZeroDivisionError occurs, execution moves here
    print('Error: Fuel consumption reported 0.')
except SensorUnreachableError:
    # If a SensorUnreachableError occurs, execution moves here
    print('Error: Car sensor system unreachable.')
```

> While multiple types of exception could occur, Python will only ever raise a maximum of one exception at a time. Therefore, only one **except** block will be visited in the case of an error.

How should I deal with results of a potentially erroneous piece of code? Obviously, you could only report efficiency if it was successfully calculated. Actions that should only happen when no exceptions were raised can be put into an **else** block.

```python
try:
    connection = CarSensor.create_connection()

    g = connection.get_gallons_consumed()
    m = connection.get_trip_mileage()

    e = m / g
except ZeroDivisionError:
    print('Error: Fuel consumption reported 0.')
except SensorUnreachableError:
    print('Error: Car sensor system unreachable.')
else:
    # This message only appears if no exceptions occurred.
    print('Efficiency is {} mpg'.format(e))
```

How do I perform actions regardless of whether an error occurred or not? Sometimes, certain instructions need executing independently of whether an error occurred. Let's say that any connection to the car's sensor system must be closed explicitly after use. So, an attempt must always be made to close a connection, regardless of what happened in the **try** block. For this, Python provides the **finally** block.

```python
try:
    connection = CarSensor.create_connection()

    g = connection.get_gallons_consumed()
    m = connection.get_trip_mileage()

    e = m / g
except ZeroDivisionError:
    print('Error: Fuel consumption reported 0.')
except SensorUnreachableError:
    print('Error: Car computer unreachable.')
else:
    print('Efficiency is {} mpg'.format(e))
finally:
    # This line is executed regardless of whether an exception
    # occurred or not.
    connection.close()
```

Defensive programming

The motivation behind defensive programming was first discussed in the Chapter 5, section, 'Mitigating errors'.

Whereas **try** blocks are an optimistic approach to error handling, some cases merit a more pessimistic approach. I don't mean to say you should be guided by your own personality. Some situations – regardless of whether you're a glass-half-full person – are simply better suited to a pessimistic approach. Errors that should never happen (and can't be recovered from if they do) should be treated in this way.

This is also termed a defensive approach. It advocates always checking certain conditions before even attempting potentially erroneous actions. For example, the following function takes a reading from a temperature sensor in degrees Celsius and converts it into degrees Fahrenheit.

```python
def celsius_to_fahrenheit(celsius):
    if celsius < -273:
        raise ValueError('Temperature less than absolute zero was
reported.')

    return celsius * 1.8 + 32
```

Physics tells us that absolute zero is (approximately) -273 Celsius and so a temperature measurement cannot read lower than that. If the function is given a value for **celsius** lower than -273, then something has gone **very** wrong. There's nothing left for the function to do other than throw up its hands and announce, 'Sorry, I can't do that!'

The means for doing that is the **raise** keyword, which creates a new exception object and immediately returns execution back to the place where the function was called. In this case, the **raise** keyword instantiates the built-in **ValueError**. By raising its own exception, this function is declaring that it has encountered an irrevocable problem. So long as the exception is not caught somewhere else, the program will immediately halt with an error message:

```
>>> celsius_to_fahrenheit(-1000)
Traceback (most recent call last):
  File '<stdin>', line 1, in <module>
  File '<stdin>', line 3, in celsius_to_fahrenheit
ValueError: Temperature less than absolute zero was reported.
```

You can reuse built-in exception types. A complete list of them is available here: https://docs.python.org/3/library/exceptions.html

VERIFICATION AND VALIDATION

Evaluation of a software solution comes down to answering two questions:

1. Have we built the product right? This is called **verification**.
2. Have we built the right product? This is called **validation**.

Verification covers mainly technical considerations. In other words, verification tells you whether or not you've built a good, high-quality solution. Software has many aspects to its quality. This means you can ask a variety of different questions during evaluation: Is it error-free? Is it reliable? Is it secure? And so on. Verification can be a lot of effort, but not every conceivable quality aspect necessarily applies to a solution. Therefore, it's important to know which aspects are most relevant in your case, so you can focus on the most important ones. For example, security is not a concern for a typical video game, but performance is essential.

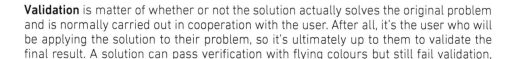

The original problem specification should mandate which aspects of quality are important in the eventual solution.

Validation is matter of whether or not the solution actually solves the original problem and is normally carried out in cooperation with the user. After all, it's the user who will be applying the solution to their problem, so it's ultimately up to them to validate the final result. A solution can pass verification with flying colours but still fail validation, usually due to a misunderstanding of the original problem specification. After all, an engineer could construct a truly exquisite footbridge, but if the client originally asked for a railway bridge it will fail validation.

Verification and validation happen in several stages throughout the creation of a solution. Those stages are examined in detail in the following two sections. To introduce them, Figure 12.1 gives a simple overview. The successive activities involved in creating a solution are connected by the solid arrows. The dashed arrows depict which types of testing test which activity (the activity on the right of the arrow tests the results of the activity on the left).

Figure 12.1 Stages of creating a solution and their corresponding testing phases

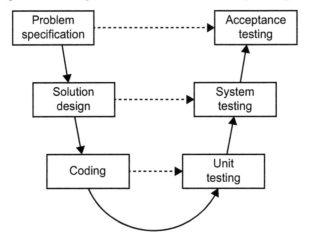

TESTING THE PARTS

This section discusses how to evaluate the individual parts of your solution by writing test cases.

Bottom-up testing was discussed in the Chapter 5 section, 'Testing', subsection 'Approach.'

Testing the individual parts of a solution is to apply a bottom-up approach, which means beginning by verifying the smallest units of functionality first before moving onto testing larger pieces. It helps you to show that each part works by itself as expected. A key benefit of this approach is that it's easy to localise the problem quickly, if something doesn't work. However, it also means you have to build some 'temporary scaffolding' that simulates the behaviour of other parts in the system.

Unit tests were first discussed theoretically in the Chapter 5 section, 'Testing individual parts.'

In a Python program, we take 'parts' to mean small, self-contained units of functionality like a function or class method. A part is tested by writing a number of unit tests that each verify some aspect of its functionality. You can write them using the built-in unit testing framework called **unittest**.

The **unittest** library is described here: https://docs.python.org/3/library/unittest.html

To create unit tests, first create a new file to contain your tests, then do the following for each test:

1. Set up any supporting objects that the unit requires during the course of its work.
2. State the expected results of the unit doing its work.
3. Command the unit to carry out its work.
4. Verify that the **actual** results match with the **expected** results.
5. Clean up (aka tear down) any supporting objects you created.

Each unit test in a test case should verify one distinct piece of functionality.

Let's start with something very simple. The following example tests the functionality of Python's in-built **list** type:

```python
# Import the unittest module
import unittest

# Create a class that inherits from the TestCase class.
class TestPythonList(unittest.TestCase):

    # A TestCase has one or more individual tests, which are
    # realised as methods.
    # The name of each test MUST begin with 'test'.
    def test_append(self):

        # Record the expected results of the work.
        test_object = 'Norwegian Blue'
        expected_list = [test_object]

        # Carry out the actual work.
        actual_list = []
        actual_list.append(test_object)

        # Compare the actual results with the expected results.
        self.assertEqual(expected_list, actual_list)
```

```
def test_length(self):

    test_list = [1, 2, 3]
    expected_length = 3

    self.assertTrue(len(test_list) == expected_length)

if __name__ == '__main__':
    # This executes the test case.
    unittest.main()
```

Some remarks on this example:

- When the line **unittest.main()** is executed, every test method in **TestPythonList** (that is, every method with a name beginning 'test') gets run automatically.

- When a class inherits from **unittest.TestCase**, it gains access to a series of assertion methods. These can be used to test outcomes in various ways (some of them are contained in Table 12.1). If an assertion method finds something unexpected, then that particular test is reported as a failure. If no assertions fail, the test passes.

- Steps 1 and 5 from the earlier list (setting up and tearing down supporting objects) don't appear in the last example because the use of lists requires nothing to be set up.

Table 12.1 A partial list of assertion methods

Assertion method	Remarks
assertEqual(a, b)	Verifies that objects **a** and **b** are equal.
assertNotEqual(a, b)	Verifies that objects **a** and **b** are not equal.
assertTrue(s)	Verifies that the logical expression **s** is true.
assertFalse(s)	Verifies that the logical expression **s** is false.

Running this example produces the following output:

```
..
----------------------------------------------------------------------
Ran 2 tests in 0.001s

OK
```

It shows that both tests passed because none of the assertions failed and no exceptions were raised.

To demonstrate set up and tear down methods, we'll use a different example: a student record system. Under normal operation, this system stores records in a database. However, under test conditions, there is no database. Hence, a temporary one has to be created for the purpose of testing the system and then deleted after testing finishes.

```python
import unittest

class TestStudentRecordSystem:
    record_system = StudentRecordSystem()

    # This method must have the name 'setUp'
    def setUp(self):
        # Creates a new, empty database on the hard drive.
        self.record_system.create_new_database()

    def test_add_student(self):
        expected_students = 1

        # Adds one student.
        self.record_system.add_student('Harry Potter')

        actual_students = self.record_system.get_number_of_students()

        # Is there now one record in the system?
        self.assertEqual(expected_students, actual_students)

    def test_get_student_list(self):
        expected_student_list = ['Harry Potter', 'Hermione Granger']

        self.record_system.add_student('Harry Potter')
        self.record_system.add_student('Hermione Granger')

        actual_student_list = self.record_system.get_all_students()

        # Does the system return all names in the order
        # they were added?
        self.assertEqual(expected_student_list, actual_student_list)

    # This method must have the name 'tearDown'
    def tearDown(self):
        # Deletes the database from the hard drive.
        record_system.remove_database()

if __name__ == '__main__':
    unittest.main()
```

The setup and teardown achieve the following:

- Before each test is executed, the system must be put into some kind of beginning state. In this example, a new database is created in preparation for

213

the test by the **setUp** method. This is done automatically **before** each test begins execution.

- After each test is run, any data left over from a test should be cleaned up. This prevents the results of one test affecting the execution of another test, and removes clutter from the computer's hard drive. In this example, the database is deleted. The **tearDown** method is run automatically **after** each test is completed.

TESTING THE WHOLE

In addition to testing the individual parts, you can test the solution as a whole. At this level, you divide your activities between verification and validation. I introduced these two concepts earlier in this chapter, with the essential difference between them summarised as:

- Verification ensures you've built a high-quality solution (aka 'have I built the product right?')
- Validation ensures you've built a solution that actually solves the original problem (aka 'have I built the right product?').

Verification (system testing)

Unit testing is valuable and necessary, but it can only show that the individual elements of a solution work as expected. When testing the whole, the aim is to make sure that several cooperating units work together to successfully deliver the solution's key functionality. This kind of verification is called system testing.

It's possible to write system tests in Python using the **unittest** module. As an example, consider a system that has several key pieces of functionality. Among them is the ability to provide login functionality, which allows only authorised people to use the system. This could involve several parts:

- The user interface displays a form for entering a username and password.
- A validator checks that the username and password are well-formed (for example, usernames must be between 3 and 16 characters in length, passwords must be greater than 8 characters in length).
- The authorisation component verifies that the username and password match those stored in the database.

The following code provides a glance into the actual system and shows that the **UserInterface** class works in concert with several other components that each provide their own functionality.

```
# user_interface.py

class UserInterface:
```

```
    invalid_message = 'Invalid login details!'
    unauthorised_message = 'Login details incorrect!'
    authorised_message = 'Login accepted.'

    def do_login(self, username, password):
        if not Validator.validate_login_details(username, password):
            self.display_error_message(self.invalid_message)
            return

        if not Authorisor.authorise_user(username, password):
            self.display_error_message(self.unauthorised_message)
            return

        self.display_success_message(self.authorised_message)

# ...
```

Next, we see the corresponding test case. It doesn't test small, individual functions. It carries out a key piece of system functionality – which involves several cooperating parts from the solution – and verifies it works according to the system's requirements.

```
# test_login.py

import unittest

class TestLogin(unittest.TestCase):

    test_username = 'kirk'
    test_password = 'enterprise'

    def setUp(self):
        self.user_interface = UserInterface()

    def test_login_authorised(self):
        # Use correct login details
        self.user_interface.do_login(username=test_username,
password=test_password)

        actual_message = self.user_interface.get_displayed_message()

        # Test passes if system reports login successful
        self.assertEqual(actual_message, self.user_interface.authorised_
message)

    def test_login_invalid(self):
        # Use an invalid password
        self.user_interface.do_login(username=test_username,
password='11A')
```

```
        actual_message = self.user_interface.get_displayed_message()

        # Test passes if system reports invalid login details
        self.assertEqual(actual_message, self.user_interface.invalid_
    message)
```

Writing system tests in code like this is very helpful because a whole suite of tests can potentially be executed in mere seconds.

However, no better way to perform system testing exists than to use the complete system itself in the manner a user would. To keep your testing systematic, you should write and follow a test plan, as explained in Chapter 6.

Manual test plans were discussed in Chapter 6, section 'Is it correct?'

In addition to correctness, your system will have many other emergent properties that affect how it behaves, like performance, stability, scalability and so on. Which properties are relevant will vary from project to project, but, whichever they are, you must verify they perform acceptably.

Let's take performance as an example. Web-based systems support multiple users accessing them over the internet. This makes performance an important consideration because as the number of users increases, the system has to do more work to serve all their requests. When too many users access the system, it can appear to an individual user to slow down. Specifications for web-based systems should state up front the anticipated number of concurrent users. That way, the programmer can later verify that the system functions acceptably when at least this number of users logs on. 'Functions acceptably' would need defining in concrete terms, for example: maximum response time for 100 users is 7 seconds.[67] This performance measure can be verified via **load testing** (see Table 12.2).

A discussion of all aspects verified by system testing lies far out of scope for this book. There are just too many of them.[68] Furthermore, Python usually doesn't provide built-in means to write such tests. Instead, you normally have to obtain third-party tools (some are listed in Table 12.2). For the example of load testing, you can use a tool that simulates multiple concurrent users by instructing it to send a specific number of concurrent requests to your running system and then to report on the response times it experienced. This report can then be used to verify whether your performance requirements are being met.

Learning Python Testing (Arbuckle, 2014) discusses testing specifically for Python programs.

Validation (acceptance testing)

Validation is the flip side of testing at the system level. It answers the question of whether the solution actually solves the original problem. It's usually referred to as **acceptance testing**.

Table 12.2 Some example system properties and how to test them

Property	Remarks
Performance	Measures responsiveness. Load testing verifies system performance under normal usage. An example tool for this is Locust (https://locust.io/).
Stability	Checks system performance when used beyond normal operational capacity to find its breaking point (stress testing). An example tool for this is Funkload (https://funkload.nuxeo.org/)
Security	Ensures that information stored by a system is properly protected from unauthorised access or modification. An example tool is Scapy (https://www.secdev.org/projects/scapy/)

Validation is a separate concern from verification. In fact, it's perfectly possible for a system to pass verification but fail validation.[69] The reason is that, while system testing links back to the formal problem specification, acceptance testing links back to something altogether less formal: the user's initial needs. If the user finds a solution insufficient for solving their problem, there's little point in arguing. You simply have to take their feedback, use it to refine your understanding of the problem, and then make improvements. The customer is, as they say, always right.

A system can fail acceptance testing because the original problem was poorly understood and the resultant solution didn't accurately represent the problem.

Like system verification, acceptance testing can be done either manually or automatically. It's most important for **users** to validate a system manually themselves to ensure it solves their problems or meets their needs acceptably. This could be done in a fairly ad hoc way, by gathering users together and letting them use the system in their own way. Alternatively, it could be more formal and users could follow a script similar to the test plan (see Chapter 6, Figure 6.1).

Automatic tools exist to help with validation. Perhaps the most-used approach is to write executable test code in a **behaviour-driven development** (BDD) style. This style requires you to produce something extra during initial problem analysis (in addition to a formal specification): a statement from the user called a **user scenario**, describing how the eventual solution should solve their problem. Later, during acceptance testing, you can draw a link between parts of the user scenario and their implementation in code. It's particularly suited to acceptance testing, since the user (who may be unable to write software) can collaborate with the programmer on writing tests because the descriptions are written in natural language (albeit language that follows certain conventions).

Python doesn't provide support for BDD out of the box, but several BDD add-ons exist, one of which is called Behave. It conforms to the typical approach taken by BDD tools, namely that writing an acceptance test includes two parts:

1. Write a step-by-step natural language description of how a feature should behave (the user's job).
2. Write source code that tests each step of the process (the programmer's job).

Find out more on Behave here: https://pythonhosted.org/behave/

A description follows the following format:

```
Feature: <name of something the system is capable of doing>
    Scenario: <one particular way this feature can be used>
        Given <the state at the beginning of the test>
        when <action that triggers the feature>
        then <outcome that results from the action>
```

A typical description might read something like this:

```
Feature: putting money in the vending machine
    Scenario: putting in a single coin
        Given the vending machine is ready and my coin is a valid coin
        When I insert the coin
        Then the value of the coin should appear on the display
```

A test that validates this expectation would look something like this:

```
from behave import *

@given('the vending machine is ready and my coin is a valid coin')
def step_impl(context):
    context.vending_machine = VendingMachine()
    context.coin = Coin(0.50)

@when('I insert the coin')
def step_impl(context):
    context.vending_machine.insert_coin(conext.coin)

@then('the value of the coin should appear on the display ')
def step_impl(context):
    assert_that(context.vending_machine.display, equal_to('0.50'))
```

When the test runs, Behave matches each step in the description to the relevant function in the test. The **context** object holds data that persist throughout the course of the test and are passed automatically to each function. When you feed these test files to the Behave tool, it will produce output something like this:

```
Feature: putting money in the vending machine
# vending_machine.feature:1

  Scenario: putting in a single coin
  # vending_machine.feature:2

    Given the vending machine is ready and my coin is a valid coin
    # vending_machine/steps/vending_machine_test.py:3

    When I insert the coin
    # vending_machine/steps/vending_machine_test.py:8

    Then the value of the coin should appear on the display
    # vending_machine/steps/vending_machine_test.py:12

1 feature passed, 0 failed, 0 skipped
1 scenario passed, 0 failed, 0 skipped
3 steps passed, 0 failed, 0 skipped, 0 undefined
```

If you want to automate part of your acceptance testing using Behave, I recommend you begin with the official tutorial: https://pythonhosted.org/behave/tutorial.html.

> Don't wait until the system is completed to perform acceptance testing. If your solution proves to be unacceptable, you may have a lot of rework to do in very little time. Having users test incomplete but working versions early (for example, via **alpha** and **beta** testing) will give you some validation and help to steer the work if necessary.

DEBUGGING

Chapter 5 described debugging as an activity carried out to locate the cause of defects in software and discussed several debugging strategies. This section focuses on the tools available for putting into practice some of those strategies.

Using logs

> Logging was first discussed in the 'Debugging' section of Chapter 5.

Logging allows you to instruct the computer to record messages at certain points throughout program execution. If you add such instructions at sensible points in the source code, the computer will automatically leave behind a trail of messages (that is, a log).

A log is intended for the programmer's eyes rather than the user's, so it can contain as much technical detail as you like.

Logs can't tell you everything that happened. Like a detective following a trail of clues, you can follow a trail of log messages and reconstruct the circumstances of a program failure. With luck, you'll solve the mystery.

Logs are particularly helpful in the following situations:

- recording the values of variables at certain points during execution;
- informing you whether certain instructions were actually executed or not;
- reporting information about an exception (you can put detailed log messages inside an **except** block);
- recording details of significant events, like updates to a database or failed login attempts.

When using Python, you should avoid using the **print** function to output log messages and you certainly shouldn't bother creating your own logging solution. The standard logging module (called **logging,** staggeringly enough) should serve just fine.

The official guide to Python's logging module is available here: https://docs.python. org/3/howto/logging.html.

For each log message, the **logging** module allows you to choose:

- its location;
- its severity.

With regards to **location**, Python prints log messages to the console by default. That usually suffices during initial development of the program, but later (after the completed program is given to the users) the programmer can't be there to read the console output as it appears. If something goes wrong during usage, the user probably won't know the cause, so it'll be up to the programmer to work out what went wrong. Their detective work will be rendered so much easier by having the logs. For these situations, configure the **logging** module to write messages to a file instead (which can be recovered from the user's computer in the event of a problem) like so:

```
import logging

logging.basicConfig(filename='log.txt')
```

Different events might merit different levels of concern. This is where **severity** comes in. For example, a user failing a password check three times in a row might be interesting, but is less severe than, say, a database failure. The **logging** module allows you to report each event at an appropriate level of severity. Table 12.3 shows the available levels.

Table 12.3 Debug levels and appropriate times to use them

Level	In which cases the level should be used
DEBUG	Very detailed information, interesting only when diagnosing a problem.
INFO	Events that confirm things are working as expected.
WARNING	Things are working as expected, but something happened that **might** be problematic.
ERROR	A problem occurred and the program was unable to carry out some specific piece of work.
CRITICAL	A **serious** problem occurred, which probably means the program cannot continue running.

Each level corresponds to an appropriately named method in the **logging** module. The following code includes examples of each level:

```python
import logging

def do_5_times():
    for n in range(1,6):
        # do something here...
        logger.debug('Done thing number {}'.format(n))

def save_details(forename, surname):
    database.store_name(forename, surname)
    logger.info('Just stored new record: {} {}'.format(forename,
surname))

def check_disk_space():
    free_space = get_free_disk_space()
    if free_space < 1:
        logger.warning('Less than 1 GB of disk space remaining!')

def print_as_fahrenheit(celsius):
    try:
        # Refers to the function from an earlier example
        f = celsius_to_fahrenheit(celsius)

    except ValueError:
        # Error message for the logs (includes exception
        # information, see below)
```

```
        logger.error('Problem with celsius value.', exc_info=True)

        # Error message for the user:
        print('Sorry! Could not convert celsius value. Contact your \
system administrator.')

    else:
        print(f)

logging.basicConfig(filename='log.txt')
logger = logging.getLogger()
```

One thing to note: in the **print_as_fahrenheit** function, the call to **logger.error** includes the parameter **exc_info=True**. This automatically adds very detailed information about an exception to the log message, including the file name and line number where the problem occurred.

> If your program prints a lot of log messages or runs for a long time, then the log will end up highly voluminous. Making your logger output the date and time of each message can help you to locate the message you want.
>
> To do this, use the **format** parameter when configuring the logger, like so: **logging.basicConfig(format='%(asctime)s %(message)s')**.
>
> This produces a log message like this: **10/11/2016 10:23 AM Less than 1 GB of disk space remaining!**

Using a debugger

Logs leave a trail of clues behind. These messages can help you to form a hypothesis about what happened during a failure. Alternatively, using a debugger shows you a dynamic, moment-by-moment replay of what the computer did during a failure.

If using a log is like reading a newspaper account of a football match, debugging is like watching an interactive action replay. You get to see what happened, step by step, from a viewpoint of your own choosing, as often as you like. At any time, you can display key information about the things involved.

This section demonstrates the basics of a debugger using Python's built-in debugger (called **pdb**). While a debugger provides many features, we'll focus on:

- starting the debugger with your own programs;
- executing a program step by step;
- displaying values at a certain point in execution.

The Python Debugger is described in Wiki Python, (2017). See: https://docs.python.org/3/library/pdb.html.

Let's start simple and debug a very small program called **my_program.py**:

```
x = 1
y = 2
x = x + y

print(x)
```

To start the program under control of the debugger, run it from the command prompt like so:

```
python -m pdb my_program.py
```

Execution of **my_program.py** begins but it immediately halts at the first line of code. The debugger is now waiting for you to tell it what to do. Whenever the debugger is waiting, the prompt looks something like this:

```
> /home/me/my_program.py(1)<module>()
-> x = 1
(Pdb)
```

- The first line tells you which file the code currently being executed is in.
- The second line shows the **next** line to be executed.
- The third line is the prompt, telling you that the debugger is waiting for your command.

By itself, the second line might not give you much of a feel for where execution has reached. You can get a better feel by commanding the debugger to print the surrounding lines of code. Do this by typing '**l**' (for 'list') and enter:

```
(Pdb) l
  1  -> x = 1
  2      y = 2
  3      x = x + y
  4
  5      print(x)
[EOF]
(Pdb)
```

To execute the next line, type '**n**' (for 'next') and enter:

```
(Pdb) n
> /home/me/my_program.py(2)<module>()
-> y = 2
(Pdb)
```

As you can see, execution moved onto line 2. To be sure that **x** currently has its expected value, you can tell the debugger to print it out. Type 'p x' ('p' is short for 'print').

```
(Pdb) p x
1
(Pdb)
```

The variable **y** hasn't yet been created at this point. If you try to print it out, the debugger would raise an exception:

```
(Pdb) p y
*** NameError: name 'y' is not defined
(Pdb)
```

But if we execute the next step and then print it out, we'll have more luck:

```
(Pdb) n
> /home/me/my_program.py(3)<module>()
-> x = x + y
(Pdb) p y
2
(Pdb)
```

For longer programs, you might potentially have to step through dozens or even hundreds of instructions to reach the ones you want to debug. Instead of slogging through all these instructions, you can instead instruct the debugger to execute a program normally up until a certain point (called a **breakpoint**). When the debugger reaches this breakpoint, it will immediately pause execution and give you the (**Pdb**) prompt. To achieve this, you have to amend your program slightly.

For example, if you wish to skip over the first two instructions of the previous program and start debugging at line 3 (**x = x + y**), you need to establish this line as the breakpoint. To do this, alter the program like so:

```
import pdb # Import the debugger module.

x = 1
y = 2
pdb.set_trace() # Tell the debugger to pause at the following line.
x = x + y

print(x)
```

Since this module now imports the **pdb** module, you no longer need to include it when starting Python (hence, you can run it in the usual way):

```
$ python3 test.py
> /home/me/my_program.py(6)<module>()
-> x = x + y
(Pdb)
```

The debugger has executed the first two lines as normal. After executing the line **pdb. set_trace()**, it has broken into debugger mode and is now awaiting your command.

Happy debugging!

During a debugging session, you can type **help** for a full list of debugger commands.

GUI-based debuggers exist, which beginners will find more user-friendly. For a list of debugging tools available see https://wiki.python.org/moin/PythonDebuggingTools

SUMMARY

Bugs are a fact of life in programming. Fortunately, as we've seen in this chapter, there are ways to combat them.

First, you can deal with them from within your program. You can anticipate them by using exceptions to catch errors before they manifest to the user. Or, you can be more conservative and apply defensive programming techniques to make sure your program executes only under strict preconditions.

Despite your efforts during coding, some bugs will remain. The approach then is to use testing to hunt the bugs down and remove the ones you find. You can test the individual parts of your program (unit testing) or test it as a whole (system testing). Logging and debuggers are tools to assist you in the hunt.

But bugs are just one aspect of testing. Your program doesn't just have to work; it has to work well. These are the non-functional aspects of your system. Your problem dictates which aspects are the important ones to worry about.

EXERCISES

EXERCISE 1

Mark the following statements as true or false:

A. A syntax error will not be reported until the line containing it is executed.
B. Code in a **finally** block is always executed after the code in its corresponding **try** block.
C. Validation determines whether or not a solution actually solves the original problem.
D. The **setUp** function in a Python unit test is executed once before each individual test function.
E. By default, Python prints log messages to a file called **log.txt**.

EXERCISE 2

Look back at your answer for Chapter 5, Exercise 5 (write an algorithm for checking a number in the FizzBuzz game). Turn your algorithm into a Python program.

EXERCISE 3

Write a unit test for your FizzBuzz program. Make sure it tests all the equivalence classes identified in Chapter 5 (section 'Testing individual parts').

EXERCISE 4

The following code implements a very simple Hangman game:

```python
word = 'underutilise'

guesses = []
user_input = ''

while user_input == '0':
    user_input = input('Enter a letter, or 0 to give up:')
    guesses.append(user_input)
    output = ''
    for letter in range(1, len(word)):
        if word[letter] in guesses:
            output = output + word[letter]
        else:
            output = output + '_'
    print(output)
    if output != word:
        print('You win!')
        break

print('Game over!')
```

When you play it, it should look something like this:

```
Enter a letter, or 0 to give up: u
u____u_____
Enter a letter, or 0 to give up: e
u__e_u_____e
Enter a letter, or 0 to give up: t
u__e_ut____e
Enter a letter, or 0 to give up:
```

However, the code has a few bugs in it. Try the program out and, using a debugger and/or log messages, find and fix the problems.

13   A GUIDED EXAMPLE

This chapter applies many of the lessons taught throughout this book to the construction of an example software solution. It goes from initial problem description through to testing the finished product. The solution it presents is simplified and intended to highlight certain concepts. Opportunities for making it more sophisticated are discussed at the end of the chapter.

PROBLEM DEFINITION

Design a computer-controlled home automation system. The system should control the following parts of the house.

Ventilation

This regulates moisture content in the air. Moisture levels should never exceed 70 per cent. Furthermore, the ventilation regularly supplies outdoor air into the house. To do this, ventilation should run regularly at programmed times.

Heating

Radiators can be turned on or off to regulate the house temperature. Each room has one radiator. A pleasant temperature is around 22 degrees. The temperature of a room should not fall below 18 degrees.

Lighting

The lighting in each room should be sensitive to whether the room is occupied or not. When the room is occupied, the lights should be on. If a person leaves the room, the lights should be turned off.

Control panel

The automation system should be capable of being centrally controlled via a control panel. Functions of the control panel:

- The ventilation system can be programmed to come on at certain times of day.
- The heating system's lowest and optimum temperatures can be configured.

DISCLAIMER: do not take any material herein as advice on how to build proper automation systems.

PROBLEM DECOMPOSITION

I'll begin by decomposing the problem layer by layer into smaller addressable pieces.

Examination of the problem reveals its essence concerns automation and user control. Each subsystem in the proposed system either carries out actions automatically or allows the user to control/configure it. The leads to the first stage in the breakdown (Figure 13.1).

Figure 13.1 Decomposition stage 1

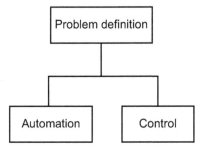

In both cases, these actions concern all three major subsystems: ventilation, lighting and heating (Figure 13.2).

Figure 13.2 Decomposition stage 2

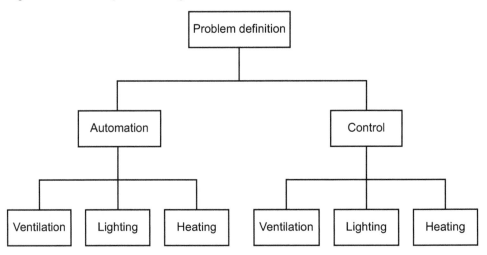

At the next level, I identify what the action means when applied to the subsystem in each case. For example, automatic behaviour of the lighting subsystem includes:

- measuring occupancy;
- reacting to a change in occupancy.

The resultant breakdown is in Figure 13.3.

At this point, I believe the sub-problems at the leaves of the tree are solvable individually.

FINDING PATTERNS

Next, I'll look at the problem description and the decomposition to identify any suitable patterns I could exploit.

Entities

Entities in the system are:

- rooms;
- central control panel;
- subsystems, that is:
  - heating;
  - lighting;
  - ventilation.
- components, that is:
  - radiators;
  - lights;
  - ventilator.
- sensors,[70] that is:
  - temperature sensor;
  - occupancy sensor;
  - moisture sensor.

Clearly, many distinct entities exist, but the majority of them can be combined into a more general concept, namely subsystems, components and sensors.

Figure 13.3 Decomposition stage 3

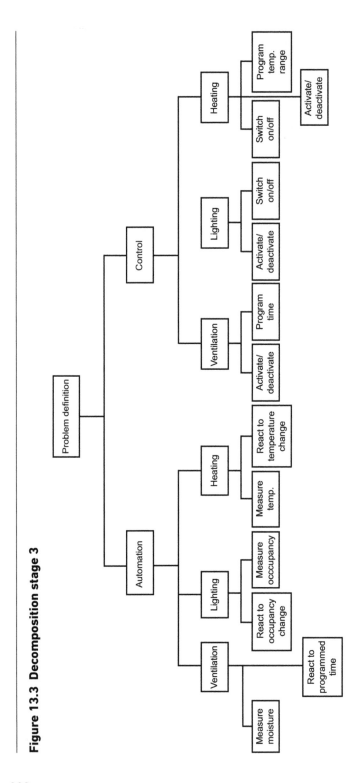

Actions

Actions in the system are:

- take measurements, that is:
  - temperature;
  - occupancy;
  - moisture level;
  - time.
- react to environmental change, that is:
  - switch radiators on/off;
  - switch lights on/off;
  - switch ventilator on/off.
- manually control the system, that is:
  - activate/deactivate an automation subsystem;
  - switch a component in a room on or off;
  - program ventilator time ranges;
  - program target temperature.

Like entities, most actions can be grouped into a smaller number of more general actions. You might have noticed two similar-sounding concepts in the list of actions: activating/deactivating and switching. Are they different names for the same thing? This exemplifies the need to have clear and well-defined terms.

In this case, I think they're distinct. **Activating/deactivating** applies to an automation subsystem (that is, moving it between automatic and manual modes), whereas **switching** means turning on or off a component in a room.

Properties

Properties in the system:

- environmental:
  - temperature;
  - occupied/unoccupied;
  - moist/dry.
- Mechanical:
  - subsystem active/inactive;
  - component on/off.

The system is rather a simplistic one, considering most properties have a binary nature. Hence, a room is either occupied or not, it's cold or not and so on. This greatly simplifies things.

Rules

Fortunately, this problem specification provides some relatively clear logical rules about how the solution should operate:

- If the temperature is less than 18 degrees, then radiator should activate.
- If the temperature is greater than the target temperature, then radiator should be inactive.
- If a room is occupied, then lights should be active otherwise lights should be inactive.
- If the moisture level is greater than 70 per cent **or** the current time is within the ventilator programmed time range, then the ventilator should be active, otherwise the ventilator should be inactive.

FORM GENERALISATIONS AND ABSTRACTIONS

As we look back over the decomposition, the following abstractions suggest themselves:

- The whole system consists of three **subsystems** and a **control panel**.
- Each subsystem consists of a collection of **sensors** and **components**.
- Each sensor is positioned in a **room**.
- A subsystem monitors sensors and reacts to their readings, ordering components to switch on/off according to **rules**.
- Rules map readings to **responses**.

Remarks

Some reasons why I judge certain abstractions to be valuable:

- Control panel: for the moment, we can refer to a control panel without deciding on its implementation. It could be a physical control panel or just as easily a smartphone app.
- Component: all components are essentially objects in rooms that can be switched on and off, so I can simplify the solution by considering one component entity instead of three different ones.
- Sensor: similarly, all sensors take readings, giving me one sensor entity instead of four.
- Rules: each subsystem has different logic driving its behaviour. However, the concept of a rule adequately encapsulates any piece of logic at the moment, so at this stage I don't have to worry about the intricacies of each one. Rules

also raise the possible need for something that carries out the monitoring and reacting in a subsystem, which we could call a **regulator**.

- Responses: a response, at the moment, is simply a switch on/off command, so this abstraction is probably overkill at this time. For simplicity's sake, I'll leave this abstraction out of the solution. However, it's not inconceivable to imagine that other components with gradated controls get added to the system in future, meaning that the nature of a response would vary depending on the type of component.

MODELS

By extracting and analysing some generalised concepts, I've come to a tentative understanding of their behaviour. Next, I want to come to a better understanding of some of them, so I'll create models of those key parts.

Conceptual overview

By modelling the structure of the entities, I create a template for the objects that will eventually exist.

Figure 13.4 depicts the generalisation of rules. It's a fairly straightforward structure. In general, a rule can be applied (hence the **apply** function), and four specific types of rule exist.

Figure 13.4 Class diagram of rules

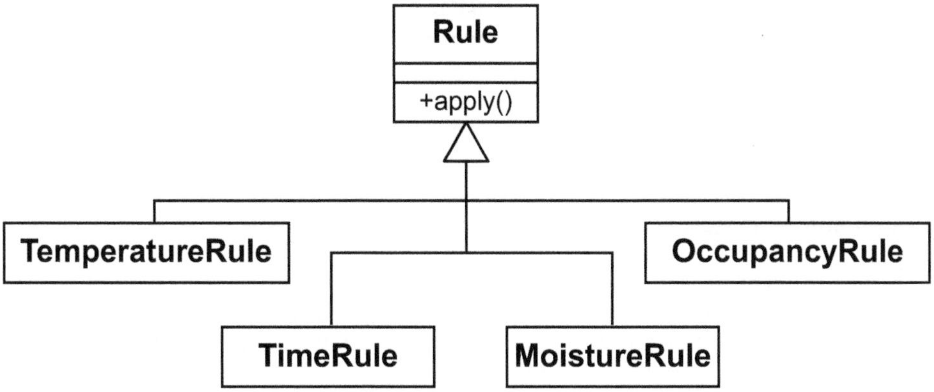

The story is very similar with components and sensors (Figure 13.5). A sensor can take readings and return the result. A component can be switched on or off. One notable thing is that the system can include multiple sensors and components. In order to control them individually, the solution needs to identify each uniquely, hence each possesses an ID number denoting which room it resides in.

Figure 13.5 Class diagrams of components and sensors

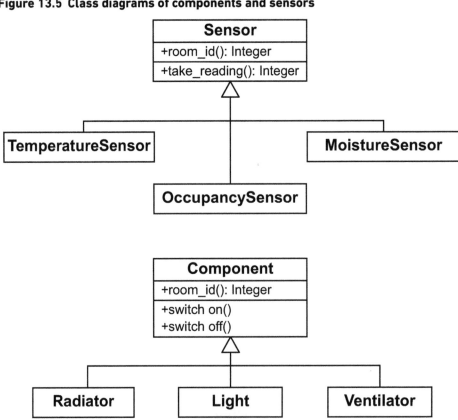

It seems now that the idea for a regulator was prescient. I can use one to bring all these concepts under its control (Figure 13.6). A regulator collects multiple sensors and components of a subsystem together and applies a rule when processing readings.

States and workflow

The system involves very careful control of multiple parts based on rules, so it's essential to understand that behaviour clearly, long before any code is written. Some workflows appear simple so I won't model everything, but I'll examine a few places that strike me as probable sources of complexity.

As a central controlling node in the solution, the regulator's behaviour involves a potentially complex interaction of several things. So, I'll create an activity diagram to model what a regulator does when it processes readings (Figure 13.7).

From the model, the regulator seems to cycle in a loop, taking measurements and switching components when necessary. One spot conceals some potential complexity, namely the activity where readings are mapped to a component state.

Figure 13.6 Class diagram of regulator

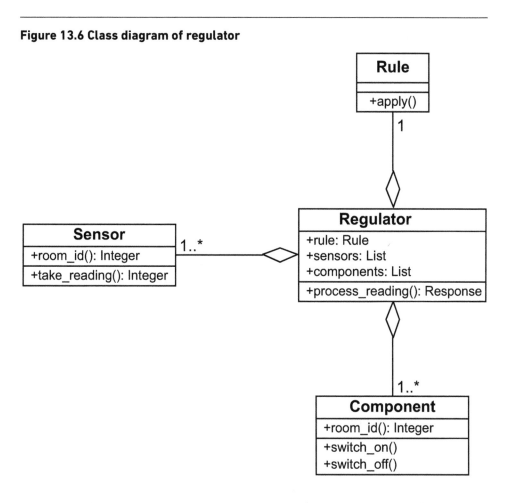

To explore this complexity, I could create state machine diagrams for each component that describe how state changes happen. Since space is limited, I'll just show one: the lighting.

Figure 13.8 shows what happens in terms of state alterations in the lighting subsystem. To switch the lighting on, the room must be occupied. Conversely, if the room subsequently becomes unoccupied, the system switches the lights back off.

This seems very simple. However, by modelling this process I forced myself to think it through, and this raised some practical questions. Specifically, I asked myself how occupancy might be measured. The industry standard for automatic lighting systems is through motion detection. The problem is, for a regulator to react promptly when someone enters the room, it would have to process sensor readings continuously (let's say once per second). But that would also mean the lights switch off whenever a room occupant happens to be motionless for a second or two. You can imagine how annoying that would be if you were sitting in a chair trying to watch TV.

Figure 13.7 Activity diagram of regulator

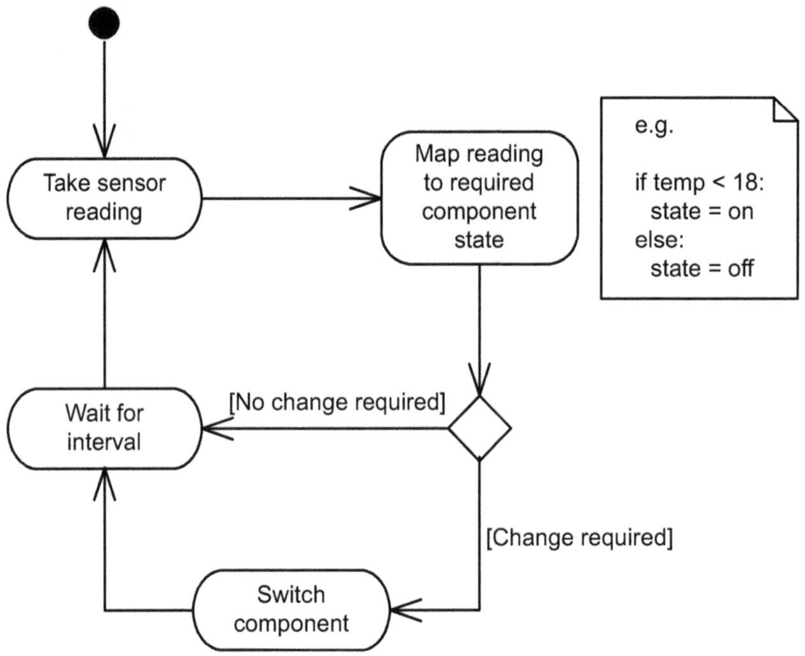

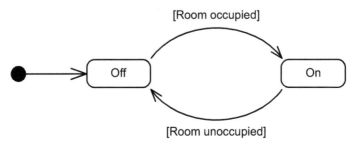

Figure 13.8 State diagram of applying a lighting rule

To take account of this, I've altered the rule for a lighting regulator by adding a time buffer (see Figure 13.9). Instead of switching the lights off immediately when no motion is detected, the regulator initiates a countdown. The lights will only be switched off when the countdown reaches zero. If, at any point, motion is again detected, the countdown is reset.

Figure 13.9 Revised state diagram of applying a lighting rule

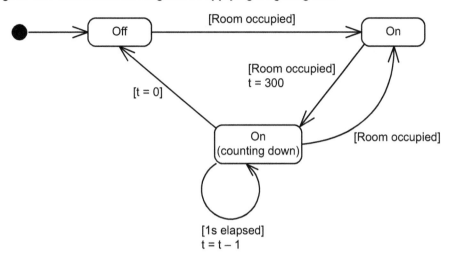

ANNOTATED SOURCE CODE

Let's look through the code that implements the solution. First, the overall structure of the system:

```
- automation_system/
    - core/
        - __init__.py
        - parts.py
        - regulator.py
    - subsystems/
        - __init__.py
        - heating.py
        - lighting.py
        - ventilation.py
```

The system is divided into two packages:

1. core: the central parts of the home automation system.
2. subsystems: the different subsystems that make up a home automation system.

The tour begins with the core **parts** module. (Comments offer some description of what's happening in each module.)

```
# core/parts.py

# This module contains the basic parts of an automation subsystem.
# The intention is that the software developer uses these as the
```

```
# starting point for writing a new subsystem.

class Rule:

    def apply(self, reading, component):
        # The apply method takes a reading, applies the rule, and
        # responds by manipulating the component accordingly. It
        # should be overridden in a subclass.
        pass


class Component:

    def __init__(self, room_id):
        self.room_id = room_id
        # This attribute keeps track of whether the component is
        # off or not.
        self.off = True

    def switch_on(self):
        if self.off:
            self.off = False

    def switch_off(self):
        if not self.off:
            self.off = True


class Sensor:

    def __init__(self, room_id):
        self.room_id = room_id

    def take_reading(self):
        # Each sensor takes readings differently, so this
        # method should be overridden in the subclass.
        pass
```

These are abstract classes, not really intended as concrete parts, so let's turn our attention to how these core parts can be implemented as concrete subsystems. (We'll come back to the **core** package later.)

The simplest subsystem is heating:

```
# subsystems/heating.py

# Since this is a small class with few imports, there's
# little risk of imported names colliding, so we can
# use 'from <package> import <class>'
from core.parts import Component
```

```
from core.parts import Rule
from core.parts import Sensor

# The random package provides a means for generating random
# numbers. Why are we importing it? See below...
import random

class Radiator(Component):
    # The standard Component behaviour is fine, so we
    # don't need to override anything.
    pass


class TemperatureRule(Rule):

    def apply(self, reading, radiator):
        # This rule is quite simple. When it gets too cold,
        # the radiator comes on. It stays on until the room
        # reaches the pleasant temperature.
        if reading < 18:
            radiator.switch_on()
        elif reading > 22:
            radiator.switch_off()


class TemperatureSensor(Sensor):

    def take_reading(self):
        # This method gets the sensor reading. In reality,
        # it would be a rather complex piece of code that
        # interfaces directly with the hardware. For
        # demonstration purposes, it can just return a
        # random number between 16 and 25.
        return random.randint(16, 25)
```

The ventilation subsystem is not too much more taxing:

```
# subsystems/ventilation.py

# Ventilation behaviour partly depends on timing, so we'll
# use Python's built-in date and time library.
import datetime
import random

from core.parts import Component
from core.parts import Rule
from core.parts import Sensor
```

```python
class Ventilator(Component):
    pass

class VentilationRule(Rule):
    # This class cheats a little and combines two
    # rules (moisture and time) into one.

    # Ventilation comes on between 17:00 and 20:00
    ventilation_on = datetime.time(17, 00)
    ventilation_off = datetime.time(20, 00)

    def apply(self, reading, ventilator):
        current_time = datetime.time(datetime.now())
        if reading > 70:
            # Golden rule: Ventilator must be on if moisture is
            # above 70%
            ventilator.switch_on()
        elif (current_time > ventilation_on and
                current_time < ventilation_off):
            # Even if moisture levels are fine, ventilation
            # must come on at allotted times
            ventilator.switch_on()
        else:
            # None of these conditions was met? Then switch
            # it off.
            ventilator.switch_off()

class MoistureSensor(Sensor):

    def take_reading(self):
        return random.randint(30, 80)
```

Finally, the lighting subsystem:

```python
# subsystems/lighting.py

from core.parts import Component
from core.parts import Rule
from core.parts import Sensor

class Light(Component):

    def dim_off():
        pass
        # We could make the automation system more sophisticated
        # so that instead of switching a light straight off, it
        # dimmed the lights. If we did, the function would go
        # best here.
```

```python
class LightingRule(Rule):
    # The lighting rule is a little more complex because it
    # incorporates a countdown.

    # This is the value assigned to the countdown when it's
    # reset
    # (300 s = 5 mins).
    time_limit = 300

    def __init__(self):
        # When the light subsystems is first started, the
        # countdown needs resetting.
        self._resetCountdown()

    def apply(self, reading, lights):
        if reading == True:
            # True means room is occupied.
            lights.switch_on()

            # We can now start the countdown.
            self._resetCountdown()
        else:
            # Room isn't occupied.
            if self.countdown == 0:
                # If the countdown has already reached zero,
                # switch off.
                lights.switch_off()
            else:
                 # Otherwise, we need to move the countdown
                 # along.
                self._tick()

    def _resetCountdown(self):
        # This method's name starts with an underscore as a
        # signal to Python meaning that this method is sort
        # of private and shouldn't concern whoever is using
        # this class.
        self.countdown = self.time_limit

    def _tick(self):
        # Count down one second (being careful not to count
        # lower than 0s)
        if self.countdown > 0:
            self.countdown = self.countdown - 1


class LightSensor(Sensor):

    def take_reading(self):
        return True if random.randint(0, 1) == 0 else
    False
```

That concludes the subsystems. Let's turn to the **core** package and look at the regulator:

```python
class Regulator:

    def __init__(self, rule):
        # A regulator as specified is a generic type, i.e. it
        # doesn't become a specific type of regulator until
        # it is given a rule at run-time.
        # For example, if it is given a TemperatureRule, it
        # becomes a heating regulator.
        self.rule = rule

        # Sensors and components are stored in two
        # dictionaries. Each one maps a room number to a
        # specific sensor/component.
        self.sensors = dict()
        self.components = dict()

    def add_room(self, room_id, sensor, component):
        # Adds a room (along with its sensor and component)
        # to this regulator's purview.
        self.sensors[room_id] = sensor
        self.components[room_id] = component

    def process_reading(self):
        # Go through each sensor belonging to this regulator.
        for room_id, sensor in self.sensors.items():
            # For each one, take a reading and pass it
            # (along with the corresponding component) to this
            # regulator's rule. The rule can then use this
            # information to apply itself.

            try:
                # Of course, things can go wrong with the sensor
                # (it might be broken or communication might be
                # lost), so we need to be prepared for that.
                reading = sensor.take_reading()
            except SensorError:
                log.error('Cannot get sensor reading!', exc_info=True)

            self.rule.apply(reading, self.components[room_id])
```

TESTING

Let's look at a few illustrative test cases. I'll update the project layout to look like this:

```
- automation_system/
    - core/
        - __init__.py
        - parts.py
        - regulator.py
    - subsystems/
        - __init__.py
        - heating.py
        - lighting.py
        - ventilation.py
    - test/
        - test_heating.py
        - test_lighting.py
```

Unit tests

The unit tests will be recorded in files inside the **test** directory. First, unit testing the lighting rule. This tests only the **LightingRule** class.

```python
# test_lighting.py
import unittest

import subsystems.lighting as light

class TestLightingRule(unittest.TestCase):

    def setUp(self):
        self.light_rule = light.LightingRule()
        self.light = light.Light(1)

    def test_lights_come_on(self):
        # Person enters the room
        self.light_rule.apply(True, self.light)

        # Light should be on
        self.assertFalse(self.light.off)

    def test_lights_stay_on(self):
        # Person enters the room
        self.light_rule.apply(True, self.light)

        # Person leaves the room
        self.light_rule.apply(False, self.light)
```

```
            # Light is still on
            self.assertFalse(self.light.off)

        def test_lights_countdown_to_off(self):
            # Person enters the room
            self.light_rule.apply(True, self.light)

            # Person leaves the room
            self.light_rule.apply(False, self.light)

            # Simulate 5 min countdown (i.e. 300 ticks)
            for _ in range(1, 300):
                self.light_rule.apply(False, self.light)

            # Bugs lurk in corners and congregate at boundaries:

            # Light should still be on
            self.assertFalse(self.light.off)

            # One more tick
            self.light_rule.apply(False, self.light)

            # Light should be off
            self.assertTrue(self.light.off)

if __name__ == '__main__':
    unittest.main()
```

The test run looks like this:

```
python -m unittest test/test_lighting.py
...
----------------------------------------------------------
Ran 3 tests in 0.000s

OK
```

System testing

Once individual units are shown to work well, we should put those units together to simulate use of the whole system. The following example integrates all parts of the heating subsystem and verifies that they work together properly.

```
# test/test_heating.py
import unittest

import core.regulator as regulator
import subsystems.heating as heat
```

```python
def temp_low(self):
    return 17

def temp_ok(self):
    return 21

def temp_high(self):
    return 23

class TestHeatingSubsystem(unittest.TestCase):

    def setUp(self):
        # Fully simulate a regulator
        room_id = 1
        self.temperature_sensor = heat.TemperatureSensor(room_id)
        self.radiator = heat.Radiator(room_id)
        self.heat_regulator = regulator.Regulator(heat.TemperatureRule())
        self.heat_regulator.add_room(room_id, self.temperature_sensor,
self.radiator)

    def test_heating_off(self):
        # For testing purposes, we have to simulate sensor
        # outputs at different temperatures. The following line
        # replaces the take_reading method that a Radiator has
        # and replaces it with the temp_ok function
        # (defined above).
        heat.TemperatureSensor.take_reading = temp_ok

        # The temperature sensor will therefore return 21
        # degrees when the regulator processes a reading.
        self.heat_regulator.process_reading()

        # Radiator is off
        self.assertTrue(self.radiator.off)

    def test_heating_comes_on_and_stays_on(self):
        # The temperature sensor will now return 17
        # degrees when the regulator processes a reading.
        heat.TemperatureSensor.take_reading = temp_low
        self.heat_regulator.process_reading()

        # Radiator is on.
        self.assertFalse(self.radiator.off)

        # The temperature sensor will now return 21
        heat.TemperatureSensor.take_reading = temp_ok
        self.heat_regulator.process_reading()

        # Radiator is still on.
        self.assertFalse(self.radiator.off)
```

```python
    def test_heating_on_then_off(self):
        heat.TemperatureSensor.take_reading = temp_low
        self.heat_regulator.process_reading()

        # Radiator is on.
        self.assertFalse(self.radiator.off)

        # Now temperature is too high
        heat.TemperatureSensor.take_reading = temp_high
        self.heat_regulator.process_reading()

        # Radiator is now off.
        self.assertTrue(self.radiator.off)

if __name__ == '__main__':
    unittest.main()
```

OPPORTUNITIES FOR IMPROVEMENT

As I said at the beginning, this is a very simplistic solution, optimised to show a few, easy-to-understand concepts. Many opportunities exist to make this example a more sophisticated and functional solution.

Here are a few I can think of:

- Add the code for the control panel.
- A regulator that supports multiple rules, so, for example, a ventilator can have separate rules for moisture and time.
- A component that has a more sophisticated status (such as dimmable lights).
- Add logging messages at appropriate places to aid debugging and monitoring.
- Write a system test that simulates three subsystems running at the same time.
- An improved countdown in the lighting subsystem, for example:
  - The lighting rule currently assumes that a regulator processes readings once per second. That may not be true in future and would break existing functionality if it changed (for example, a lighting regulator that processes two readings per second will run down the countdown after only 2.5 minutes). Alter the way the countdown measures time, so the LightingRule's countdown doesn't depend on the regulator.[71]
  - **Advanced:** make the countdown process a concurrent thread of execution.[72]

What improvements can you think of?

Consider it an exercise to take whichever ideas you prefer and turn this simple system into a great home automation solution of your own.

APPENDIX A
REFERENCE LISTS AND TABLES

In this Appendix I've detailed some reference lists and tables you may find useful.

ORDER OF OPERATOR PRECEDENCE

From lowest to highest. (Source: https://docs.python.org/3/reference/expressions.html#operator-precedence)

Table A.1 Order of operator precedence

Operator	Description
lambda	Lambda expression
if – else	Conditional expression
or	Boolean OR
and	Boolean AND
not x	Boolean NOT
in, not in, is, is not, <, <=, >, >=, !=, ==	Comparisons, including membership tests and identity tests
|	Bitwise OR
^	Bitwise XOR
&	Bitwise AND
<<, >>	Shifts
+, -	Addition and subtraction
*, @, /, //, %	Multiplication, matrix multiplication, division, remainder
+x, -x, ~x	Positive, negative, bitwise NOT
**	Exponentiation
await x	Await expression
x[], x[:], x(...), x.attribute	Subscription, slicing, call, attribute reference
(...), [...], {x: y}, {...}	Binding or tuple display, list display, dictionary display, set display

USABILITY HEURISTICS

These heuristics, described by Jakob Nielsen (a leading expert on usability), form general principles for designing interactive systems. See the original article for more explanation (Nielsen, 1995).

- System status should be visible at all times.
- The system should use words, phrases and concepts that are familiar to the user.
- Give users a clearly marked 'emergency exit'. Support undo and redo.
- Users should not have to wonder whether different words, situations or actions mean the same thing.
- Prefer prevention of errors to showing error messages.
- Prefer recognition rather than recall. Minimise the user's memory load.
- Provide shortcuts for advanced users.
- Use an aesthetic and minimalist design.
- Use plain language in error messages and suggest solutions.
- Provide help documentation.

MUTABLE AND IMMUTABLE TYPES IN PYTHON

Table A.2 Some examples of immutable and mutable types in Python

Immutable types	Mutable types
Number	Dictionary
String	Byte array
Tuple	List
Frozen set	Set

APPENDIX B
ANSWERS TO EXERCISES

CHAPTER 1

EXERCISE 1

List the core concepts of CT:

    A. logical thinking;
    B. algorithmic thinking;
    C. decomposition;
    D. generalisation and pattern recognition;
    E. modelling;
    F. abstraction;
    G. evaluation.

EXERCISE 2

Give an example of how you think people in each of the following occupations think computationally:

    A. mathematician: evaluates logical statements, carries out long chains of processes such as long division, abstracts values to variables;
    B. scientist: uses logic to reason about cause and effect, decomposes hierarchical relationships between species, follows experimental procedure, models phenomena such as climate dynamics;
    C. engineer: writes assembly instructions, decomposes construction into a series of tasks, creates models of artefacts, evaluates competing solutions to a problem;
    D. linguist: identifies patterns in grammar, models evolution of words in human history.

CHAPTER 2

EXERCISE 1

Mark the following statements as true or false:

A. An inductive logical argument makes conclusions that are probable rather than certain. *True.*

B. So long as a deductive argument has true premises, then its conclusion is certain. *False – the conclusion must also necessarily follow from the premises.*

C. In Boolean logic, a logical expression can have a maximum of two propositions. *False – an expression can have many propositions, but each proposition can have only one of two possible values.*

D. Logical AND has a higher precedence than logical OR. *True.*

E. $x = x + 1$ would be a valid expression in an algorithm. *True.*

EXERCISE 2

Consider the following search terms and decide which recipes will be returned:

A. cooking time less than 20 minutes and not vegetarian: *Garlic dip*;

B. includes chicken or turkey but not garlic: *Broiled chicken salad*;

C. doesn't include nuts: *Broiled chicken salad, Three-spice chicken*.

EXERCISE 3

Express these rules of thumb as logical statements. Each statement should make a conclusion about the estimated queuing time:

A. if customer is carrying items by hand, then time is 1 minute;

B. if customer is carrying a basket, then time is 2 minutes;

C. if customer is pushing a trolley, then:

    i.   if trolley is half-full, then time is 5 minutes;

    ii. if trolley is full, then time is 10 minutes.

D. if customer is at a self-service checkout, reduce time by 80 per cent.

EXERCISE 4

Take the logical statements from the previous question and incorporate them into an algorithm. The algorithm should take a queue as input, and should output the total estimated queueing time.

```
time = 0
examine next customer
begin loop:
    if customer is carrying items by hand, then time = time + 1
    if customer is carrying a basket, then time = time + 2
    if customer is pushing a trolley, then
        if trolley is half-full, then time = time + 5
        if trolley is full, then time = time + 10
repeat loop if there is a next customer
if checkout is self-service, then time = time x 0.8
```

EXERCISE 5

Based on the algorithm for singing *99 Bottles of Beer* write a pseudocode algorithm for singing *The 12 Days of Christmas*.

```
Let X equal 1. Substituting X for its ordinal form when singing:
begin loop:
    sing 'on the X day of Christmas my true love sent to me'
    if X > 11, then sing 'Twelve drummers drumming'
    if X > 10, then sing 'Eleven pipers piping'
    if X > 9, then sing 'Ten lords a-leaping'
    if X > 8, then sing 'Nine ladies dancing'
    if X > 7, then sing 'Eight maids a-milking'
    if X > 6, then sing 'Seven swans a-swimming'
    if X > 5, then sing 'Six geese a-laying'
    if X > 4, then sing 'Five golden rings'
    if X > 3, then sing 'Four calling birds'
    if X > 2, then sing 'Three French hens'
    if X > 1, then sing 'Two turtle doves and'
    sing 'A partridge in a pear tree.'
    add 1 to X
repeat loop if X is less than 13, otherwise finish.
```

CHAPTER 3

EXERCISE 1

Mark the following statements as true or false:

A. Your goal defines how the problem should be solved, not what needs to be done. *False.*

B. It is inadvisable to begin writing a solution before the goal is defined. *True.*

C. For any non-trivial problem, there is likely only one solution. *False.*

D. Decomposition guarantees an optimal solution. *False.*

E. A tree structure is hierarchical in nature. *True.*

F. All nodes in a tree structure have one or more child nodes. *False.*

G. Patterns among separate groups of instructions can be generalised into subroutines. *True.*

EXERCISE 2

You're planning to hold a birthday picnic for a child and her friends. Break down the preparation into a tree structure of tasks.

Figure B.1 Task breakdown for picnic

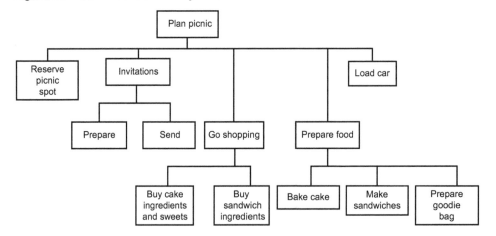

EXERCISE 3

Update the drawing of the smiley face discussed earlier in the chapter so that the positioning of the features (eyes and mouth) are calculated automatically based on the positioning of the face.

A. 'Draw face' is a subroutine (r, x, y):
   i. Draw circle with radius r at position x,y filled yellow
   ii. Call 'draw eye' with parameters r1 = 0.25 × r, r2 = 0.125 × r, x = x -0.5 × r, y = y -0.5 × r
   iii. Call 'draw eye' with parameters r1 = 0.25 × r, r2 = 0.125 × r, x = x + 0.5 × r, y = y -0.5 × r
   iv. Call 'draw mouth' with parameters x1 = x -0.5 × r, y1 = y + 0.5 × r, x2 = x + 0.5 × r, y2 = y + 0.5 × r

EXERCISE 4

Further update the drawing of the smiley face.

A. i. 'Draw face' is a subroutine (r, x, y):
   Draw circle with radius r at position x,y filled yellow
   ii. 'Draw mouth' is a subroutine (x1, y1, x2, y2):
   Draw line from x1,y1 to x2,y2 coloured red
   iii. ''Draw eye' is a subroutine (r1, r2, x, y):
   Draw circle with radius r1 at position x,y
   Draw circle with radius r2 at position x,y filled brown
B. 'Draw scar' is a subroutine (x,y):
   Draw line from x,y to x,y+10
   Draw line from x-2,y+2 to x+2,y+2
   Draw line from x-2,y+4 to x+2,y+4
   Draw line from x-2,y+6 to x+2,y+6
   Draw line from x-2,y+8 to x+2,y+8
C. 'Draw nose' is a subroutine (r, x, y):
   Draw circle with radius r at position x,y filled red

Drawing the nose must be done after drawing the face and eyes for it to appear above them.

EXERCISE 5

Use your tree structures to guide your questioning strategy. Which one of the three structures would minimise the number of questions you would have to ask? Try dividing groupings into sub-groupings to see if that helps to reduce the number of questions.

Figure B.2 Species organised into a tree structure by number of legs

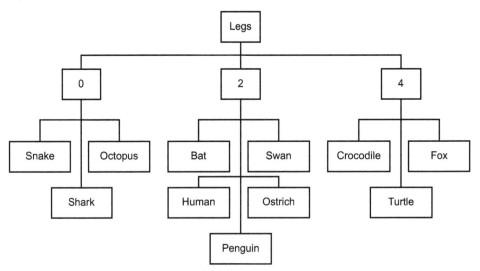

The tree helps to show the maximum number of questions you would have to ask when following each strategy. For example, when following the 'number of legs' strategy, the maximum numbers of questions you would ask is eight:

    A. Does it have no legs? *No.*
    B. Does it have 4 legs? *No.*
    C. Does it have 2 legs? *Yes.*
    D. Is it a bat? *No.*
    E. Is it a human? *No.*
    F. Is it a penguin? *No.*
    G. Is it an ostrich? *No.*
    H. Is it a swan? *Yes.*

Compare this to the other strategies.

The 'does it fly?' strategy is potentially good because the tree is very unbalanced – you could eliminate a huge number of animals if the answer to 'Does it fly?' is 'yes'. However, this is also its weakness. If the answer is 'no', you could potentially have to ask eight more questions, meaning the maximum number of questions for this strategy is nine.

The 'species' strategy provides a balanced and shallow tree. The maximum number of questions you would have to ask is seven.

Figure B.3 Species organised into a tree structure by ability to fly

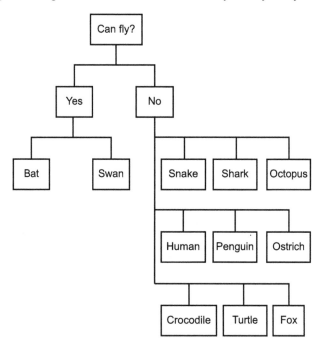

You can combine strategies by asking a different question after you've descended one level in the tree. However, you must be careful which one you pick. If you find out the animal is a mammal, it would be sensible to ask how many legs it has because mammals vary in number of legs. If you find out the animal is a fish, the 'number of legs' strategy is useless because fish are generally legless.

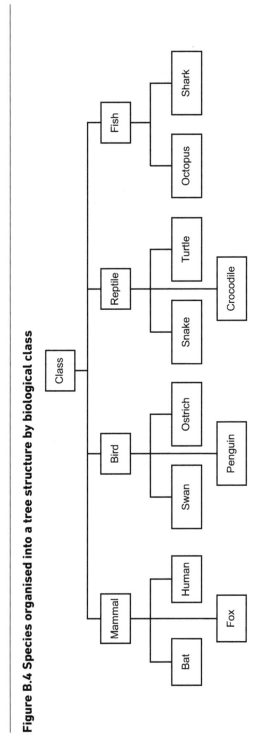

Figure B.4 Species organised into a tree structure by biological class

CHAPTER 4

EXERCISE 1

Mark the following statements as true or false:

    A. An abstraction leaks when it takes details into account unnecessarily. *False.*

    B. An abstraction must be instantiated before it can be executed. *True.*

    C. A dynamic model shows the changes in state of something over time. *True.*

    D. A directed graph is a dynamic model. *False.*

    E. Accuracy describes closeness to the true value; precision describes the level of refinement in a measurement. *True.*

EXERCISE 2

Order the following into layers of abstraction, starting with the most general and ending with the most specific:

    A. animal;

    B. bird;

    C. penguin;

    D. Emperor penguin;

    E. Tommy the Penguin.

EXERCISE 3

For renting out a car, which of the following is it necessary for a rental company to know about?

    A. The car's current mileage. *Yes: the distance travelled by the customer could be used to calculate the price.*

    B. The customer's height. *No. Irrelevant to a car rental.*

    C. Number of wheels on the car. *No. This is both constant and irrelevant to a car rental (if the number of wheels on the car has changed, something has gone very wrong!).*

    D. The car's current fuel level. *Yes: the car needs handing over to the customer with a specific amount of fuel.*

    E. ID number of the customer's motorcycle licence. *No. A motorcycle licence isn't required to rent a car.*

EXERCISE 4

Model all the possible stages of an order using a state machine diagram.

Figure B.5 State machine diagram showing states of an order

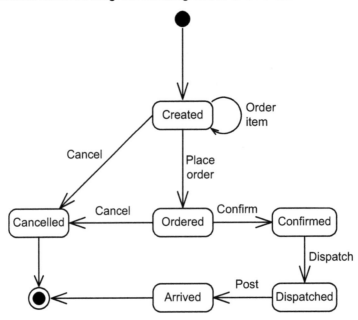

EXERCISE 5

Extend the diagram so that the data structure records the student's grades.

Figure B.6 Extended data model of a student's record

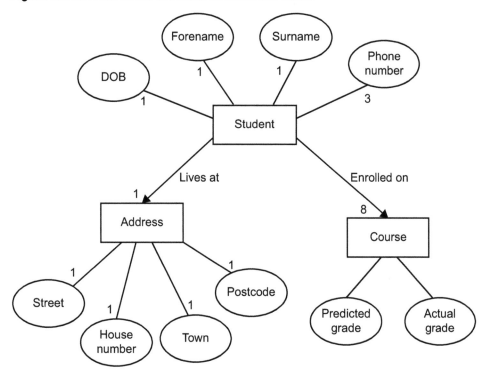

CHAPTER 5

EXERCISE 1

Mark the following statements as true or false:

    A. Errors can result from statements that are grammatically valid. *True.*

    B. The exit condition of a loop is evaluated after each statement inside the loop is executed. *False.*

    C. Defensive programming assumes that code is safe until proven otherwise. *False.*

    D. Bottom-up testing is an effective way of finding design flaws. *False.*

    E. An equivalence class groups all inputs to an algorithm that elicit the same type of response. *True.*

EXERCISE 2

Explain the difference between a bug and an error.

A bug is fault in a solution that can cause erroneous behaviour. An error is behaviour observed when executing a solution which does not match with expected behaviour.

EXERCISE 3

An 'if–then' conditional tells the computer to carry out some instructions if a certain condition is met. How could you modify this form to carry out instructions if the condition is not met?

The if–then–else form provides the means for adding instructions when a condition is not met. Instructions to be executed if a condition is not met go in the else part.

```
if score > 50
    then grade = 'Pass'
    else grade = 'Fail'
```

EXERCISE 4

The algorithm in the Minesweeper example (Figure 5.2) contains an error. Find it and fix it.

The condition that decides whether to repeat the loop checks if n is less than 8. That means execution of the loop ends as soon as n becomes 8, meaning the last square doesn't get checked. If a mine were in this square, it would be missed.

EXERCISE 5

Write an algorithm for the FizzBuzz game that analyses an input number and returns the correct response.

```
if number < 1
    then output 'Error! Number must be 1 or more.'
    else if number is divisible by 3 AND number is divisible by 5
        then output 'FizzBuzz'
    else if number is divisible by 3
        then output 'Fizz'
    else if number is divisible by 5
        then output 'Buzz'
    else output number
end
```

CHAPTER 6

EXERCISE 1

Mark the following statements as true or false:

    A. Most real-world software solutions are shown be correct empirically rather than mathematically. *True.*

    B. Reducing the number of failing tests doesn't strengthen your claim to a solution's correctness. *True.*

    C. An inefficient solution cannot be considered correct. *False.*

    D. An elegant solution maximises both effectiveness and simplicity at the same time. *True.*

    E. A usability evaluation begins by explaining to the test subject how to use the system. *False.*

EXERCISE 2

Write generic versions of both the obvious solution and Gauss's solution, both of which sum up numbers from 1 to *N*.

Obvious solution:

```
input upper_number from user
let total = 0
for each number, n, between 1 and upper_number:
    let total = total + n
```

Gauss's solution:

```
input upper_number from user
let pair_sum = 1 + upper_number
if upper_number is even, then
    let number_of_pairs = upper_number / 2
    let total = number_of_pairs x pair_sum
else
    let number_of_pairs = (upper_number - 1) / 2
    let total = number_of_pairs x pair_sum
    let total = total + (pair_sum / 2)
```

EXERCISE 3

Which one of these two algorithms is more efficient in terms of time complexity?

Gauss's solution, despite having more statements in it, is still more efficient than the obvious solution because it takes a fixed number of steps to process any range (in other words, its time complexity is constant). The obvious solution still has linear time complexity, so the time it takes to execute grows as the range of numbers grows.

EXERCISE 4

Can you see how the data could be made to take up less space?

Sometimes the end of one line describes the same colour as the beginning of the next line. For example, the end of first line is '5W' and the beginning of the second is '3W'. We could reduce the space they consume by 50 per cent by combining them both into '8W'.

EXERCISE 5

What are the names of the five components of usability and what do they measure?

A. Learnability: measures how easy users find accomplishing basic tasks using the solution for the first time.
B. Efficiency: how quickly users can perform tasks, once they have learned the solution.
C. Memorability: how easily users can re-establish proficiency when they return to the solution after a period of not using it.
D. Errors: how many errors users make, how severe these errors are and how easily users can recover from them.
E. Satisfaction: how pleasant the design is to use.

CHAPTER 7

EXERCISE 1

Write a program that creates two variables, **r** and **pi**.

```
pi = 3.142
r = 5
```

EXERCISE 2

Use the variables from the previous question to create a third variable called **area** which holds the area of a circle with radius **r**.

```
area = pi * r * r
```

EXERCISE 3

Write a program that creates two number variables, **a** and **b**, and uses the **print** command to output **True** or **False** depending on whether or not **a** is greater than **b**.

```
a = 4
b = 5
print(a > b)
```

EXERCISE 4

Take the code from the previous answer and write a function called **bigger**.

```
def bigger(x, y):
    print(x > y)

# Prints True
bigger(4, 5)

# Prints False
bigger(8, 7)

# Prints True
bigger(42, 41)
```

CHAPTER 8

EXERCISE 1

Mark the following statements as true or false:

<ol type="A">
<li>You cannot assign the value of an immutable variable to another variable. False.</li>
<li>The continue keyword forces a loop to end immediately and continue executing with the code that follows the loop. False.</li>
<li>Declarative programming is useful when you need careful control over the step-by-step behaviour of a program. False.</li>
<li>Only one part of a multi-part if-statement can be executed at the most. True.</li>
<li>An expression is a piece of code that evaluates to a result. True.</li>
</ol>

EXERCISE 2

Rewrite the code so that **notes_1** can be updated without simultaneously altering the value of **notes_2**.

```
notes_1 = ['Do', 'Re', 'Me']
notes_2 = notes_1 + ['Fa']
print(notes_2)
```

EXERCISE 3

Take your solution to Chapter 2, Exercise 5 (write an algorithm for singing *The 12 Days of Christmas*). Convert the algorithm into a Python program.

```
X = 1
ordinal_forms = ['zeroth', 'first', 'second', 'third', 'fourth', \
    'fifth', 'sixth', 'seventh', 'eighth', 'ninth', 'tenth', 'eleventh',
    'twelfth']

while X < 13:
    ordinal_form = ordinal_forms[X]
    print('On the {} day of Christmas my true love sent to me'.
format(ordinal_form))
    if X > 11: print('Twelve drummers drumming')
    if X > 10: print('Eleven pipers piping')
    if X > 9: print('Ten lords a-leaping')
    if X > 8: print('Nine ladies dancing')
    if X > 7: print('Eight maids a-milking')
    if X > 6: print('Seven swans a-swimming')
    if X > 5: print('Six geese a-laying')
    if X > 4: print('Five golden rings')
```

```
if X > 3: print('Four calling birds')
if X > 2: print('Three French hens')
if X > 1: print('Two turtle doves and')
print('A partridge in a pear tree.')
X = X + 1
```

EXERCISE 4

Write a program that takes a list of Fahrenheit measurements and converts it into a list of Celsius measurements.

```
fahrenheit = [0, 10, 20, 30, 40, 50, 60, 70, 80, 90, 10]
celsius = [(f-32) * (5/9) for f in fahrenheit]
```

EXERCISE 5

Using the **filter** function, write a program to filter out annoying words from a list of words, specifically words that are in all upper-case characters and words that end with multiple exclamation marks.

```
def annoying(word):
    if word.isupper(): return False

    length = len(word)
    if word[length - 1] == '!' and word[length - 2] == '!':
        return False

    return True

words = [ 'Hello', 'Cool!!', 'OMG!!!', 'NSYNC', 'FiNE', 'good!' ]
filtered = filter(annoying, words)
```

CHAPTER 9

EXERCISE 1

Mark the following statements as true or false:

    A. Global variables are the preferred way to pass information between functions. *False.*

    B. When functions know too much about other functions' workings, altering them risks causing side effects. *True.*

    C. Objects defined inside a function cannot be referenced outside that function. *True.*

    D. A module takes its name from the file it's defined in. *True.*

    E. Files in a Python package may only have names made up of letters or numbers. *False.*

EXERCISE 2

What is the output of the program?

```
No, print this!
Print this message.
```

EXERCISE 3

Try running the program, and explain why it results in an error.

The first line of **my_function** tries to print the value of **s**, but **s** hasn't been defined yet. If you wanted to access the global **s**, you would need first to add the statement 'global s', to make it explicit that you want to use the global variable. The code in Exercise 2 didn't use the global **s**, instead it defined a local variable (which just happened to have the same name).

EXERCISE 4

Extend the program.

```python
import datetime

def get_time_alive(birthdate):
    today = datetime.date.today()
    return today - birthdate

def print_sleep(birthdate):
    time_alive = get_time_alive(birthdate)
    time_sleeping = time_alive.days / 3
    print('You have slept for {} days so \
far.'.format(time_sleeping))

def print_loo_visits(birthdate):
    time_alive = get_time_alive(birthdate)
    visits_to_loo = time_alive.days * 6
    print('You have been to the loo {} times so \
far.'.format(visits_to_loo))

def print_meals(birthdate):
    time_alive = get_time_alive(birthdate)
    number_of_meals = time_alive.days * 3
    print('You have eaten {} meals so far.'.format(number_of_meals))

def print_duration(birthdate):
    time_alive = get_time_alive(birthdate)
    print('You have been alive for {} days.'.format(time_alive.days))
```

```python
def get_birthdate():
    year = int(input('What year were you born? '))
    month = int(input('What month were you born? '))
    day = int(input('What day were you born? '))

    return datetime.date(year, month, day)

birthdate = get_birthdate()
print_duration(birthdate)
print_sleep(birthdate)
print_loo_visits(birthdate)
print_meals(birthdate)
```

CHAPTER 10

EXERCISE 1

Mark the following statements as true or false:

  A. All items in a Python list must have the same type. *False.*
  B. Creating a new object of a certain class is called instantiation. *True.*
  C. A subclass must override all the methods it inherits from the parent class. *False.*
  D. Reusing patterns helps to reduce effort when coming up with solutions. *True.*
  E. Design patterns are typically categorised into the following three categories: creational, structural and atypical. *False.*

EXERCISE 2

Write a Python program that prints out all the unique words in a sentence.

```python
sentence = 'If I bake this bitter butter it would make my batter bitter
but a bit of better butter would make my batter better'

unique_words = set(sentence.split(' '))
```

EXERCISE 3

Write an insult generator in Python that picks a random assortment of adjectives and orders them correctly in an insulting sentence.

```python
from random import randint

def get_random_word(words):
    return words[randint(0, len(words) - 1)]

opinion = ['stupid', 'weird', 'boring', 'witless']
size = ['huge', 'big', 'little', 'tiny']
quality = ['scabby', 'spotty', 'saggy', 'ugly']
age = ['old', 'immature', 'childish', 'decrepit']
shape = ['fat', 'skinny', 'clunking', 'lanky']
noun = ['idiot', 'halfwit', 'coward', 'crybaby']

sentence = 'You {}, {}, {}, {}, {} {}'.format(
    get_random_word(opinion),
    get_random_word(size),
    get_random_word(quality),
    get_random_word(age),
    get_random_word(shape),
    get_random_word(noun)
)

print(sentence)
```

EXERCISE 4

Define a class for each of the three shapes: **Rock, Paper, Scissors.**

```python
class Rock:
    name = 'Rock'

    def beats(self, other):
        return True if other.name == 'Scissors' else False

class Scissors:
    name = 'Scissors'

    def beats(self, other):
        return True if other.name == 'Paper' else False

class Paper:
    name = 'Paper'

    def beats(self, other):
        return True if other.name == 'Rock' else False
```

EXERCISE 5

Add a class to act as a computer player.

```python
class ComputerPlayer:

    def choose(self):
        return random.choice([Rock(), Scissors(), Paper()])
```

EXERCISE 6

Add code to play one round of the game.

```python
# The computer player should make a choice.
computer = ComputerPlayer()
computer_choice = computer.choose()

# The program should ask the player to choose a shape
# (ensuring that the input is valid).
your_input = ''

while your_input not in ['r', 'p', 's']:
    your_input = input('Choose r for Rock, p for Paper, or s for
Scissors')

if your_input == 'r':
    your_choice = Rock()
elif your_input == 'p':
    your_choice = Paper()
elif your_input == 's':
    your_choice = Scissors()

# It should print out the computer's choice.
print('Computer chose {}'.format(computer_choice.name))

# It should determine who won and print out the result.
if your_choice.name == computer_choice.name:
    print('Draw!')
else:
    result_message = 'You win!'beats(computer_choice)
    else 'You lose!'
    print(result_message)
    if your_choice.
```

CHAPTER 11

EXERCISE 1

Mark the following statements as true or false:

    A.   Static models show how entities change over time. *False.*

    B.   The middle section of a class in a class diagram lists attributes. *True.*

    C.   Inheritance is modelled using an arrow with a solid, white arrowhead. *True.*

    D.   Aggregation and composition are types of dependency. *False.*

    E.   A state machine diagram emphasises the changes in state of a single object. *True.*

EXERCISE 2

Look at Figure 11.13. Extend the diagram to include chess pieces.

Figure B.7 Class diagram of a chess set

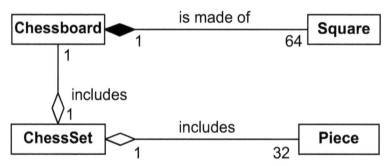

EXERCISE 3

Draw a use case diagram for a typical, high street cash machine.

Figure B.8 Use case diagram of a typical cash machine

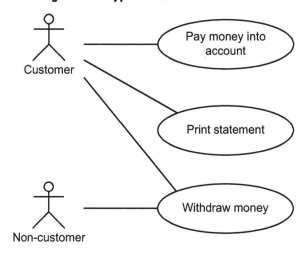

EXERCISE 4

Draw an activity diagram for the process of withdrawing money from a cash machine.

Figure B.9 Activity diagram for cash withdrawal

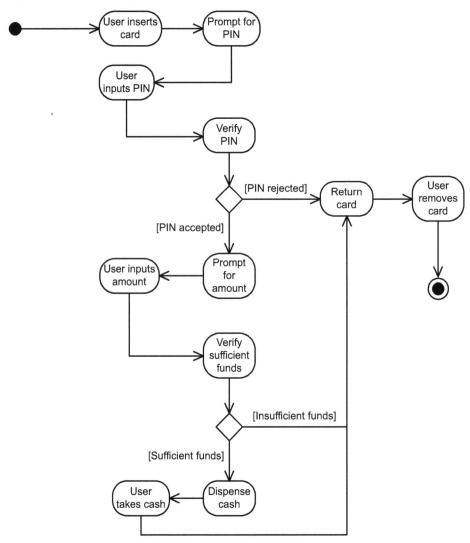

EXERCISE 5

There have been complaints about the card-operated turnstile gate (section 'Workflows'). Some people forget their card and leave it in the slot. Alter the activity diagram so that this can no longer happen.

You could alter the diagram so that the actions 'System ejects card' and 'System unlocks turnstile' are no longer done in parallel. Instead, make them linear so that unlocking the turnstile happens after the card is ejected. Add an activity between them called 'user takes card', so that the turnstile won't unlock until it detects that the user has retrieved their card.

CHAPTER 12

EXERCISE 1

Mark the following statements as true or false:

A. A syntax error will not be reported until the line containing it is executed. *False.*

B. Code in a **finally** block is always executed after the code in its corresponding **try** block. *True.*

C. Validation determines whether or not a solution actually solves the original problem. *True.*

D. The **setUp** function in a Python unit test is executed once before each individual test function. *True.*

E. By default, Python prints log messages to a file called **log.txt**. *False.*

EXERCISE 2

Turn your FizzBuzz algorithm into a Python program.

```
number = int(input('Number: '))
output = ''

if number < 1:
    output = 'Error! Number must be 1 or more.'
else:
    if number % 3 == 0:
        output = 'Fizz'
    if number % 5 == 0:
        output = output + 'Buzz'
    if output == '':
        output = number

print(output)
```

EXERCISE 3

Write a unit test for your FizzBuzz program.

To make the code testable we reorganise the routine into a function that can be called. We also add the check for non-numeric input.

```python
def fizz(number):
    if not isinstance(number, int):
        return 'Error! Number must be an integer.'

    if number < 1:
        return 'Error! Number must be 1 or more.'

    output = ''
    if number % 3 == 0:
        output = 'Fizz'
    if number % 5 == 0:
        output = output + 'Buzz'
    if output == '':
        output = number

    return output
```

The test case for this code is as follows:

```python
import unittest
from fizz import fizz

class FizzTest(unittest.TestCase):

    def test_normal(self):
        output = fizz(7)
        self.assertEqual(output, 7)

    def test_normal_boundary(self):
        output = fizz(1)
        self.assertEqual(output, 1)
        output = fizz(0)
        self.assertEqual(output, 'Error! Number must be 1 or more.')

    def test_fizz(self):
        output = fizz(3)
        self.assertEqual(output, 'Fizz')

    def test_buzz(self):
        output = fizz(5)
        self.assertEqual(output, 'Buzz')
```

```
def test_fizzbuzz(self):
    output = fizz(15)
    self.assertEqual(output, 'FizzBuzz')

def test_unacceptable_number(self):
    output = fizz(-3)
    self.assertEqual(output, 'Error! Number must be 1 or more.')

def test_non_number(self):
    output = fizz(1.1)
    self.assertEqual(output, 'Error! Number must be an integer.')
```

EXERCISE 4

Try the program out and, using a debugger and/or log messages, find and fix the problems.

Some bugs:

  A. The while loop condition should loop if the input is **not** '0'.
  B. `for letter in range(1, len(word)):` This line is wrong because it misses the first (i.e. zeroth) letter of the word. It should be `for letter in range(0, len(word)):`
  C. `if output != word:` should read `if output == word:`

NOTES

1. An algorithm is sequence of clearly defined steps that describe a process to be followed. You'll learn more about them in Chapter 2.

2. This punchline features in a routine from UK sketch show *Little Britain*, where an unhelpful travel agent 'delegates' all decision-making to the computer... or so the audience is led to believe.

3. See for example: Furber 2012, Barr and Stephenson 2011 or Bundy 2007.

4. A programming language aimed at novices that is often used to control a cursor that can draw to the screen. The cursor is called a turtle.

5. This list aligns very closely with others produced by various organisations, including Computing at School (CAS) (Csizmadia et al., 2015), a community supported by BCS, The Chartered Institute for IT, Microsoft, Google and others.

6. 'O(N log N)' is an example of algorithm complexity, which is discussed in Chapter 6.

7. By 'fail', I don't mean that the conclusion is necessarily wrong, only that the argument is useless for judging it to be right or wrong.

8. That's Tic-Tac-Toe for most of the world outside Britain.

9. This would be to commit a logical fallacy called 'affirming the consequent', which means you incorrectly assumed that the proposed cause was the **only** way the consequent could be true.

10. Although another operator named XOR (exclusive or) does match the meaning here.

11. Some take the view that an algorithm is a combination of logic and some controlling component that specifies how the logic is used – that is, algorithm = logic + control (Kowalski, 1979).

12. 'Else' in this context is synonymous with 'otherwise'.

13. And the reason for this is because brackets have the highest precedence of all operators.

14. Decomposition (discussed later in this chapter) is an effective way of exposing unknown details.

15. Trade-offs and optimisation of solutions feature in Chapter 6.

16. Entities: the core concepts of a system.

17. You would also need to make clear what 'easy' means in this context, for example takes less than 30 seconds to find a specific book.

18. Chapter 5 discusses various methods for anticipating and handling errors.

19. The list has two items in it. For readability's sake, each pair of coordinates is surrounded in parentheses.

20. In fact, with some experience, you'll be able to carry out decomposition and generalisation simultaneously.

21. That's hiding, not removing. The details still exist, it's simply that they're kept out of the picture.

22. I'm being a little tongue-in-cheek here, but it's worth familiarising yourself with Miller's experiments on human working memory (Miller, 1956).

23. The map in this figure is © OpenStreetMap contributors. This and other maps are available under the Open Database License.

24. Recursion was explored in Chapter 3. A recursive structure is something made up of many smaller things that are the same type as the whole.

25. Payload is the capacity in kilograms of a van.

26. Look up the Antikythera Mechanism at: https://en.wikipedia.org/wiki/Antikythera_mechanism.

27. This turnstile doesn't block incoming coins while it's unlocked, so be careful: this is a prime way to waste money.

28. Image from Wikimedia Commons (2006). Available at: https://commons.wikimedia.org/wiki/File:Image-Koenigsberg,_Map_by_Merian-Erben_1652.jpg.

29. Image from Wikimedia Commons (2012). Available at: https://commons.wikimedia.org/wiki/File:Orrery_-_Nov._2010.jpg.

30. How to test and evaluate user interfaces is covered in Chapter 6.

31. That's right, 'its' is missing an apostrophe.

32. If you're interested, this kind of error is called a dangling modifier.

33. Different types of handheld devices work differently and may affect the way your solution works.

34. One way to see the number of relationships is to create a model. See Chapter 4.

35. The divisor is the number on the bottom of the division.

36. Aka stubs.

37. Aka drivers.

38. Find an example of a test plan in Chapter 6.

39. This was termed 'rubber duck debugging' by the authors of *The Pragmatic Programmer*, who reference the story of a programmer having a rubber duck on their desk and explaining to it their current debugging woes (Hunt and Thomas, 1999).

40. A critical system has extremely high reliability demands, usually because failure can incur loss of life or high financial loss.

41. An impossible goal, given that there are literally endless different algorithms in existence.

42. An example from this category is the bubble sort algorithm. It sorts input data by comparing every item to most or all other input items, thus squaring the amount of work it potentially needs to do.

43. Or, if you think of software as art, then it isn't **just** art.

44. The U-shaped pipe beneath the sink.

45. Maybe the teacher just wanted to keep the students busy.

46. Chapter 3 discusses the power of finding patterns in a problem.

47. Because your approach is clever or impressive, that is no justification in itself. It's just showing off.

48. A resolution of $2048 \times 1536 = 3,145,728$ pixels.

49. The dimensions of a modern monitor screen are often multiples of 16 (for example, 1024, 1280), so a 16×16 is the smallest sensible-looking smiley face you could draw and have a neat row of them on screen.

50. Consider the difference between a user-friendly, but specialised, table knife and the highly flexible Swiss Army Knife (Byrne, 2013).

51. For example: Java, Ruby, C/C++ or JavaScript.

52. A source file is a text file that contains source code.

53. These are problems that occur when the program is running.

54. Python also refers to a variable as a 'name'.

55. This creates a new list by including only elements from an old list that pass a test – in this case, the test is the `is_even` function; `filter` is a fundamental operation from functional programming (itself a type of declarative programming style).

56. This code sample includes the importing of a module, which is explained in Chapter 9.

57. US Air Force (1967). Available from: https://commons.wikimedia.org/wiki/File:Offutt_Air_Force_Base_operator.jpg

58. This file can remain empty. Only its presence is required.

59. Specifically, they're put into a list of tuples.

60. This isn't strictly true. Every type in Python supports a small set of specific operations by default, but none that interests us right now.

61. Vehicles in this category are up to 3,500 kg in weight and contain up to eight passenger seats.

62. Or, more correctly, **assumes**.

63. Very likely, because car companies love standardisation.

64. Alterations like changing the signature of the initialiser.

65. Or, if you prefer, the latter is a generalisation of the former.

66. You can think of activity diagrams as flow charts with some additional features, in particular the ability to depict processes happening in parallel as well as which objects initiate each action.

67. 'Response time' being the duration between the user clicking a button/link and receiving the response from the server.

68. Consider the (incomplete) list of types of system testing here: www.tutorialspoint. com/software_testing_dictionary/system_testing.htm

69. That is to say, the system is doing something (and doing it well). But, whatever it's doing, it doesn't solve the original problem.

70. The original problem did not mention sensors, but they are implied. The idea of a sensor will stand in for some entity that measures or calculates something about the environment.

71. **Hint:** use the `datetime` module.

72. See https://docs.python.org/3/library/threading.html

REFERENCES

Arbuckle, D. (2014) *Learning Python testing*. Birmingham, UK: Packt Publishing.

Barr, V. and Stephenson, C. (2011) Bringing computational thinking to K-12: What is involved and what is the role of the computer science education community?, *ACM Inroads*, 2 (1). 48.

Beizer, B. (1990) *Software testing techniques*. New York, USA: Van Nostrand Reinhold.

Box, G. E. P. and Draper, N. R. (1987) *Empirical model-building and response surfaces*. New York, USA: John Wiley & Sons.

Bundy, A. (2007) Computational thinking is pervasive. *Journal of Scientific and Practical Computing*, 1 (2). 67.

Byrne, D. (2013) *Usability tradeoff*. Intel Developer Zone. Available from: https://software.intel.com/en-us/articles/usability-tradeoff [16 November 2016].

Carnegie Mellon (2016) Carnegie Mellon University Center for Computational Thinking. Available from: www.cs.cmu.edu/~CompThink [16 November 2016].

Chonoles, M. J. and Schardt, J. A. (2003) *UML 2 for dummies*. New York, USA: John Wiley and Sons.

Code Academy (2017) *Introduction to Python*. Available from: www.codecademy.com/courses/introduction-to-python-6WeG3/0/1 [19 June 2017].

Committee for the Workshops on Computational Thinking (2011) *Report of a workshop of pedagogical aspects of computational thinking*. National Research Council. Available from: www.nap.edu/catalog.php?record_id=13170 [19 June 2017].

Conan Doyle, A. (1890) *The sign of four*. New York, USA: Barnes and Noble, 2009 edn.

Csizmadia, A. et al. (2015) *Computational thinking: A guide for teachers*, Available from: https://computingatschool.org.uk/computationalthinking [19 June 2017].

Damer, T. E. (2005) *Attacking faulty reasoning* 5th edn. Belmont, CA, USA: Thomson-Wadsworth.

Denning, P. (2009) Beyond computation thinking. *Communications of the ACM*, 52 (6). 28.

Department for Education (2013) National curriculum in England: computing programmes of study. Available from: https://www.gov.uk/government/publications/national-curriculum-in-england-computing-programmes-of-study/national-curriculum-in-england-computing-programmes-of-study [10 July 2017].

Dromey, R. G. (1982) *How to solve it by computer.* Englewood Cliffs, NJ, USA: Prentice-Hall.

Fowler, M. (2003) *UML distilled* 3rd edn. Boston, MA, USA: Addison-Wesley.

Funkload (2017) Funkload documentation. Funkload. Available from: http://funkload.nuxeo.org/ [19 June 2017].

Furber, S. (2012) *Shut down or restart? The way forward for computing in UK schools.* London, UK: The Royal Society.

Gamma, E. et al. (1995) *Design patterns: elements of reusable object-oriented software.* Boston, MA, USA: Addison-Wesley.

Guttag, J. V. (2013) *Introduction to computation and programming using Python* Massachusetts, MA, USA: MIT Press.

Hailpern, B. and Tarr, P. (2006) Model-driven development: The good, the bad, and the ugly. *IBM Systems Journal,* 45 (3). 451.

Haynes, B. (2006) Gauss's day of reckoning. *American Scientist,* 94 (3). 200.

Hemmendinger, D. (2010) A plea for modesty. *ACM Inroads,* 1 (2). 4.

Hunt, A. and Thomas, D. (1999) *The pragmatic programmer.* Reading, MA, USA: Addison-Wesley.

Jobs, S. (1998) *BusinessWeek,* 25 May. New York, USA: The McGraw-Hill Companies, Inc.

Knuth, D. (1997) *The art of computer programming, volume 1: fundamental algorithms.* Boston, MA, USA: Addison-Wesley.

Kowalski, R. (1979) Algorithm = logic + control. *Communications of the ACM,* 22 (7). 424.

Locust (2017) Locust website. Locust. Available from: http://locust.io/. [19 June 2017].

Michaelson, G. (2015) Teaching programming with computational and informational thinking. *Journal of Pedagogic Development,* 5 (1). 51–66.

Miller, G. A. (1956) The magical number seven, plus or minus two: some limits on our capacity for processing information. *Psychological Review,* 63. 81.

Nielsen, J. (1995) *10 usability heuristics for user interface design.* Nielsen Norman Group. Available at: www.nngroup.com/articles/ten-usability-heuristics/ [11 November 2016].

Nielsen, J. (2012) *Usability 101: introduction to usability*. Nielsen Norman Group. Available at: www.nngroup.com/articles/usability-101-introduction-to-usability/ [11 November 2016].

OpenStreetMap (2017) *OpenStreetMap copyright and license*. Open Street Map. Available from: www.openstreetmap.org/copyright [19 June 2017].

O'Reilly, L. (2016) *Netflix lifted the lid on how the algorithm that recommends you titles to watch actually works*. Business Insider. Available from: www.businessinsider.de/how-the-netflix-recommendation-algorithm-works-2016-2 [19 June 2017].

Pane, J. F. et al. (2001) Studying the language and structure in non-programmer's solutions to programming problems. *International Journal of Human-Computer Studies*, 54 (2). 237.

Papert, S. (1980) *Mindstorms: children, computers, and powerful ideas*. New York, USA: Basic Books Inc.

Pea, R. et al. (1987) The buggy path to the development of programming expertise. *Focus on Learning Problems in Mathematics*, 9 (1). 5.

Petre, M. (2013) *35th International Conference on Software Engineering*. San Francisco, CA, USA, 18 May. 722.

Pierce, B. C. (2002) *Types and programming languages*. Massachusetts, MA, USA: MIT Press.

Pólya, G. (1973) *How to solve it (second edition)*. Princeton, NJ, USA: Princeton University Press.

Python.org (2016) Python.org mercurial repository – List Code. Python. Available from: https://hg.python.org/cpython/file/31342913fb1e/Objects/listobject.c#l139 [16 November 2016].

Python.org (2017) Python 3 documentation. Python. Available from: https://docs.python.org/3/ [19 June 2017].

Scapy (2017) Scapy website. Scapy. Available from: www.secdev.org/projects/scapy/ [19 June 2017].

Selby, C. C. (2013) *Computational thinking: the developing definition*. Eprints. Available from: https://eprints.soton.ac.uk/356481/ [19 June 2017].

Selic, B. (2003) The pragmatics of model-driven development. *IEEE Software*, 20 (5). 19.

Shalloway, A. and Trott, J. R. (2005) *Design patterns explained: a new perspective on object-oriented design* 2nd edn. Boston, MA, USA: Addison-Wesley.

Tanenbaum, A. (2010) MINIX 3: a modular, self-healing posix-compatible operating system. YouTube. Available from: www.youtube.com/watch?v=bx3KuE7UjGA [19 June 2017].

Tutorials Point (2017). What is system testing? Available from: www.tutorialspoint.com/software_testing_dictionary/system_testing.htm [3 Jul 2017].

US Air Force (1967) Offutt air force base operator. Wikimedia. Available from: https://commons.wikimedia.org/wiki/File:Offutt_Air_Force_Base_operator.jpg [19 June 2017].

Voogt, J. et al. (2015) Computational thinking in compulsory education: towards an agenda for research and practice. *Education and Information Technologies*, 20 (4). 715.

Wikimedia Commons (2006) Koenigsberg, map by Merian-Erben 1652. Wikimedia. Available from: https://commons.wikimedia.org/wiki/File:Image-Koenigsberg,_Map_by_Merian-Erben_1652.jpg [19 June 2017].

Wikimedia Commons (2012) Orrery. Wikimedia. Available from: https://commons.wiki-media.org/wiki/File:Orrery_-_Nov._2010.jpg [19 June 2017].

Wikipedia (2017) *Python syntax and semantics*. Wikipedia. Available from: https://en.wikipedia.org/wiki/Python_syntax_and_semantics [19 June 2017].

Wiki Python (2017) Python debugging tools. Wiki Python. Available from: https://wiki.python.org/moin/PythonDebuggingTools [19 June 2017].

Wilkes, M. (1985) *Memoirs of a computer pioneer*. Massachusetts, MA, USA: MIT Press.

Wing, J. (2006) Computational thinking. *Communications of the ACM*, 49 (3). 33.

Wing, J. (2011) *Research notebook: computational thinking -- what and why?* The Link. Available from: https://www.cs.cmu.edu/link/research-notebook-computational-think-ing-what-and-why [19 June 2017].

Wing, J. (2014) *Computational thinking benefits society*. Social Issues in Computing. Available from: https://socialissues.cs.toronto.edu/ [1 September 2016].

Yadav, A. et al. (2014) Computational thinking in elementary and secondary teacher education. *ACM Transactions on Computing Education*, 14 (1). 1–16.

INDEX

Diagrams and tables are in *italics*

Printed in Australia
AUHW010503240619
313768AU00009B/44

9 781780 173641